MANHOOD

MANHOOD

The Masculine Virtues America Needs

JOSH HAWLEY

Regnery Publishing
WASHINGTON, D.C.

Regnery® is a registered trademark and its colophon is a trademark of Salem Communications Holding Corporation

Cataloging-in-Publication data on file with the Library of Congress

ISBN: 978-1-68451-357-4
eISBN: 978-1-68451-430-4
Library of Congress Control Number: 2022950138

Published in the United States by
Regnery Publishing
A Division of Salem Media Group
Washington, D.C.
www.Regnery.com

Manufactured in the United States of America

10 9 8 7 6 5 4 3 2 1

Books are available in quantity for promotional or premium use. For information on discounts and terms, please visit our website: www.Regnery.com.

Some names and identifying details have been changed to protect the privacy of individuals.

To my sons, Elijah and Blaise

CONTENTS

PART I

CHAPTER ONE
In the Beginning   3

CHAPTER TWO
A Man's Mission   15

CHAPTER THREE
A Man's Battle   31

CHAPTER FOUR
A Man's Promise   45

PART II

CHAPTER FIVE
Husband   61

CHAPTER SIX
Father   85

CHAPTER SEVEN
Warrior   103

CHAPTER EIGHT
Builder   129

CHAPTER NINE
Priest   151

CHAPTER TEN
King   177

EPILOGUE
Of Temples and Men   205

Author's Note   213
Notes   215
Index   241

PART I

CHAPTER ONE

IN THE BEGINNING

For a time I worked as a law professor, in Missouri, and my job naturally afforded me ample opportunity for conversation with students. They came to see me about papers and exams and difficult-to-understand law cases and all manner of other things that students want or need, and sometimes, more often than you might expect, they would tell me about what was going on in their lives.

Those were interesting conversations. I was barely over thirty years old at the time and can't say I was in much of a position to offer sage life counsel, but I did soon enough begin to notice a pattern. Many of the young men who came to see me were struggling, and in ways they found hard exactly to define. Some lacked confidence, some lacked direction; others could not seem to get motivated. They were afraid to fail, to venture out and take a risk, but felt at the same time dissatisfied with their lives as they knew them. One after another said, in one way or another, *I'm not sure what I'm supposed to do with my life.* And yet they felt they were failing at whatever that was.

I think of one law student in particular, I'll call him John.* He was a computer scientist by training, a bright and talented young man, sociable, witty, a person of faith—by all appearances well-positioned to succeed in life. But he seemed unable to take the next step out into life itself—to leave behind his family and school and actually *live*, as an independent adult, as a grown man. The prospect paralyzed him. And that very paralysis produced a profound sense of shame. He was failing as a man before he had even begun. *What should I do with my life*, he wondered. *What if I fail at it?* And then: *Why can't I get myself together?* Sadly, John tried to commit suicide twice in the years I knew him.

His case may be extreme. But the general pattern is by no means atypical. The numbers tell the tale, on one measure after another. More and more young men are living at home with their parents, apparently incapable of coping with life on their own. One recent survey found that among twentysomething young men considered "lower-skilled" workers, more than 50 percent are still living with parents or close relatives. That figure includes young men who have a job. For those who don't, fully 70 percent are living at home.[1]

As for jobs, fewer and fewer young men have them. In 2015, nearly a quarter of men between the ages of twenty-one and thirty, historically a cohort strongly attached to work and the labor force, had no work to speak of. These men had not engaged in labor during the previous twelve months. *At all.*[2] Meanwhile, those who are working are earning comparatively less than their fathers did at the same age. In 1970, 95 percent of thirty-year-old men earned more than their fathers had. By 2014, only 44 percent of thirty-year-olds could say the same.[3]

---

* Here and throughout, where I draw from my experiences as a teacher or from personal acquaintances, I have changed names and some of the details to protect the privacy of those involved.

Those are two measures of male malaise, living habits and work. Here's a third. Increasing numbers of boys and younger men are under-performing at school, if not opting out of education altogether. Boys earn the overwhelming number of the *D*s and *F*s handed out in primary and secondary school in America, 70 percent worth. By eighth grade, a bare 20 percent of boys are proficient in writing in this country; by the same age, merely 24 percent can earn proficient scores on reading exams. Boys meanwhile compose two-thirds of the students in remedial education programs—not, researchers point out, because their average intelligence is lower. But because they aren't trying.[4]

Not trying is becoming a theme for young men when it comes to education. More of them are choosing to drop out of college or forgo it entirely. Men now account for only 40 percent of college students in America, well below historical averages and well beneath their propor-tion of the college-aged population. Between the 2015 and 2020 aca-demic years, college enrollment in the United States fell off by 1.5 million students, with men constituting 71 percent of that drop. There are plenty of qualified male candidates for college, admissions officers say. They just aren't applying.[5]

What are these young men doing with their time? Screens, leisure, porn. "By far the biggest difference between the daily schedules" of men not in the labor force and those who are is the time spent in what researchers label "socializing, relaxing, and leisure."[6] Sitting around, in other words. On average, men not working spend almost eight hours a day on leisure, nearly twice the time as men who have a job.[7] And "leisure" does not mean visiting museums or listening to books on tape. The vast majority of men's leisure time is screen time, including video games and pornography.[8]

Perhaps not surprisingly, these same young men are often battling depression, like my friend John, or drug abuse, both of which are at historic levels. The number of men—of all ages—committing suicide in America leapt by more than 25 percent between 1999 and 2017. Some thirty-five thousand men in this country now die by their own hands every year, amounting to one suicide every fifteen minutes.[9] No sector of society is exempt: the young and the old, urban and rural, civilians and members of the military—the burgeoning crisis of suicide has found them all.[10] So have surging levels of drug abuse. Drug over-doses among men soared 250 percent between 2000 and 2017.[11] This burden of drug addiction bears down especially hard on men who have never been married. They make up about one-third of males between the ages of twenty-five and fifty-four, but account for two-thirds of the deaths involving drugs.[12]

I wish I could say that these troubles were confined to younger men only, like my former students, that these are hardships of youth that get left behind. But that is not the case. The same afflictions that followed the students I knew also beset men who are fully adults, far past college age. Older men, too, are working less than ever before, spending more time in front of screens than ever before, taking more drugs, leaving their families or failing to form them, and dying by suicide at alarming rates.[13]

All is not well with men in America. And that spells trouble for the American republic.

It has been a perennial question of political philosophy, since the first republics were formed, whether a free nation could survive without soundness of character in its people. The old-fashioned word for that is virtue, meaning not just moral uprightness but the personal fortitude and vision such uprightness produces—strength, in other words. Machiavelli called it *virtù*. Practically everywhere one looks in America now, male *virtù* is crumbling, and the consequences for the country are grave.

Crime is on the rise, overwhelmingly committed by men. Disinterest in work is becoming commonplace. And in perhaps the starkest example of male weakness, fatherlessness abounds. The percentage of children living with only their mother—no father present—has doubled since 1968.[14] Today, the majority of children born to women under thirty are born into fatherless homes—a new, ignominious milestone in American history.[15] The epidemic of absent fathers is a social solvent, dissolving the future. Boys raised in fatherless homes face increased odds that they will use drugs, commit crimes, perform poorly in school, and live in poverty—and then become absent fathers themselves.[16]

Much has been said in recent years of the divisions in American society, the dangers to our democracy, and our growing polarization. Surely it is no coincidence that these ills have proliferated while American men have struggled. As the anthropologist David Gilmore once wrote, "Manhood is the social barrier that societies must erect against entropy, human enemies, the forces of nature, time, and all the human weaknesses" that threaten social life.[17] No menace to this nation is greater than the collapse of American manhood, the collapse of masculine strength.

To be frank, some welcome that collapse: namely, those on the American left. In fact, they have helped drive it. In the power centers they control, places like the press, the academy, and politics, they *blame* masculinity for America's woes. The tribunes of elite opinion long ago decided that male strength is dangerous—toxic, leading inevitably to oppression and a hateful patriarchy. To be admitted to polite society in America today, one is supposed to confess—and I say "confess" advisedly, for the left it is a type of religious incantation—that masculinity is an arbitrary social construct that has made the world a much more terrible place. As one liberal author summed up the conventional wisdom, "talking about 'healthy masculinity' is like talking about 'healthy cancer.'"[18]

Not long ago I was sitting in a hearing of the Senate Judiciary Committee, of which I am a member. The topic was women's rights, but as I waited my turn to ask questions, I noticed that the other side's star witness, a highly accomplished professor at an elite university, refused to use female-gendered terms, such as "mother." Rather than take that apparently verboten word upon her lips, she kept saying, over and over again, "people with the capacity for pregnancy." I started keeping count on my notepad of the number of times she said it. When my turn came, I couldn't help but start by addressing this strange—yet revealing—verbal tic. What did she mean, I asked, by the phrase "people with the capacity for pregnancy"? Why wouldn't she just say "mother"? The witness promptly instructed me, in an exasperated tone that perfectly reflected the left's condescending intolerance for anyone who disagrees with its dictates, that transgender "men"—meaning biological women who now identify as male—can get pregnant, too. When I suggested this answer was, not to put too fine a point on it, absurd, and erased the reality of biological sex—you know, *men* and *women*—the professor informed me I was "transphobic" and that views like mine led to violence. *Violence.* In other words, shut up and don't question the official line. Finally, irritated with my queries, she demanded to know: "Do you believe men can get pregnant?"[19]

The answer, of course, is obvious. Or should be. No, men cannot get pregnant, as every person in recorded human history from the dawn of time has understood, until now. That today's left not only finds this "question" urgent, but is determined to vilify and ultimately silence those who answer it truthfully, shows just how radical they have become. To leftists, manhood is fake. Womanhood, too. Both are merely social confections that society made up and can remake at will. And today's left is determined to remake American men.

The left's disdain for masculinity flows from what remains of modern liberalism, which isn't much—an assortment of complaints about Western society being unequal, unjust, and corrupt to its foundations, masculinity being one of those foundations. Liberals historically claimed to prize liberty above all else. The members of today's left have pushed liberty into nihilism, defining it as the right to live free from biological sex, family, tradition, and God—free from reality. They paint every inherited structure, every moral duty and social obligation, as a shackle that must be smashed, by government if necessary, so the individual can be made "free."

Men have been told this nonsense for decades now by the press and politicians. They have been taught it in schools: that to be a man is to be an oppressor; that to display the masculine traits of assertiveness, independence, and risk-taking is to make society unjust; that to work hard at a blue-collar job is a loser's game for those who can't learn to code. America's policymakers have acted on this same ideology, medicating boys into submission in their school years, then shipping the manufacturing jobs many men once performed as adults off to foreign countries. In these circumstances, under the influence of this creed, is it any wonder that so many men now feel adrift, bereft, and—yes—ashamed to be men?

But the warning signs of trouble are becoming too glaring to ignore. Amid the suicides and drug abuse and epidemic of absent fathers, amid the collapse of work and explosion of crime, even some on the left are now expressing alarm. Men feel it. Those with sons know it. We cannot go on like this.

Modern liberalism, however, offers no path forward. It is, in fact, much the source of our present troubles. We must look elsewhere for renewal, farther back and deeper—to a more profound source of truth.

■   ■   ■

There was a movement in the 1980s, I understand, that promoted something called the "deep masculine." This was before my time, but I'm told the general idea was to recover a healthy vision of masculinity

from beneath the rubble of modern liberalism. Adherents of the movement placed a great deal of emphasis on the power of myth and story
as keys to unlocking truths about manhood—and the human condition
more generally—that our sterile modern ideologies obscure.[20]

There may be something to that part about stories. My observation
in teaching young men and in talking with men of all ages from all
walks of life is that many of them cannot say what their lives are about.
They have no template, no vision for what it is to be a man. Our contemporary culture certainly doesn't offer one, beyond blame and guilt.
Today's liberalism is in many ways an anti-story; it teaches that life is
meaningless, that there is no God, no heaven or hell or eternity, that
we must each do our best to make our lives bearable in this passing
moment in this cold and pointless universe, knowing full well it will
amount to nothing in the end.

It was not always this way. The West was formed by a powerful
story that had a good deal to say to men. It happens to be the oldest
and most profound story there is. It is the story of the Bible.

We are not supposed to say that today, of course; the Bible is
off-limits. Schools are not to mention it. Politicians are not to speak of
it. The chattering class cringes at the Bible's many appearances in
American history. They want to erase all of that—the Bible is too much
a part of the American story of which we are supposed to be so deeply
regretful. But I, for one, have no regrets when it comes to the Bible. The
Bible is *the* moral source of the Western tradition: it is the fount of our
most cherished moral ideas, from equality to freedom. It has shaped
our notions of God and earth, of time and future, of what it means to
be an individual, and yes, what it means to be a man. From Jewish
antiquity to the Roman Empire to the present, the Bible has sparked
social and personal transformation. It powered the rise of the monasteries and the early universities; it fueled the founding of the first hos-
pitals and the birth of modern science; it led to the invention of the

nation, the church, and constitutional government.[21] Of special note to Americans, the Bible inspired the English revolutionaries of the seventeenth century, who hoped to make of their nation a "Hebrew republic" where all men would be equal and free. Those revolutionaries in turn inspired our own.[22] That is another way of saying that the Bible invented America as we know it.

It is a shame, then, that the story of the Bible is so little known today. The Bible story is an epic that speaks directly to the purpose of men. Indeed, from the Christian perspective, the story comes to center on a Man. The story, in thumbnail form, is this. From chaos and nothing, God created the world for a purpose. He created it to be a temple. Why a temple? The world was to be a place filled with his presence. And man was to have a role making it so. At the center of his creation God placed a garden, and in the garden a man. And he instructed the man to cultivate that garden, to protect it, and to build it outward—to expand it into all the world. That was the man's calling, his sacred duty, and his purpose in life. Man was to be God's representative on the earth, to serve God by helping build the earth into an Eden, the temple it was meant to be, a place of beauty and order, liberty and peace, a dwelling for God himself.

This was the first man's mission, according to the Bible, and now the mission of all men. For when the first man abandoned it, God made the work his own, and continues it even now, inviting every man to discover the meaning of his life by joining in. To do so, to take up this ancient mission and perform this sacred work, will involve a man in hardship and sacrifice. It will implicate him in danger and love. It will lead him to the true meaning of freedom. In short, it will change his soul. The Bible's mission for men is an invitation to matter. And it is, at its core, an invitation to character.

For to become the servant of God the Bible says man is meant to be, each man must become what God's call will demand of him. He must shape his soul. He must acquire the character of a husband and father, a warrior and builder, a priest and king. The man who has character like that is a man indeed. America needs more men like that. And that is what this book is about.

The "depth psychologists," the disciples of Sigmund Freud and, particularly, Carl Jung, are fond of saying that when chaos and confusion threaten, opportunity awaits. This is because chaos is often founded in the breakdown of culture and the waning of its moral sources. So chaos spells danger, yes, but also—possibility, the chance for new breakthroughs, fresh vision. Chaos impels us back to our first guides, back to the sources that generate life. And there we may find something new.[23] Certainly this has been true in my own life. The Bible is the story I know best. It has shaped my life from the days my mother began reading it to me, and that began as early as I can remember. The Bible's epic has forged my sense of meaning and purpose and reality, so much so that when it comes to life's guides, it is nearly the only guide I can think to offer. And so I offer it here, with hope, and without apology.

It's a perfect match, in one sense. Masculinity is a taboo subject. And the Bible is, for some, a taboo book. But my claim is this: The Bible can inspire men today, guide them, and disclose new possibilities for their souls—new purpose, new strength. And that means renewal for the American republic. Much of today's left seems to welcome men who are passive and tame, who will do as they are told and sit in their cubicles, eyes affixed to their screens. That would be the ruination of America. Theodore Roosevelt once observed that long before ancient Rome became a dictatorship, the Roman republic had ceased to exist, because the hearty Roman yeoman had ceased to be capable of liberty.[24] That might be America's fate. But it need not be, if American men will shoulder their responsibilities and develop again the strength of character needed for self-government. There is no better place to learn of that character than the Bible.

I begin with Adam, the first of men, and follow his story across the Bible's pages. I say across the Bible because Adam's project begins but does not end with Adam. The commission God gives him is one the Bible says God means for all men. The Adam story is actually a series of stories, running from the Garden of Eden and well beyond, up to the present even, stories that unfold as the men of the Bible struggle to do what God made them to do: expand the garden, subdue the darkness without and within—as they struggle to become men. My hope is that in telling again these Adam stories, we will find our own story written there and discover new vision for our lives.

These are troubled times. But trouble may lead to renewal. If the Bible is right, the mission of Adam beckons, and the possibility of something better—for men, for America—awaits us.

_____

CHAPTER TWO

A MAN'S MISSION

My grandfather was a farmer who raised wheat, soybeans and corn, and also some milo, which is sometimes called sorghum, on the north plains of Kansas. He was the first member of our family on my mother's side born in the United States. His father was a Norwegian immigrant from a family of fishermen, but when they came to America they took up farming. It was from him, my grandfather, that I first learned about love of the land—to appreciate a straight-rowed, well-kept field of corn; to notice the beauty of common things like sunflower fields and a pasture after rain. He loved to work, and when I was a boy he did me the great good service of taking me along with him out to the fields whenever we would visit. (My family lived in Missouri, "in town," albeit a small one, and my mother, farm girl that she was, wisely thought it very important that my sister and I spend as much time on the farm as we could.)

One of the things I remember doing with him was laying irrigation pipe—this was during the summer months—pipe being the principal means on his farm of delivering water to the otherwise forbiddingly dry land. The pipes came equipped with gates along their sides, small doors that slid open or closed to regulate the flow of water into the rows of corn or soybeans or what have you. The gates had to be manually "changed," that is, tapped open or shut, usually with the side of a hammer or some similar implement, on a set schedule. My grandfather changed them twice a day. I remember doing this with him, and I remember how sometimes he would stand, when we finished the last field of an evening, leaning on his shovel and admiring his work, taking it in, a field of grain that stretched out to the horizon in the fading summer sun. "Mother Nature," he would sometimes say, "she does have a way."

Years later I realized he had taught me in those times together something very fundamental about manhood. He taught me that a feeling of purpose in life comes from the work one does, and that this is the right and natural way of men. As to work, he cultivated the earth. He farmed. Day in and day out he worked the ground, and he showed me that all work worth doing is cultivation in some sense: it brings forth the possibilities that are there in the world and uses them to supply and sustain others. It brings fruitfulness from void and chaos. It pushes forward the frontier of life. That is dignified work, and doing it dignifies the worker. Certainly my grandfather was a dignified man, despite holding no position of particular social importance. He was not wealthy or well-connected or politically significant. But he was respected by the other men of the region, who also made their living from the ground and recognized his skill at what he did, and by most all who knew him, of whatever walk of life. He had the dignity that came from work well done.

He had his share of struggles in life. Crops that failed, relatives who did him wrong, drought, disease, blight. Though a farmer his life long, he never owned much land himself. Most of what he farmed, he leased. But when he died, twenty years ago now, the multitude of kith and kin who gathered to memorialize him revealed that he had in fact acquired much. He had made possible the lives of a good many others, including my own.

The Bible begins its discussion of men with a story about a man who is a farmer of sorts—Adam, from the Hebrew *adamah*, earth. Like my grandfather, the Bible says this first man was a tiller of the soil. And in telling his story, the Bible makes this point, that all men are to work the earth, as my grandfather did, and in this sense: each man is appointed to bring forth creation's possibilities, to help perfect the world and build it into what it could be. That work begins with his own soul. The left does not care to hear that message today, and certainly not from the Bible. But it has the advantage of being true. Adam's story is a grand narrative of chaos and order, light and darkness: an origin story. And from it, we learn the origins of man's purpose.

THE MAN AND THE GARDEN

> In the beginning, God created the heavens and the earth. The earth was without form and void, and darkness was over the face of the deep. And the Spirit of God was hovering over the face of the waters. (Genesis 1:1–2)

The world was a chaotic place at first: no day and night, no land and sky, no order. Just "the deep," an ancient symbol of chaos, ever-churning, without form and in darkness—disorder itself. There are many creation stories in the literature of the ancient Near East, and most of them begin with chaos and darkness, followed by an account of how the first gods emerged from it, out of the deep. Not so in Genesis. When it begins, God is there—already, forever—standing apart from the churning depths. He does not emerge from them, he moves out over them in a show of command. And to do what? To bring forth order. Order from chaos, light from darkness: night and day and land and sky and sun and stars and seasons. God is subduing, he is pushing back the deep, he is building. It will become a pattern. What God does at the first he will ask man to help continue.

The story gets at that almost immediately, when it introduces us to the first man and his wife, the primal pair, brought into the world on the sixth day of creation. You may remember how it goes.

> Then God said, "Let us make man in our own image, after our likeness. And let them have dominion over the fish of the sea and over the birds of the heavens and over the livestock and over all the earth and over every creeping thing that creeps on the earth."
>
> So God created man in his own image, in the image of God he created him; male and female he created them.
>
> And God blessed them. And God said to them, "Be fruitful and multiply and fill the earth and subdue it...." (Genesis 1:26–28)

God creates man after his own likeness, which means many things, but already here the story hints at one of them: that man will continue doing what God is doing, that he will join God, somehow, in his labors.

There are actually two distinct creation accounts in Genesis, one right after the other, and while the first is famous for the declaration that man and woman are made in the image of God, the second story picks up in a different place and adds a new dimension to the picture of this creature, man. The second account emphasizes where Adam lives and what it means: that he comes from earth, and is meant to make the earth into something magnificent. "[T]hen the LORD God formed the man of dust from the ground and breathed into his nostrils the breath of life, and the man became a living creature. And the LORD God planted a garden in Eden, in the east, and there he put the man whom he had formed."[1]

In this second narrative, God fashions Adam from the soil. Thus his name, *Adam*, "of the earth." (Significantly, the woman, Eve, arrives later in this account, and is not formed from the soil, but from Adam himself.) The point we are meant to see is that this man of earth is formed for the purpose of the earth; the two go together. This is why after God forms Adam, he brings him immediately to a place no doubt familiar in name, but one that turns out to hold a deeper significance for Adam, and for us, than we may appreciate. God brings Adam to Eden.

What is Eden? Well, it is a garden, of course—that is the term Genesis uses—though the sense of the term is something more like a park than a bed of roses or turnips.[2] But the Bible suggests almost at once that Eden is far more even than that.

For starters, Genesis says God populated Eden with "every tree that is pleasant to the sight and *good for food*."[3] The garden can sustain life. The Bible says a great river watered Eden and flowed out of it, the river being an ancient symbol of fertility. So: the garden is a source of life. Eden is Eve's home—God creates her there, in the story—she is the mother of life. And at the garden's center, we learn, God planted a tree of knowledge and, yes, a tree of life.[4]

Eden is not a mere idyll, not in Genesis. It is far more significant than that. Eden is a place of wonder, of beauty, and above all, of life. Indeed, it is the home of life's author, God himself. The Bible reports in Genesis 3, almost offhandedly, that God walks in the garden, "in the cool of the day."[5] Eden is a temple.[6]

Temples are homes of gods, of course. They were common in the ancient Near East, in both fact and literature. Creation stories that feature them abound. In one of the most ancient of these, the *Enuma Elish* from Mesopotamia, the god Marduk completes his conquest and reconfiguration of the cosmos by building the city of Babylon as, yes, a temple, which the gods could inhabit. "We shall lay out the shrine," Marduk says, "let us set up its emplacement, when we come thither…we shall find rest therein."[7] There is a hint of similarity to Genesis: "And on the seventh day God finished his work that he had done, and he rested…" (emphasis added).[8]

Rest meant to take up residence—to come home. What is happening in the ancient stories and in Genesis? God builds the world to be a place where he can dwell. And from there, *rule*. Temples in the ancient world were throne rooms, control centers. They were frequently pictured in ancient literature as the center points of the cosmos, the places joining heaven and earth, mounts of power from which the god's influence emanated. "[M]ake the house grow like a mountain range," sings the cylinder of Gudea, the oldest known account of temple-building in the ancient world—"let it soar into the midst of heaven like a cloud…. Make it raise [its] head over all lands…."[9] Temples were sources of order. As one biblical scholar explains, a temple "was considered the center of power, control, and order from which deity brings order to the human world."[10] By joining heaven and earth together, temples sustained the structure of the cosmos.[11]

And that is what Eden is in the Bible: God's temple and dwelling place, the center of the universe and source of its life. What does this have to do with men? Plenty.

Consider. Temples were for the gods—or for the next best thing, their *images*. Another early report of temple-building records Pharaoh Seti I of Egypt constructing a house for the god Osiris, lord of the underworld. He finishes the construction by placing a statue of Osiris inside. The Egyptians believed the sun god Ra enabled the various Egyptian deities to inhabit the stone images the builders made for their temples. The stone likeness, in other words, represented and somehow hosted the presence of the god, or so they believed.[12] This was a common motif. From the ancient Egyptians to the Assyrians to the Babylonians, worshippers built temples and placed images of the gods inside them to symbolize the gods' presence.

Now to the Bible. Something similar takes place there, in Genesis. God subdues the chaos, makes a temple (Eden), and places an image in its midst. But in Genesis, the likeness of God in Eden is not a statue. The likeness of God is mankind.

Now we see even more sharply the significance of the garden—and of man. If Eden is a temple, Adam and Eve are its icons, the living statues of God placed in the garden sanctuary to represent him. And just as the statues of gods within the temples of the ancient world symbolized the presence and rule of the god of the temple, so too in Genesis, Adam and Eve preside over earth in God's stead. They represent his presence. They reflect him. And they are there to continue God's work on his behalf.[13]

In no other creation story in the world do the humans figure so prominently. Adam is the representative of God on earth. Eve, too. This is the Bible's opening claim about a man's life and the world he lives in. The universe has an order and a purpose, a destiny, if you like—and men are integral to it. Each of us. A man need not scout about to find his significance. He is born with it, to a position of consequence; that's the message of the Bible. He is born into a story underway. And his choices and his life will help determine the outcome. What a man does and how he lives will affect the destiny of the world.

That brings us back to the question of Adam's mission, his job as a man. Genesis supplies the first half of the answer by telling us Eden is a temple, and Adam (like Eve) is God's image inside that temple. But what is it exactly that Adam is supposed to do from there? The Bible has something to say on that score as well. Genesis reports that God "took the man and put him in the garden of Eden to *work* it and *keep* it" (Genesis 2:15; emphasis added).

God has made all the world, but it seems there is more work yet to be done. There is chaos yet to subdue, darkness to confront. Creation is an unfinished project. Men are there to help finish it.

BUILDING THE TEMPLE

My grandfather's father was named Lars, and he came to this country as a teenager, along with his mother and half a dozen brothers and sisters. They came through Ellis Island and then went on to Kansas, where Lars's father was waiting on the homestead. Those early years were difficult. Not long after he arrived in Kansas, Lars married and my grandfather Harold (a good Scandinavian name) was born—in a house of rough-hewn timber, which Lars built himself. When my grandfather kept down his mother's milk on the second day, they knew he would live. Homesteading was perilous business—the crops might fail, the weather was unforgiving, the money short—and exceptionally difficult work. To plant the fields, Lars and his father first had to claim them from the prairie. The fields had to be *made*.

Something akin to this happens in the story of Adam. Especially if we have read the Bible's Genesis stories before, perhaps hearing them as children, we are tempted to think of the entire creation effort as a neat and tidy episode that spans seven days and is done with. Adam and Eve come upon the scene and all the work is done for them, much like the farmer coming to fields already prepared. But that is not the picture Genesis in fact paints. Genesis says God spent six days bringing order from chaos, light from darkness, land from sea; filled what he had made with fish, fowl, and beasts—*and then* charged the humans to follow his example, "subduing" and "filling" after him.

What can this mean but that the earth was not yet fully finished, not yet fully subdued or filled, the work of God not yet fully done? That is what man is there to do.

Look closely. In the Genesis story, Eden is the only place of order and flourishing the Bible describes. It is the only park, the only garden, the only outpost of peace. When we learn anything of the land beyond Eden's borders, it appears untamed, wild. Dark forces lurk there. A sly and wicked serpent will enter the story a chapter later in Genesis, and from where? Beyond the garden's edge. That place, the place beyond, looms as a site of potential development, yes—God has made it and brought it forth from the deep—but also of darkness and disorder. It is, as yet, unfinished. Adam's job is to help finish it, to bring it into order. His job is to *expand* the garden temple.[14]

The story gets at this in several ways, beginning with the fact that Adam himself comes from beyond the garden. Genesis says God first formed Adam from the dust and then brought him to Eden afterward— "And the LORD God planted a garden in Eden, in the east, and there he put the man whom he had formed" (Genesis 2:8). The idea is that just as Adam's destiny began outside the garden, his vocation will take him beyond it.

Above all, there are the specific tasks God assigns Adam once he gets to Eden. Genesis says God designates Adam to work the garden and keep it. Work is *abad* in Hebrew, meaning, most basically, to till the soil, like my grandfather did, to put back and muscle into it. But Eden itself is already cultivated; God did that part. If Adam is to till, he must till what is not tilled already. He must subdue what is yet wild; he must claim land from the wilderness.

And there is plenty of land to cultivate beyond Eden's borders. The Bible notes that the river (of life) that watered Eden did not stop at Eden's boundaries. It flowed out beyond the garden to the wider world.

Ancient Jewish commentators found in this imagery evidence that the garden temple was to expand into all the earth.[15]

Consider a final story from the garden. The Bible says one of the first things God does once he has fashioned Adam and installed him in Eden, even before he creates Eve, is to bring the animals to Adam to be named.[16] In the ancient world, the rite of naming was itself an act of creation. To name was to designate a thing's nature and purpose, to order its destiny. God had formed the animals already, but he gave Adam the task of naming, and thus completing, them.

Just as God brought order from chaos and placed a temple at its center, now Adam is to take up God's labors after God's pattern. He is to cultivate the lands beyond the temple that are still unsettled, yet disordered, and bring order there, after the model of Eden. Adam is to be a co-laborer with God, helping to fulfill the destiny of creation.

The earth beyond the garden may be unkept, there may be malevolence there in some form, but Genesis insists God created even this world and called it good. It is not desolate; it is merely unfinished. It will respond to man's work. And Adam is to work it. His effort will bring forth the hidden purposes of the world.

And here we come to the heart of a man's mission. The Bible has been speaking of Adam, but at the same time it is speaking of all men, those whom Adam represents. Man's mission is to expand "the garden" into all the world. Man's sacred mission is to cultivate the world, order it, and bring forth its potential: make it a temple.[17]

Abraham Kuyper was a journalist and one-time pastor who became prime minister of the Netherlands in the early 1900s. He devoted a good deal of his life to meditating on these very passages from Genesis, which became for him a cornerstone of his personal and political philosophy. He summarized them like this: "We with our own human nature are placed in a nature *around* us, not to leave that nature as it is, but with an urge and calling within us to work on nature through human art, to ennoble and perfect it."[18]

This says quite a lot about men and about the world. About men it says this: they are the partners of God. They are no mere bystanders. Man is not a pawn of fate or chance or history. His work matters. God built the universe for it to matter, and for man to matter.

My older son, Elijah, is, as I write this, nine years old, and a great lover of cars. That includes designing them. He keeps a sketch pad near him at most times to rough out ideas he has for new vehicles. He has produced multiple sketches improving on the truck I drive, for example. He has also designed entirely new vehicles equipped with features previously unknown to mankind. He is a surprisingly good artist for someone aged nine, better than his father will ever be, and his sketches— to include interiors, frame and body, as well as engines—are detailed and fascinating. I recognize in this boyish work of his the impulse to cultivate and build, already apparent at a young age. He is fitted to venture out and improve the world. He is a temple builder. All men are meant to be.

About the world, Genesis says this: it was not made to be a wasteland. It was made to be a cathedral. The Hebrew prophet Isaiah would put it this way, "For thus says the LORD, who created the heavens (he is God!), who formed the earth and made it (he established it; *he did not create it empty, he formed it to be inhabited!*)."[19] The world we know can be better, much better; it can be a place of goodness and beauty and life. It can be a place that reflects God himself. For anyone who has glanced at the world recently, that might seem implausible. But it might also seem hopeful. And it should. That is the point. As men, we are supposed to do something to make hope reality.

The work begins within. It is not the exterior world only that men are called to work upon, far from it. There can be no change in the world that does not begin with the soul. The mission of temple-making is a call to build our characters, to shape our souls. Abraham Kuyper made just this point. To be what God made him to be, a man must improve his nature, Kuyper said; he must work upon himself.[20] Unlike some later philosophers who would idealize the "state of nature" as perfect and complete, the Bible never romanticizes either the past or man's own character. The Bible says man's destiny is grand, to be sure, his mission sacred. But he must reform himself to realize what he could be. He must conform his character to God's purposes for his life.

Men know this, instinctively, whether they express it in those terms or not. It is why they respond to coaching and discipline and challenge. I once had a student who came to law school quite young, at just twenty-one, and though he had graduated from college, he was only beginning to learn to be an adult, to get to places on time, to keep commitments he had made. He asked for my help in creating a study schedule and setting academic goals, which I was happy to provide. But then he surprised me. Almost immediately thereafter, he asked for my advice in setting other, less academic goals: fitness goals, spiritual goals, a personal improvement reading list. Having got a taste for order and discipline, he wanted more. He wanted to shape his soul.

LIFE WITHOUT PURPOSE

The message of Genesis—what a man is and what he can do—cuts against the loudest voices in our contemporary culture and the philosophy behind them. That philosophy is a modern form of liberalism, though it draws on ancient sources. It sees no inherent purpose in any human being, whether man or woman. It sees no inherent meaning in the universe.

Modern liberalism comes to these conclusions by way of an alternative origin story, a rival account to Genesis about the beginning of all things. This alternative story was best told by an ancient philosopher, a Greek, named Epicurus. He lived before Christ in the days of the Greek city-states and died around 270 BC, though he would claim influential followers long after.[21] The creation story Epicurus told goes something like this: The universe is neither planned nor orderly. It is composed of infinitesimally small atoms that move and spin entirely at random. Study the atoms and you will find no purpose, no plan, only a series of uneven movements, generating random, disconnected events and a history that means, of itself, nothing.

From this "physics," Epicurus drew the following conclusion: If there are gods—and Epicurus was somewhat ambivalent on this point—they mean nothing good for human life. The gods are either subject to the same spinning atoms as the rest of us, and therefore not qualitatively different or more powerful than humans, or they simply take no interest in human beings. Or maybe they don't exist at all. Any way you parse it, the gods contribute nothing useful to the lives we lead. In fact, the only thing the gods really inspire is fear. The possibility of their existence terrorizes mankind, causing us to invent rules and arbitrary standards about who qualifies for the afterlife. We worry about what the gods think of us and what they might do.

All needlessly, according to Epicurus. His advice was direct. Mankind should put the gods aside and focus on what really matters, which is, he said, pleasure, happiness. Happiness is *all* that matters, on Epicurus's view, and this present life is all there is: no immortal soul, no great beyond, none of that. What counts now, what life is truly about, is being happy for as long as one can, any way one reasonably can.[22]

For Epicurus, the cosmos was an empty place, and certainly not a temple. Humans were meaningless creatures, and certainly not God's icons. The only destiny humans had was the one they chose for themselves. The trick was to arrange one's life, and society, in such a way as to allow maximum choice for pursuing pleasure and personal satisfaction. There was, simply put, nothing more.

If all that sounds familiar, it should. Epicurus's ideas have exerted enormous influence on the modern mind. Today's popular culture instructs us to prioritize self-fulfillment over duty, pleasure over sacrifice. It tells you to find "your truth" and choose your own values. Like Epicurus, today's thought leaders reject religious faith in favor of atheism and materialism. Modern liberals say there are no permanent truths, only "constructs." And now they want to deconstruct masculinity on the basis that the demands of manhood prevent individuals from doing what Epicurus said was the only thing worth doing, achieving personal happiness.

But behind the modern cheerleading for pleasure and choice looms the dark specter of emptiness. Meaninglessness. The reason the search for enjoyment is so urgent, the reason our culture instructs us to pursue pleasure so frantically, is because without these things there is nothing worth living for at all. At least according to modern, Epicurean liberalism, that is. And this is the plight of our age. People pursue happiness relentlessly because they are so desperately unhappy and so desperately without hope for the future.

Against this emptiness, Genesis tells a different tale. It says man was created as God's image and called to perform God's work. And that high and noble task gives man's life meaning and direction.

Genesis encourages every man who struggles to see the point of his life, who feels that his work is a waste, or who wonders whether he will amount to anything to think again. Your work matters. Your life matters. Your character matters. You can help the world become what it was meant to be. And that is no small thing.

THE POWER OF PURPOSE

The Bible offers a purpose that summons each man, a purpose that will transform him. A man cannot stay as he is, not if he is to take on the mission of manhood. He cannot live for himself alone. He must grow and learn and acquire the qualities of character his mission requires. That is how one truly becomes a man, according to the Bible. The call to be God's servant will be a journey of transformation.

The Greeks and Romans said something similar on this point. They also believed achieving manhood required personal change and the forging of character. They held that manhood was a vocation that each man must struggle to assume. On this point, the Romans distinguished between a true man (a *vir*) and a mere male (*mas*).[23] Boys were born as males, but not yet as men. One became a man only by acquiring certain character traits. A man, a *vir*, was willing to bear pain, for instance, willing to give his life for others, willing to act boldly, to face death. The Roman Cicero pointed to Gaius Marius, a Roman general, who once required surgery but refused to be held down during the operation. Rather, he willed himself to equanimity as the surgeon cut. "Being a *vir*," Cicero concluded, "he bore the pain."[24] Roman warriors frequently admonished their soldiers in similar fashion to act "like men" on the field of battle. Seneca's Achilles, the ultimate mythic hero, is just such a case in point. Seneca says the great fighter might have avoided battle and lived to old age, but "chose the sword and professed himself a man."[25]

The Roman word for manliness was *virtus*, which is the ancient ancestor of our word for excellence of character, virtue. One became a man by becoming virtuous, by forming oneself to be what manhood demanded.

And it is not only the Romans who have said this. Plenty of American men have preached the same doctrine, not least Theodore

Roosevelt, who connected manhood and its virtues to liberty. "Self-government is not an easy thing," he said.[26] It demands men who are "bold, self-reliant, and energetic."[27] Roosevelt understood that a man's struggle to answer the call on his life and become all he might carries implications well beyond himself. The future of the republic depends on it. Only men who can practice the virtues of "self-command, of self-restraint, and of wise disinterestedness," Roosevelt said, could hope to be free. And only those men could hope to sustain a free nation.[28]

The Adam story and the mission it reveals offer us the chance to live with purpose, to leave behind the meaninglessness that afflicts so much of the modern world and to venture out boldly with fresh hope and confidence. But the mission does not leave us where we are. It summons us to greater things and personal change. And that requires we face hard truths. For according to the Bible, God's plan to make all the world a temple faces opposition. There are dark forces that resist this mighty work, and that will resist us if we take up Adam's call. To fulfill our purpose, we must struggle against the evil in the world—and in ourselves. This is the next installment of man's creation story.

CHAPTER THREE

A MAN'S BATTLE

When I was fourteen years old, I began attending a Catholic high school about an hour away from the small town where my family lived. This was a seismic shift in my life. I suppose going to high school is often a major episode in one way or another, but the change seemed especially momentous to me. I had only rarely ventured beyond the town where we lived, which boasted a population of five thousand souls, and then usually to visit relatives. Now there would be a long commute every day, a new school, and entirely new classmates. We had a family friend who taught there, and my parents knew another couple who sent their son to the school, but he was two years ahead of me and I didn't know anyone else at all. Instead of my old class of sixty-odd students, most of whom I had known since kindergarten, my incoming freshman class would have approximately two hundred. The prospect was at once hugely exciting—new frontiers, adventure—but also, to my young self, daunting.

I signed up to play freshman football, a sport I had been playing since I was nine. That proved to be a saving grace. Lots of boys at the school played football, but not all two hundred, and being part of the team gave me the opportunity to meet new people in a smaller setting and identify a group of friends early on to call my own. I also turned out to be pretty decent at it (for a fourteen-year-old), which gave me confidence that spilled over into my academic studies.

One of the people I met first on the team was Jake.[1] He was a big guy, tall, even as a freshman, with a shock of thick brown hair. I remember how he was always smiling; that was in fact my first impression of him. On the football field, though, he didn't smile. He was tough. He hit hard. We became fast friends, for freshman year and the rest of high school.

He was a devoted Christian and possibly the first person my age I had known who felt comfortable talking about his spiritual life. He would tell me what he was reading in the Bible or thinking about, his questions about God and faith and life. He listened to me do the same. I loved it. I spent a goodly amount of time at his house, where I was treated like another son. He had seven siblings—two brothers, five sisters—and his house hummed with activity. Jake and his family were great lovers of animals, and I never ceased to be amazed at the lizards and snakes and parakeets and fish I seemed to encounter in every room, sometimes confined to tanks and cages, sometimes not. His house was a fabulous place.

We played football together all four years and spent lots of time playing other games besides—one-on-one basketball in his driveway, games of tennis, a little golf in the backyard, if memory serves (before the neighbors put a stop to it). He grew to be six foot three or four, a truly hulking individual, but was always agile and quick. I don't think I beat him in one-on-one basketball even once.

When we went off to college, we stayed in regular touch and visited each other in the summers and for birthdays. Jake wanted to be a doctor, like his father, which suited him. He was quite possibly the gentlest man I knew, despite his towering size and ferocity on the football field. He loved people and cared for them; he was an attentive listener. He majored in biology and kidded me endlessly about my choice to study history. Not a serious subject, he said. Not rigorous.

Then something began to go wrong our senior years. I first noticed it the summer before senior year started, before we headed back to our respective campuses. I had invited Jake to a family get-together of mine in Arkansas, a hiking trip, and toward the end of the weekend he said to me cryptically, "I don't know if this med school thing is going to work out." I was surprised. I knew medical school had long been his aim. And he was a good student, sharp, intellectually curious, and a hard worker. But I didn't pursue it. I wish I had.

Ten months later, after graduation, I left to spend a year teaching in England, a gap year of sorts between college and law school. Jake meanwhile stayed on for a fifth year of college. While I was away, we talked very little. We chatted a bit over Christmas break on the phone or over email, I can't now remember which, but I remember he seemed down, still uncertain about medical school and uncharacteristically bleak. He told me he was reading a lot in the book of Job. I recall a stray comment he made, the context for which I forget, saying, "I don't want you to lose whatever respect for me you have left." It was a strange statement. There was no one I respected more.

Then one night about four months after that, in April, while I was back home in Missouri for spring break, the phone rang, the one in the kitchen attached to the wall, those being the days before ubiquitous cellphone use. Even now I can remember the exact spot where I was standing, leaning against the kitchen counter that was topped with green tile. On the other end was the father of another of my close high school friends. "Josh, you're home," he said, surprised I had been the one to pick up. "Have you heard about Jake?"

I knew immediately. He didn't need to say anything more. I knew at that moment, in the pit of my stomach, before I could give it voice or even form the thought, that my friend was gone. My boyhood companion, my first truly close friend in life, had put a gun to his head earlier that day and pulled the trigger. He was twenty-two.

It never made any sense to me. It still does not. I got to be present for his burial several days later and I remember reflecting, as I watched his casket inch into the ground, on all that we would miss. He wouldn't be at my wedding one day. I would not be at his. Our children would not play together. Our lives, once intertwined, would no longer be. And even now, all these years later, I still miss him and grieve. I grieve that the world lost the wonder of who he was. I grieve that I wasn't a better friend, that I wasn't there with him or for him in the end. I wish I had been.

His death was shattering in many ways, and among the things it destroyed in my life was any illusion that all is well with the world, or with me. The world is not as it should be, nor am I, nor is any man. There is darkness in the world that resists what is good and strains to destroy it. There is darkness within us. This is a reality each man must face. This is his battleground.

Our modern, Epicurean culture has trouble facing it. It wants to insist that human nature is inherently good and that evil, if there is any such thing, is a product of corrupt social systems. It's the fault of "the patriarchy" or systemic racism or capitalism or the like. By the same token, Epicurean liberals flee from trial and pain. They have nothing useful to say about these things—other than to avoid them. The Epicurean idea of character formation comes down to this: ignore your vices, pursue pleasure, and prioritize happiness—and be a generically "nice person" who won't stand in the way of anyone else pursuing self-gratification.

One of the reasons the Bible is so out of favor with the left is that it takes a very different view. The Bible has much to say about evil, and much more to say about a man's duty to confront it, in himself above all. Man's commission to subdue the earth's chaos and bring forth its potential means confronting the evil the chaos conceals. And that begins with himself. The battle with evil is the proving ground of a man's character. Genesis is direct about this. To build the world into a temple, he must stand in evil's way, starting in his soul. That is truth today's men need to hear.

THE DUTY TO GUARD

God assigned Adam two tasks when he brought him to Eden. The first was to work the garden. The second was to "keep" it, as in to guard.[2] A perimeter needs guarding only when there is danger, and God's instruction to Adam to "keep" the garden indicates danger waits beyond Eden's boundaries. This is the reality of evil. It is present, beyond our ability to comprehend or explain. It threatens us and what we hold dear. It threatens the good work of God.

In the ancient world, priests guarded the temples they served. Their responsibilities included keeping out intruders who might defile what was inside.[3] In Genesis, the garden is the temple and Adam its priest. Guarding the sanctuary was his duty. One early Jewish commentary put it this way: "And [God] said that [he] would make a man for this world as guardian over [God's] works."[4]

Which is to say: at the heart of Adam's mission was the obligation to place himself between the good things God had given him—his wife, his family, his home—and evil. Adam was to be part of God's solution to the danger in the world. If evil would enter the garden, it had first to contend with him. That was the plan.

And what was true for him is true for us. Men are part of God's solution to danger in the world. Like Adam, we are called to expose ourselves to danger to protect others and to serve what is right. With regard to others: Life is an exquisite, exceptionally fragile gift. Every parent knows this, viscerally. The life of a child can be extinguished in a moment. The sanctity of a home can be disrupted in mere seconds. Someone must stand between the ever-present threat of evil and the gift of life. That someone is a man.

The Bible does not shy away from powerful men. On the contrary, it teaches that powerful men are necessary. Genesis says that God gave Adam power: strength to be used in the holy task of expanding the garden. But God gives Adam no authorization to dominate or destroy. Even as he delegates Adam (and Eve) "dominion," he charges Adam to *guard* carefully the good things in his care. Adam has power for the purpose of defending others. So do we. But what happens when we do not use it that way, or do not use it at all? Genesis offers a case study.

THE POWER OF OUR CHOICES

In the face of evil, we can choose to confront the darkness or we can choose to go along, to compromise. Adam chooses the path of least resistance, which is to say he does nothing, as men are often tempted to do. He does not place himself between his family and danger; he does not challenge the dark impulses of his soul. The consequences are disastrous—for him, of course. But Adam led a consequential life, and so do you. His choices are disastrous for the world.

"Now the serpent was craftier than any other beast of the field that the Lord God had made. He said to the woman, 'Did God actually say, "You shall not eat of any tree in the garden?"'" (Genesis 3:1).

The serpent was widely portrayed in cultures across the ancient Near East as an agent of destruction and evil.[5] It lives up to that billing in Genesis. The snake convinces Eve to disobey God's instructions and eat from the tree of knowledge, one of the holy trees planted personally by God. The choice of tree is significant. God planted the trees of knowledge and life together, suggesting the way to life everlasting comes by way of knowledge, and knowledge by way of obedience to God. The trees represented God's promises, but the humans were not to eat of them until God said so.[6]

The serpent challenges that, of course. It tells Eve to eat of the tree of knowledge now, that if she does she will be a god herself. Now remember, Eve and Adam were already God's icons at the center of his temple, which itself sat at the center of the cosmos. But the snake challenges Eve to forgo her status as mere servant; he challenges her to forgo discipline and obedience and reach for gratification now.

The serpent is the voice of envy and resentment, the voice of selfish ambition. Perhaps Eve would have heard this voice at some point in her life irrespective of what Adam did. Perhaps she would have had her reckoning with evil no matter what. But that is not the impression Genesis leaves. How precisely the snake managed to find its way into Eden the story does not say, but the implication is that the serpent is there because Adam did not do as God instructed. He did not guard the perimeter. His negligence exposed his wife to darkness.

Things go rapidly downhill from there. Eve accepts the serpent's invitation. Rather than resist, confront the snake or push back, Adam does the same. He gives in. He chooses himself. And then in a part of the story that underlines the power of human choices, the darkness that was once outside the garden comes rushing into the garden itself. Indeed, it comes into the humans' very souls. Genesis reports that for the first time, Adam feels anger and shame—and promptly shifts blame and lies. Confronted by God, who arrives perhaps in a storm to symbolize the disruption the humans have let loose,[7] Adam first hides—fleeing responsibility—then accuses his wife.

Genesis does not suggest Adam's decisions created evil, any more than ours do. But they did embolden it. They let it loose in the world in a new and powerful form. And this is a warning to every man. Your choices matter, for better or worse. For Adam, in this instance, it was worse. God tells Adam the earth itself will be cursed because of him: "cursed is the ground because of you; in pain you shall eat of it all the days of your life; thorns and thistles it shall bring forth for you" (Genesis 3:17–18). Recall God's earlier charge to Adam to "work" the garden, to cultivate and expand it, his mission to build the temple. What Adam has done is make that mission, that building and expanding and cultivating, much more difficult. He has worked against his purpose rather than for it. The curse on the ground is a curse on Adam's ability to bring forth the world's potential. It means his life's purpose will henceforth be fraught and difficult and frequently disappointing.

There is more. The curse Adam has let loose means Adam will die—he and all those he loves. "[Y]ou are dust," God tells him, "and to dust you shall return" (Genesis 3:19). When we choose evil rather than confront it, when we coddle it and side with it, we bring ourselves and those we love closer to death. There is a kind of death in lying, in blaming, in living in resentment. It is a slow death of the soul. Adam's choices brought him into this place of death, to live in the midst of it. One of Adam's sons will kill the other, and the entire human race, as it grows, will be vexed by vice and misery, part of its inheritance from Adam. The first human society Genesis describes at any length, Babel, is irredeemably wicked. By expanding the garden and God's temple, Adam was supposed to help subdue the chaos. Instead, he unleashed it.

This is the chaos and darkness in which every man lives, the disorder that ate away at my friend Jake's hope and that I never felt more deeply than when I lost him. It infects us all; it dogs our steps. In the days after Jake's death, I observed a strange pattern in myself. On the one hand, I dreaded any invitation, however well-meaning, to "talk about it." On the other, I resented those of my friends and colleagues who failed to inquire about or at least acknowledge what had happened. How could they just go on, I wondered, as if nothing was changed, as if all of this was somehow normal?

The fault was not in any of these people, of course, but in me. I was face-to-face with the disorder of the world, and I found it deeply disorienting. It seemed to affect even my physical orientation and sense of place. I remember returning home after Jake's funeral and thinking my room looked strange, as if the furniture had been shifted around. I had the same sensation upon returning to my apartment in England a week later. Nothing had in fact changed, not physically. Only in me, facing the evil that haunts all our lives.

FLEEING RESPONSIBILITY

The question is what we are going to do about it. Our modern culture absolves us of personal responsibility and urges us to blame someone or something else—society, perhaps, or "the system." This is because modern liberalism views evil very differently from the Bible. And as a result, it instructs men to mold their characters into a very different shape.

Epicurus, modernity's ancient forefather, had little to say about evil, other than that the greatest evil was to live one's brief life bereft of happiness. This was why he laid so much blame at the feet of the gods. Their legends inspired only terror, he said.[8] Against the pain of the world, best to secure whatever small happiness one could.

His later disciples took this line of thinking further. One of them was Jean-Jacques Rousseau, an eighteenth-century Frenchman whose ideas helped inspire the French Revolution and much later liberal thought. Rousseau considered himself a kind of Epicurean, and it was his contention that man in the state of nature was good, blissfully simple, and free. Man's freedom consisted in the fact that he knew no distinction between his desires and his duties. In fact, he had no duties, not to speak of. He could live for himself: his duty was to satisfy his needs.[9]

Suffering came along only when society intervened, Rousseau said. According to him, society made man self-conscious. It imposed on him arbitrary standards and intolerant moral precepts. It spoke of God and duty. It encouraged man to look on himself and criticize.

You have no doubt heard this line of reasoning before. The worst sin is the sin of intolerance, we are frequently told. The worst thing you can be is judgmental. Rousseau argued society was at fault; society made man judgmental, and this caused man pain—it divided him against himself. It gave him a sense of duty and moral obligation that was at war with his desires. This inner conflict in turn produced misery, and miserable men did miserable things. Evil, Rousseau said, sprang from a divided soul.[10]

What was needed, Rousseau said, was a kind of rehabilitation. The solution was to liberate man from the moral shackles society had forged for him by getting him back in touch with himself. Christian writers down the centuries had advised men to turn inward to hear the voice of God. Rousseau advised man to grow quiet and look within to hear...himself. When you look in your soul, Rousseau said, you discover your inner goodness.

And that brings us to the Epicureans' prescriptions for personal character. Rousseau's counsel was: Ignore the dictates of society and the moralizing voice in your head (that society spawned) and choose your own values. Only you can decide what you truly want, what is best for you. So find your true passions and serve them, whatever anyone else says. Express yourself. Create your own identity. Discover your own truth. The path to personal wholeness is personal fulfillment.

To be happy, to become authentic, you must become the author of your own self. That was Rousseau's program.

And it is today's gospel. We are taught some version of it from the time we are young; we hear it rehearsed in school lessons and television shows and self-help books and movies. We hear it in the cadences of modern liberalism, which contends that the greatest evils to be defeated are found in social "structures"—like the family, or Christianity, or manhood. The evil in these institutions, today's Epicureans say, is that they oppress the individual by preventing him from choosing what he can become. If you want less pain and suffering in the world, the argument goes, liberate individuals. Let them throw off the bonds of family obligations. Let them repudiate "gender roles." Let them flout religious ordinances regarding the sanctity of life or holy matrimony. Let them mock tradition, ignore history, and deny the immutable facts of biology. Let nothing stand in the way of their pursuit of personal satisfaction.

Rousseau took his own advice in this regard. He fathered five children in his life and abandoned all five of them to orphanages.[11] He didn't want the burden of raising them: they might interfere with his personal choices. So he gave them away, and kept himself free to be his own man, according to his own desires. It was all very Epicurean—and reprehensible. In the end, beneath the rhetoric of choice and freedom and self-creation, that's what modern Epicureanism offers—the counsel to abandon the things that make demands on you, down to your very flesh and blood, and chase pleasure. The character they lionize is relentlessly focused on self.

FROM SELF TO SACRIFICE

The Bible takes a different view. Faced with evil and pain, the answer is not to set yourself free but to give yourself up, sacrificially. To make yourself expendable.

God made Adam a guardian and charged him to watch the perimeter. Adam was to devote his life to those he was responsible for—his wife and family and their life together, as well as the good things of the garden. There could be no mission of temple-building unless someone was there to protect the temple, to protect what is good. That person was to be Adam. Those people are to be men.

Where Epicurean liberalism urges self-creation as the path away from pain, the Bible urges different qualities of character: self-renunciation and sacrifice. The Bible says meaning is found and the soul is formed in confronting the darkness and setting oneself against it, standing between other people and evil. Does this explain why there is evil in the world to begin with? Of course not. But it tells a man what he is supposed to do about it. It tells him that his pain and hardship can be turned to good if he will take up his post and stand in the gap.

For this very reason, many societies press boys through rites of suffering as a gateway to full manhood, so that the boy will learn that to become a man is to become self-sacrificial, to be willing to give one's life for others.[12] This was true of the Romans. For them, a "male was transformed into a man by the willful expenditure of energy"—more specifically, by the willful, voluntary expenditure of his life.[13] To quote the Roman poet Virgil, a true man "scorns the light of life and holds that honor you are aiming at as cheaply bought if all its price is life."[14]

When I was five or six years old, I was out one summer day in the fields with my grandfather Harold. I remember it was summer because the corn was tall and green and the day was bright. And I remember I was five or six because I was struggling with the laces on my work boots. They were thicker than the laces of my shoes, harder to hold and harder for small hands to tie. I had to ask for my grandfather's help, and as he bent down to take hold of the laces, I complained vaguely about having to wear boots at all. He replied, "You need to learn to tie your boots. You have to know how to get them on right." And then he added, "You know, soldiers wear boots." Still a little sullen, I replied to this that I wasn't a soldier, so I didn't need to put on the boots. He replied, "You may be, one day. If your country calls, you'll go."

He had something specific in mind. One of his sons, my uncle Gene, had been drafted for service in the U.S. military at the height of the Vietnam War. It was a point of pride in my family that despite potential grounds for deferment, he had served in the 101st Airborne. When I was young, my mother showed me the newspaper clippings my grandmother had carefully preserved from the county paper with pictures of Gene leaving for Vietnam. Later clippings showed pictures of his return. I knew what my grandfather was referring to that day when he said, "you'll go." That was expected. That's part of what it meant to be a man—to go stand on the line, to go and defend. To confront evil and do something about it.

In Genesis, the charge to guard Eden is certainly a duty. But it is also an invitation: to forge the kind of character that can be a solution to evil. We will have better families, better churches and places of work—a better nation—when we have men with character like that. That's the kind of character that can unlock the promise of the world.

CHAPTER FOUR

A MAN'S PROMISE

In college I took up rowing, largely by accident. On the first day of the fall quarter, freshman year, I was making my way from my dormitory to the university's main quadrangle for what they called freshman convocation. As I was walking along, an older student stopped me. *You look like you played sports in high school*, he said. I said I had, football. *Have you ever rowed?* he asked. I had no idea what he meant. I told him I'd used oars in a boat before, if that was what he was getting at. But he meant competitive rowing, in one of those long, thin boats they call shells that can hold as many as eight people. He said the college was holding tryouts for the men's rowing team the next day. He handed me a flyer and invited me to come along.

I did, out of curiosity but also because in the transition from high school to college I was feeling a certain sense of loss. I had enjoyed playing sports as a kid and in high school—it was how I belonged, and I was finding the prospect of being suddenly without a team as I began my first year away from home a strange and difficult transition to manage. I ended up joining the rowing team, though my stint was brief and uneventful. I landed a spot on the freshman boat but dislocated my left shoulder half a year in. By the time I was cleared to get back in the boat, I had settled in to my new surroundings at school—I had joined a Bible study group and made new friends and found my tribe, so to speak. I decided that perhaps I wanted to do something with my time other than rowing twice a day. So I hung up my oar.

I was glad for the experience, though, especially when I found myself back on the water a few years later, coaching a rowing team. This was in the year between college and law school when I was in England on a teaching fellowship. As part of the arrangement, the school where I taught asked the fellows to help manage a sport or activity for the students. The school didn't play football ("American football," as they called it) or baseball or other sports I knew well or had played, with one exception. They had a very active rowing team.

And thus began my coaching career. I ended up coaching the "third eight," which meant the third boat on the depth chart, basically the junior varsity team, composed of what we would call sophomores and juniors. We practiced on the water most afternoons and lifted weights twice a week.

I loved coaching. If it is possible, I think I loved it more even than playing. Some of the most important people in my life were coaches, and I felt connected to them when I coached. There was Tom Hayes, who coached me in middle school. He arrived just as my eighth-grade year began. I had never had somebody believe in me like he believed in me, aside from my parents. He was also my principal, and he used to take me along with him on his rounds through the school, visiting classrooms, picking up litter in the halls, fixing leaky windows, doing whatever needed to be done. He was like my grandpa in that way, teaching by doing, by demonstrating. He demonstrated to me that there was no task beneath his dignity. He was a gruff man, direct, sometimes stern, but he knew how to inspire. *I won't live to see you do all that you will do in this life*, he once told me, *but I know you'll change the world*. He saw what was good in me, what was possible, things I didn't see, and helped call them out.

There was Tony Severino, my high school football coach. Coach Sev, as his players called him, was already a legend when I arrived. His teams had won a spectacular number of state football championships; he had been a collegiate player at Kansas State himself. He carried himself like Sylvester Stallone and had what we boys thought was the trace of an Italian accent. Or maybe it was just his manner. In any event, it worked. He was an excellent fundamentals coach, but his greatest talent was the power to project belief. His players became what he believed they could be. I was a lineman in high school and not fast, not remotely. Coach Sev believed I could be fast. As a team, we used to run repeat forty-yard dashes in the basement hallway of the school during the winter, when it was damp and cold outside, and I can still hear Coach Sev standing at the end of the hall, stopwatch in hand, urging me on, faster, faster. The more he urged, the faster I ran.

These men changed my life, and I wanted to do that for my players, my rowers. I studied coaching videos on rowing technique and read every manual I could get my hands on. But I wasn't kidding myself, I knew that they wouldn't succeed because of my technical prowess. I had rowed competitively for only a short time, and I had never coached before. What I really wanted to give them was belief.

That was easier said than done. The thing about coaching is it's always easier on paper. On the whiteboard. In theory. When you're drawing up race plans or workout routines, it all works beautifully. Then you try to make it work with your players, who are high school students, and therefore often some version of hungry, distracted, confused, or uninterested, and things get much harder. I wanted to inspire my rowers and motivate them, like Tom Hayes and Tony Severino had motivated me, but as the months wore on, I wasn't having much luck. Instead, I could feel my irritation building. Why wouldn't they do as I said? Why weren't they getting better? And: What does this say about me as a coach? I began to wonder if any of it was worth my time.

Then one morning in the weight room, while I was barking commands at somebody on the bench press, one of the youngest rowers over in a different part of the room lost his balance while trying to perform the back squat and nearly toppled over. An older teammate, I'll call him Michael, grabbed him just in time. The more significant thing happened next. Michael, who was a strong rower and respected on the team, but generally quiet and detached, suddenly engaged. He looked at his younger teammate square in the eye and offered him a few brief words of encouragement. I watched him do it. It wasn't long, it wasn't a speech. But it was real. And I saw in that moment things I hadn't previously seen in Michael: that he was reliable in the clutch, that he had a heart to encourage others, and that his peers not only respected him but responded to him. With a few words, Michael wiped away any embarrassment his younger teammate may have felt and set things back in order. Watching him was like catching a glimpse of his future self, the man he could become.

And I knew that having glimpsed it, having seen the possibility in him, I was obligated to serve it. I was obligated to serve what he might be. I finally realized then what I was there for. If I wanted to lead these young rowers and help them achieve what they could, I had to get myself out of the way and serve the best possibilities in them. I had to stop thinking about my record and start serving what they might become.

That morning was an inflection point for us as a team, a moment that marked a quiet but powerful shift, not least because it shifted me. That morning helped me understand what I had in truth already been taught, if only I had had the sense to recognize it: that real character culminates in servanthood. After that, the rowers coalesced. They began to trust each other. And they went on to win several medals in competition (perhaps despite their coach).

Of course, mention "men," "leadership," and "power" in the same breath these days and you are liable to be swiftly denounced as a misogynist or worse. The Epicurean left sees little to praise in male leaders. On the contrary, liberal voices portray masculine power as a disease in need of curing, as a particularly virulent social toxin. To the extent they believe in something like the Fall, this is their version of it: masculinity is responsible. Their message to men is, consequently, shut up. Be passive. Abjure leadership. Work your office job, consume lots of stuff, and do as your betters instruct. Many men—too many—have complied, and America is the worse for it.

The Bible issues men a different set of directives. In the face of Adam's failure, in the face of evil and human weakness, the Bible insists man's promise remains. God's answer is not to abandon his commission to men or to do away with manhood. His solution is to retrieve true manhood, to redeem it. He passes on Adam's task to other men (and finally, the Man), and calls those men to live differently than Adam did. His solution, in short, is to call men toward the kind of character that embraces servanthood, to the subordination of self. That is the kind of character that will sustain true leadership. That is the path out of the darkness. That is the way each man must trod, the Bible says, toward a new Eden.

THE CASE AGAINST MASCULINITY

The Bible's view is not the conventional wisdom today, to say the very least. Plenty of people today argue that male leadership of any variety is the solution to nothing; it is the problem, society's original sin. These are the opponents of masculinity, and their voices have come to define an age.

In the academy, masculinity and oppression have been practically synonymous terms for years. This runs back to the liberal focus on social oppression as the source of evil in the world. Rousseau hinted at this, as we've seen. Most modern-day liberals are even more decisively influenced by Karl Marx. Marx was a dedicated materialist, following Epicurus. He believed material conditions determined man's beliefs and behavior. Sin, if we can call it that (and Marx did not), was a product of social forces. In Marx's case, the relevant social forces were economic, which he argued oppressed the working class.

By the 1900s, a newer brand of Marxists concluded Marx was only half right. Western society was structurally oppressive, they agreed, but the truer source of that oppression was culture, not economics. Modern people needed to be liberated from outdated cultural ideas and systems, especially those connected with Christianity. That's where manhood comes in.

By the 1960s, these new, cultural Marxists contended that the revolution the Western world needed would come by throwing off the sexual conventions of the past. They settled into American universities and began to take particular aim at manhood. Masculinity was just another oppressive social system, they said, a "patriarchy" that imposed male dominance through the rules of public discourse (which men allegedly set), social expectations (which men allegedly controlled), and family traditions (like male leadership in the home), all enforced by domestic abuse and other violence.[1] This "patriarchy" came with a demanding set of ideals for men to live up to, which the new Marxists and other critics said suffocated men themselves and caused them mental anguish.

But the revolutionaries eventually decided the problem wasn't just the system that produced masculinity. The problem was men. The American Psychological Association rehearsed precisely this view in

2019, opining that "traditional masculinity—marked by stoicism, competitiveness, dominance and aggression—is, on the whole, harmful."[2] The organization offered that "conforming to traditional masculinity ideology"—*ideology*, since manhood is supposedly nothing more than a social construct—can "negatively influence mental health and physical health."[3]

Other academics and expert elites added that masculinity is naturally violent and domineering. "Violence is, of course, itself regarded as a badge of masculinity," wrote one law professor, in a typical refrain.[4] And then there was the most serious charge of all, for those of an Epicurean persuasion: that traditional masculinity limited the personal choices of those influenced by it. It impinged on the treasured Epicurean right to define your own truth. "[T]raditional masculinity" has "oppressed girls and women and limited the identity construction of all boys and men," said one academic.[5] "Little wonder that masculinity is now rarely seen without its adjectives: toxic and fragile," said another, who suggested it is "reasonable to conclude that men are trash."[6]

And there you have it. To be a man is, of itself, to contribute to the supposed tyranny of the social order. It is to be trash. An entire generation of cultural Marxists and other liberals have drummed this theme into the head of anyone who will listen. Which turned out to be a lot of people. The lesson has been rehashed and recycled for decades by the media, Hollywood, and various politicians. You will find it now even in elementary schools, where proposed curricula teach the youngest children that masculinity is shameful and oppressive.[7] It has become the conventional wisdom of our Epicurean age: manhood is toxic.

THE POTENTIAL OF LEADERSHIP

Genesis says unapologetically, by contrast, that God made men for good and he meant them to lead. Genesis says God directed man—and woman—to *rule*, to "have dominion over the fish of the sea and over the birds of the heavens and over every living thing that moves on the earth" (Genesis 1:28).

The charge to lead or rule is the crowning command to humanity. It is the first thing God speaks to them on the first day they are created. And while modern liberalism says men bring dysfunction, Genesis says God intends man's leadership to bring life. Eden itself is a symbol of what that leadership can do, what it can amount to. But first a man must have the character to sustain it.

Adam did not. God called Adam to a kind of character devoted to service, and a kind of leadership to match. Adam's power, like Adam's life, was to be devoted to serving the work of the garden—protecting his family, expanding the temple, bettering the world, worshipping God. Adam elected instead to serve himself. He chose the path of self-gratification, self-importance. As a result, Adam abdicated leadership and the responsibility that attends it. Everywhere in our society we see men doing the same. They are leaving their families or failing to start them, prioritizing their entertainment or pleasure, withdrawing from responsibility. The result is the same for us as it was for Adam in the garden: disorder, decline, dysfunction.

Adam's choice, like that of many men today, was less a form of initiative than the abandonment of it. The snake offered Adam something for nothing—self-promotion without duty, self-advancement without service or obedience—and Adam took it. Most self-seeking amounts to the same sort of abdication. Putting your wants and pleasures first is almost always a form of withdrawal; it means abandoning the power to help others. Self-indulgence makes a man more passive.

The irony is, today's Epicureans offer men substantially the same bargain as the serpent. They tell men to forgo leadership responsibility and to pursue self instead. Take no initiative, they counsel, do not aspire to anything—but feel free to spend as much time as possible on screens or reconsidering your pronouns. It is a fool's bargain, as it was for Adam. And it is not the answer to the chaos and cruelty that afflict the world. It is the cause. The answer is for men to do what Adam was not willing to do, to subordinate their self-interest and turn toward God and others to serve. The key to true leadership, the Bible maintains, the leadership that brings life, that turns a wilderness into a garden, is self-giving. It is the character of servanthood.

I have a custom of reading to my two boys each night before they go to sleep. I started this ritual when my older boy, Elijah, was four or five, as an opportunity for the two of us to do something special together at the close of each day. I suppose I was trying to pass down to him something cherished from my childhood. Some of my earliest childhood memories are of my mother reading to my sister and me at night before bed. The stories she read to us—*The Chronicles of Narnia* particularly stand out; she must have read the series to us at least half a dozen times—helped feed my imagination and shape it. I wanted the same for my sons. So Elijah and I started reading together each night, first picture books when he was quite small, and by stages graduating to longer stories with chapters. His brother Blaise, my younger son, joined the nightly reading when he was old enough, and now we read all together. They clamor for it each night. There are evenings when I will be kept late at the Capitol and will quietly climb the stairs to their rooms well after their bedtimes, trying not to wake them, only to hear their voices call out, "Daddy, read!" as I walk by. And so I will.

These evening sessions have inspired me to retrieve old childhood favorites from jumbled boxes and the odd bookshelf, and not long ago I came across a small volume about King Arthur and his knights. I tried this out on the boys, who loved it. By now we have read about Camelot, Arthur, Merlin, and Lancelot and their deeds of derring-do. Which returns me to Genesis. The Arthur legend revolves around the relationship of knights and kings, of servant-warriors who pledge themselves to a liege lord. Even Arthur is a servant, a vassal, in a sense: he is to serve Camelot and God. And when he forgets that in the later cycle of legends, his reign breaks, and Camelot with it.

Man has a need to serve something other than himself. Psychologists counsel that to achieve healthy personal integration, a man's ego needs an object outside itself to venerate, a will or a cause to pledge itself to. Otherwise the ego dominates, and a man becomes a petty tyrant to those in his life.[8]

The Greeks and the Romans had their version of the same insight. True liberty, they said, begins with self-mastery, with the subordination of self. Plato famously pictured the soul as a chariot pulled by twin horses. The horses were man's base appetites (for sex and money, say) and his spiritedness (his higher passions for honor and glory). Each had its place. Each was necessary for the forward motion—the life—of the soul. But the passions of man's life required direction. For Plato and the ancients, that direction was to be found in the great order of nature, the eternal law of the universe that gave a man his identity and his purpose. Man must arrange his soul according to that permanent order, Plato said, in order truly to live—and in order to be free. Give the passions rein and the chariot would be pulled every which way, ending up nowhere—or worse, overturned. To live that way was to be enslaved to a disordered soul. Unity of soul, on the other hand, brought true freedom—the power to direct your life. And that began with submission to something greater than oneself.[9]

To be clear, the Bible rebukes men who would use their power in life to dominate, demean, or belittle. That is not the way of manhood as Genesis portrays it. The Bible's response to the dangers of power is to demand men subordinate themselves to the sacred purpose for which power exists, to God and his way.

Our Epicurean age balks at that, of course. Even as today's liberals decry male leadership and denounce men as trash, they insist on the sanctity of personal choice. The self must be sovereign! To submit to anything—any rule or order you have not created for yourself—is, they say, the very definition of submitting to tyranny.

The Bible contends the opposite. The Bible says servanthood is true power and true freedom. Only when Adam had subordinated himself to God could Adam be trusted. Only if he chose to serve could his rule bring life.

Adam did not. And the world suffered. That's where we come in.

THE JOURNEY OF MANHOOD

The Adam story is the story of a man and his possibilities, and also, famously, the story of a man who fails. That may well be its best-known part, Adam and Eve cast out of the garden, the way back barred by an angel with a flaming sword. Karl Marx once complained that the biblical account of man's meaning was itself a failure for just this reason. Ending as it does, he said, the story elides what it should explain: the presence of evil and the solution to it.[10]

But Marx didn't read closely enough. He did not understand the true claims of the Bible. Genesis is not content to tell a story about the past. The Bible tells us about the here and now. It carries a message for our lives, as men today. And that message is, in sum, that the Adam project does not end with Adam. It continues with us. The Adam mission is what manhood is about. God is still looking for men to serve, to lead, to resist evil, and to build his world into the temple it was meant to be.

And that mission begins with a man's soul. A man who would take up his vocation and realize his promise must forge his soul and shape his character: he must become something more. The Romans were right all those years ago. Manhood is something attained, not born to. It is an attainment of character.

The mission of manhood as the Bible defines it will, if we are willing to shoulder it, redefine us. It will reshape and reorient our lives. It will press us into new roles and responsibilities and demand that we grow in virtue, in humility, in service. It will be the greatest adventure of our lives, and the greatest challenge.

How are we to do it? We must read on.

After Adam leaves Eden, the Bible goes on telling the Adam story across other lives and later histories. It tells of men called to take up Adam's mission, as we are. And it uses each of these later stories, this Adam cycle, if you like, to reveal new and deeper dimensions of the Adam project, to disclose other elements, one by one, of what the character of manhood truly means.

If we would take our place in this drama, we must follow the story and learn. From men like Abraham and Joshua, David and Solomon, we learn more concretely what it is to be God's servant, to do what Adam was meant to do. God charged the first Adam to make the world into a temple. From these later Adams we see what this will truly require. It will mean to order our souls, to find new and better—deeper—ways of living. To be a man as the Bible defines it is to acquire the character of a husband and a father, a warrior and a builder, a priest and a king. These are the roles of the Adam mission. This is the character that defines manhood.

In the pages that follow, I take up each of these qualities and each of these roles in turn, with the aim of learning how to be what the Bible invites men to be—and what that might mean for our lives, our families, and our nation.

This invitation, if we take it, leads to a kind of manhood that is not defensive or strident or anxious about itself, unlike some today, whose defense of manhood sounds shrill and shot through with fear. For those who take this strident tone, manhood involves a kind of rigorous "bro code" that has to be followed in all times and in all places: if you can't drive a forklift, deadlift three hundred pounds, or sleep with the prom queen, you're not a real man. That's a serious mistake. And paradoxically, it's the same message touted by radical postmodern critics of masculinity, who insist that maleness and femaleness are just "performances" tied to the standards of a specific, time-bound culture.[11]

By contrast, the biblical story teaches that God is *Creator* first and foremost, and so his design for individual men and women is already woven into the fabric of reality. The call to manhood is no more—and no less—than a call for men to realize what they were crafted to be. It is not a summons to conform to some arbitrary social law or other, but rather a call to character.

There is a paradox here. Adam's failure in the garden is what launches the story forward, out of Eden and on toward us. And yet each of the later Adam-like figures we will encounter fails too, in one respect or another. None can fully shoulder his mandate. None is perfect. Maybe that is a warning. Or maybe it is cause for hope.

As the Bible tells and retells the Adam story, certain constants emerge: there will be hardship and trial, setbacks and pain. But perfection, in the end, is not the point. To be a man is to realize that we are, each of us, imperfect. We are wounded and flawed. We are dependent for our significance on something outside ourselves. That is no cause for shame. For in recognizing our need, we do what Adam would not. We embrace humility, we accept the call to serve, and we open our lives to the possibility of transformation. The success of a man's life turns out to depend not finally on the man. It depends on the God he serves.

PART II

PART II

CHAPTER FIVE

HUSBAND

My grandparents, Harold and Mabel, moved from their farmhouse to town just about the time my parents were married. Town was Scandia, Kansas, so named for the Scandinavian immigrants who had settled it a century and a half prior. It had three or four hundred residents. Cornfields came right up to the edges of the yards. My grandparents' house was a white, two-story "I-house," as historians call them, with second-floor gables and a deep front porch, a style popular with farmers at the turn of the last century and named for its prevalence in farming states like Iowa, Indiana, and Illinois. The house had belonged to my grandpa's sister before him and to other family members before her. It's still there.

I loved that house. I spent many a day there in my childhood, many a summer day and holiday and birthday. It was not overly large—the front door opened into a dining room, with a small sitting room or "parlor," as my grandmother called it, to the left, where she put her best furniture and treasured items. In the original house, there was a kitchen behind the dining room with a sewing and laundry room connected to that. Then three modest bedrooms directly overhead, upstairs. And that was it. But it was a gracious home and always seemed big to me, never more so than when filled up with family.

My grandparents had six children, my mother being the youngest, and fifteen grandchildren—so the family all gathered did tend to fill up a place. On holidays and like occasions, people would cram in every which way. I remember one birthday in particular, one of my own. We children sat at folding tables in the sewing room (literally—my grandmother had a sewing machine in the corner), with adults at the kitchen table and in the dining room and any other place they could find a spot. Grandma had made chicken noodle soup, her locally famous dish and my favorite, and mashed potatoes, and a birthday cake of some variety and a pound cake and homemade rye bread, which was another of her signature items, being Scandinavian. Presents were not a great feature on that side of the family, and I don't remember that we opened any, but the family sat together long and visited and told stories of the old days. And there was the singing of "Happy Birthday," and later, as the adults sat and talked, I coaxed the younger grandchildren upstairs to play a game of "lights out" hide-and-seek, which led to all sorts of hooting and hollering that the adults could hear because they were sitting in the rooms directly beneath us and which earned me a reprimand, since the game was expressly forbidden by my grandmother. (She would open the door to the stairs and call up, "Josh! Enough!"—not even bothering to ask if anyone else was responsible for the hoo-ha. She knew.)

And there were Christmases with a tree in the parlor and a fire on the hearth and summers of chasing fireflies in the front yard while the adults watched from the porch. The kitchen in that house always smelled of coffee, whatever the season, because both my grandparents drank it in the morning and my grandmother sometimes all day, and to this day when I smell it I think of that kitchen and of them. As for the house itself, I associate it with home more than any other single place of my childhood, perhaps strangely, given it was not the house that I grew up in. But it was for me a never-failing haven of joy and happy memory, a spiritual outpost in my life much as it was a physical outpost on the prairie, tucked there among the fields.

What I would only later come to appreciate is that the house and the life it harbored represented what my grandparents Harold and Mabel had built together. By the time I came along, the next-to-last of their grandchildren, they were already nearly seventy, and their life together had been long. The home I loved so much and the times we had there were really a reflection of their marriage, not that it was perfect or in some way ideal—I actually know very little of my grandparents' marriage—but the simple fact that it *was*, and that they, together, endured. If their home seemed to me like a kind of Eden, that's because in a very real sense it was.

The Bible, that taboo book for today's elites, makes a claim about marriage many of those same elites cannot understand: that it comes with a promise, the promise of Eden. In fact, the way out of the darkness Adam helps unleash in the world comes through marriage—and then children: home and family. When God calls a new Adam in the Genesis stories, to help undo what Adam did, he calls him to be a husband.

This new Adam is Abraham, the famous Father of Many Nations. And what his story reveals is that if a man wants to fulfill his mission and meet his purpose as a man, he will have to give himself away. He will have to learn to open his life to another and bind his fate to hers; he will have to go outside himself and beyond his desires, his wants, his interests. He will have to learn that his true self is found only in relationship with another. He will have to learn to acquire the character of a husband.

Not all men become husbands in fact. But all men can learn a husband's virtues. And to use the imagery of the Bible, if a man wants to subdue the darkness, if he wants to build the temple, he must.

There was a time when this message was widely affirmed by our culture. Marriage was viewed as foundational to a good life. Men expected to be husbands and were proud to be. Today our Epicurean age teaches a different set of lessons—against commitment, against sacrifice, against the idea that one can truly become oneself only by giving oneself to another. Marriage is in decline in America, and an increasingly sharp one. More and more men are delaying marriage or opting out altogether. As a result, America has more men who never really grow up, men who never see beyond themselves. This fact lies at the root of our present social troubles. The Adam stories summon men to a different path, to a manhood of sacrifice and self-giving, the manhood of a husband.

THE REDEMPTION OF MARRIAGE

On the Genesis telling, after Adam and Eve get ejected from Eden, the world is left in a sorry state. The creation that was meant to be made a temple is now in chaos. The light of Eden is extinguished. Darkness spreads, men conspire, evil abounds. This is the world as we know it, the world we inherit, all of us, from Adam. The question is what to do about it.

Genesis answers that query, strangely enough, by turning to a man named Abraham (or Abram, as he is first called), a nomadic herder who appears in the story from—nowhere. He is a nobody, a nonentity, an unimportant individual with nothing to commend him until God chooses him suddenly out of thin air and thrusts him into the story, center stage. Abraham is advanced in years when we meet him— seventy-five—married, but still living with his father's family. We don't know much about him otherwise, besides this seminal fact: he is childless. Genesis underlines that point, that Abraham has no heir, which is perhaps why he is still loitering about his father's tents at his age.

Without an heir, without a son, he has no future of his own to look to. The family inheritance will go to another kinsman when he dies, the family name will continue via another man, and Abraham's life will not be remembered. The only immortality the ancient pagans expected—family, lineage—will be denied him.

But God changes Abraham's trajectory when he selects him without warning and announces he will give him a future, a purpose: a family—and through that family, will transform the world. Abraham's story begins like this.

> Now the LORD said to Abram, "Go from your country and your kindred and your father's house to the land that I will show you. And I will make of you a great nation, and I will bless you and make your name great...and in you all the families of the earth shall be blessed." (Genesis 12:1–3)

God's announcement works a momentous shift in Abram's life, signified by a new name, a marker in the ancient world of a new destiny. Abram will become Abraham and leave his father's house to venture out on his own, to a new land God will reveal to him. He will recover Adam's mission of making the world a temple. Genesis immediately puts Abraham and Adam in parallel in this regard. God created Adam from earth, from nothing; he chooses Abraham from nothing. He took Adam to the land of Eden; God tells Abraham to leave his father and go "to the land that I will show you"—a new Eden.[1]

And for what purpose? To conquer the darkness. To renew the world. To undo what Adam did and get God's grand purposes for the world back on track. God had directed Adam to "subdue" creation, to expand the garden temple into all the earth. Adam unleashed evil instead. Now creation needs more than completing. Creation needs rescuing. God promises Abraham that through him and his family, that rescue and renewal will come. The world will be "blessed"—made right, made whole. Made into a temple, one might say.

Just so we don't miss the point, Genesis reports that the first thing Abraham does upon reaching the new land where God sends him is to build an altar—a temple in miniature—and beside an oak tree, a deliberate echo of Eden's arboreal imagery.[2] The Adam project begins anew. Through Abraham and his family, the chaos of the world will, in some form or fashion the Bible does not yet fully flesh out, be subdued, and the creation made what it could be.

And the starting point for all of this will be Abraham's marriage. "And God said to Abraham, 'As for Sarai your wife, . . . I will bless her, and moreover, I will give you a son by her.'"[3] By her, you notice. The promise to Abraham of a future, of a family, of meaning and purpose, does not come to him isolated and alone. It comes to him with his wife. God will begin to heal the evil Adam wrought and bring his creation toward fulfillment by calling Abraham *as a husband*.

We are conditioned by our Epicurean culture to consider our lives as solitary endeavors, and manhood, when we are allowed to speak of it at all, as a solitary pursuit. American writers have been preaching that gospel to men at least since Henry David Thoreau retreated to Walden Pond. That is not the Genesis perspective. A man's mission is not, it turns out, a solitary exercise. A man cannot be who he is meant to be on his own. And that is because his purpose is not ultimately about him. He must give himself away to become a man. He must lay down his life to discover what it truly means. The road to a new Eden begins with self-giving.

MAN FOR OTHERS

The Epicurean ethic that suffuses our culture insists just the opposite, that a man's life is his own creation, or should be. Here is the basic message, repeated a thousand different ways through a thousand media—

television, film, school curricula: Your identity is something you construct, alone, by yourself and for yourself. Your life is for you, your identity is made by you, and the only way to be an individual is to put the pieces of your life and identity together exactly as you want them, according to your own lights. That is how you become authentic and free. Or so the story goes.

At precisely the same time, today's Epicureans tell men they are, as men, the biggest threat our society faces; that the male longing for adventure and heroism is dangerous; that a man's desire for accomplishment is oppressive; that masculinity is toxic, inherently. So whatever identity men construct and life they make had better take all that into account; it had better screen out the objectionable elements of masculinity, which are, by the liberals' reckoning, most of them. This mixed message puts young men, especially, in a bind: they are supposed to fashion an identity entirely of their own choosing in order to be authentic, but leave out the features that have defined men for millennia. Good luck with that. No wonder young men feel bewildered.

Every action produces an opposite and equal reaction, and there is accordingly a male-specific version of the Epicurean myth that appears to rebel against the left's denigration of men. This version portrays marriage and children as dead ends, and society more generally as corrupted by female influence. The film *Fight Club* remains tremendously popular for delivering just this message. "Bourgeois" norms are poisonous, it says, emasculating. They serve only to feminize a man and destroy his soul. A man can truly be a man only by escaping society and his duties to other people, the things that tie him down.

Some men go further still and embrace with glee the left's claim that real masculinity is founded on exploitation. They revel in the idea. The case of Andrew Tate, a social media provocateur and self-styled "success coach" for men, comes to mind. Tate's idea of success apparently involved sleeping with as many women as possible, berating them, abusing them, and celebrating it all as manly, as "freedom." As reported by the *New York Post*, Tate "advised his followers to 'slap, slap, grab, choke' women in the bedroom." He counseled that "if a man in a relationship has sex with someone else, it's 'not cheating, it's exercise.'" Meanwhile, if accused of cheating himself, "It's bang out the machete, boom in her face and grip her by the neck," Tate claimed.[4]

Every man who has been in a locker room recognizes the type. The fake bravado, the endless boasting. Those aren't the words of a man; those are the words of a child pretending to be a man he thinks someone will like or respect. And his posturing is far less rebellious than Tate would like to imagine. What Tate appears to prize above all is just what the Epicureans say he should, the ability to do whatever he wants. Asked why he moved to Eastern Europe, he reportedly said, "I like the idea of just being able to do what I want. I like being free."[5] Of course. Tate and company do not challenge the Epicurean line; they merely rehearse it in a nihilistic, misogynist key. They still counsel self-indulgence as the path to fulfillment. They still put self at the center of the universe. There is no real strength, no discipline or self-command, there. No manhood. As turned out to be the case with Andrew Tate, incidentally. Police in Romania arrested him in December 2022 on charges of human trafficking: he was making a fortune, reportedly, by abusing those weaker than himself.[6] What a joke.

The Abraham narrative presents the true alternative. It says a man's purpose is not found in chasing pleasure. It is found in giving himself away. The notion of the self-creating, self-sustaining individual is the foundational myth of the Epicurean idea, but it is, finally, a myth. Men are not born to live alone or for themselves only. We are not most ourselves when holed up alone playing video games. Men are born to give their lives to others, and they discover who they are when they do. Marriage calls men to this kind of character.

Why is this the case? Because no man is complete in himself. We all know this, if we are honest. We feel it from almost the moment we are self-aware. The Bible addresses it explicitly in the story of Adam and the creation of Eve. God had brought the animals of Eden to Adam to be named, but among them Adam finds no one who can help him, the story says. The point is, Adam *needs* help. He cannot accomplish his task, his life's work, on his own. He cannot even be himself on his own. He, like all men, like all people, requires another person to activate his potential and help him realize who he is, and could be. He needs another to teach him things he does not know, to challenge him to notice what he does not see, someone to appreciate his abilities and help address his shortcomings. He needs another to listen to him and help him reflect. And he needs someone who will ask all the same from him. He needs culture, and family, and tradition—and ultimately, at the apex of these many and varied human relationships, he needs a wife. So God places Adam into a deep sleep and fashions Eve from a rib God takes from Adam's side. Eve and Adam are made to fit together.

What does this mean for men today? It means that contrary to the voices of our age, a man is built for commitment. He is built to open himself to others and to pursue life with them, to sacrifice, to curb his own self-interest, to journey out from himself. That is what we call love. Love is not an adventure in self-expression; it is an adventure in self-giving. In love, we do just the opposite of what the Epicurean myth counsels: we surrender control over our own lives to someone else. We abandon our focus on self and focus instead on someone else. More than that even, we make that other person part of who we are: we come to be defined by them, by their interests and passions, by their callings and gifts, and not simply by our own choices. Marriage exemplifies this pattern in the relationship between husband and wife. By giving himself, by breaking open the chalice of his life, a man finds what is inside him. That is the point.

Of course, to do this is to make yourself vulnerable, which is one reason the modern Epicureans so strenuously object to seeing our identity as bound up in self-sacrifice and self-giving. Other people make demands on us that we may not, strictly speaking, choose, just as our families and traditions make demands on us we have not specifically chosen. And there's the fact that to love another person and commit to her is to open your life to pain, hardship, and misunderstanding. That happened to Abraham (a good bit of which he caused). It happens to every man. But it is also the path to building something that lasts, the path to finding out who you truly are. It is what being a husband is. It is the path to manhood.

I first began to sense this in my own life in the years after I finished school. I moved around a fair bit in my twenties, as many people do—off to college, then a year teaching high school and coaching, then to law school, and each of these in different places. Having traveled little as a kid, I enjoyed moving, the adventure of it; I liked meeting new people and seeing different parts of the country. I won't say that I found it easy, however. As someone who grew up in a rural place, I had—and still have—a strong preference for home, for family and the people I know face-to-face. Moving was a challenge, and I think that's part of why I embraced it. I wanted to see if I could do it, if I could make it far from home. I found I could.

But as my twenties wore on, I noticed the thrill of new vistas diminishing. Packing the suitcase for another move may have been exciting in one way, thinking on the new possibilities waiting in the great unknown, but it became wearying in another sense. I began to wish for someone to come along with me on the journey. I felt the ache of loneliness. I had my family, of course, to whom I relayed my experiences, and the friends I'd made along the way. But these people didn't come *with* me, not every step. They cheered me, supported me, encouraged me—but I was, in a profound sense, alone. I was out on my own—as I had wanted, to be clear—and yet, somehow, without a home.

I met my wife in my second job out of law school. We both worked at the U.S. Supreme Court as clerks for a year, which means we acted as legal assistants to a Supreme Court justice, more or less. The court building was being renovated that year, and we ended up sharing an office, and that is how we got to know one another properly. We had attended the same law school but graduated in different years and knew each other only in passing. Now we were office mates and spent many an hour together.

The thing I noticed about Erin almost immediately was how much she seemed like someone I had known all my life. She was a rancher's daughter from rural New Mexico but could have been, or so it seemed to me, from my hometown in rural Missouri. In those early days, we talked across our desks about our small towns and books we liked and movies we watched and our interests in the law. I found her easy to talk to; in fact, in fairly short order I found myself going to her to share new ideas I had (to improve the Supreme Court! to change the country!) or to retell a funny story or talk out something I had read—the kinds of things I usually reserved for family.

And then one day it struck me, as we were standing around the small kitchen attached to our boss's office, getting ready to take plates and other things out to our fellow clerks for lunch—a sort of domestic scene, unintentionally, like a husband and wife standing in the kitchen together. I realized that being with Erin felt somehow like being at my grandparents' house in Kansas, filled up with family. Being with her felt like *home*. And I knew then, quite a long time before I would actually ask her, that I wanted to marry her. And I sensed then, though it would take me longer still to understand it, something more of what the Abraham story says: that home is not a place one can get to on one's own. Home—belonging, fulfillment—is found only with another. Home is a promise given to a husband, made possible only by a wife.

So: God tells Abraham it is as a *husband* he will bless him—that the promise of son, family, and a new Eden is one he will bestow on Abraham and Sarah's marriage, on their life together. Men are meant to be husbands, to form the virtues of a husband in their souls. The question becomes, how do we do it?

To start, you have to be willing to put yourself at risk.

CHEAP SEX

Married life will expose a man to hardship. You can be certain of it. Seasons of difficulty and episodes of pain and family conflict will arise. It happens in every marriage. To have the character of a husband, a man must abandon safety. He must put himself at risk.

There's a passage in Abraham's story about him and Sarah going down to Egypt. Famine strikes. Abraham confronts a choice: he can face the danger, come what may, or retreat to a safer space. He chooses safety. He leaves the land God gave him and takes Sarah and the rest of his company to Pharaoh. Once there, he pretends to be Sarah's brother rather than her husband, so that any Egyptian dignitary who might desire Sarah will leave him be. Abraham no doubt thought this gambit to be very clever. In fact, it was very pathetic. In a swift series of decisions designed to keep himself safe, Abraham managed to expose first his wife and then the rest of his clan to acute danger. God must eventually intervene to rescue Sarah, doing what Abraham should have done from the first.

There are many kinds of false security to which men retreat, many Egypts to which they flee. One that is particularly, rampantly popular with men today is pornography. This is true not least because it is rampantly available, on a scale as never before. Many of the most popular websites in the world are, by an order of magnitude, porn sites.[7] Porn traffic drives the internet: porn searches are by far some of the most popular search terms, in America and worldwide.[8] The porn industry is a multibillion-dollar business. To be sure, porn has been around in one form or another from time immemorial, but not like this, at the click of a button, at the tap of a phone, available to be watched or downloaded or streamed anywhere, at any moment, with movie-like quality. As sociologist Mark Regnerus has remarked, "Men can see more flesh in five minutes than their great-grandfathers could in a lifetime."[9] He is not exaggerating.

The result of this newfound availability is a dramatic increase in usage. By the numbers, 43 percent of American men report watching pornography in the past week. If you limit the data to men aged eighteen to thirty-nine, the number climbs to 46 percent. And fully 24 percent of men report their last porn usage as "today" or "yesterday"—that is, within the last twenty-four hours. Those averages, by the way, include both unmarried and married men.[10]

Porn use persists across age groups. The popular notion that most porn is consumed by teenage boys is simply false. The research shows porn use in fact peaks for men in their late twenties, nearly half of whom say they've watched porn in the last week, and remains at about that level until approximately age forty, when it begins a slow—very slow—decline. Even 30 percent of sixty-year-old men report watching porn at least once in the last seven days.[11]

One effect of this massive, routine consumption of porn is increased sexual addiction, not surprisingly.[12] Another is the frequency with which porn has become a regular feature of dating (or married) relationships—something women must navigate around. (Women's porn usage has risen as well, I should note, but their overall consumption is tiny compared to men's.)[13] Inevitably, many women face the unwelcome prospect of dating a man who has a porn problem.[14] And that's to say nothing of married women who must grapple with their husbands' porn issues.

Then there's this: Major porn consumption encourages some men to forgo the risk of dating and marriage altogether. The porn industry sells its wares as a daring and adventuresome experience, but the research tends to indicate the opposite is true. Men who consume large amounts of porn appear to become less confident in their interactions with women.[15] They become less confident in their physical appearance. They become more self-conscious and insecure.[16] And perhaps as a consequence, some number of them stop dating entirely.

In a recent survey of men under age fifty, none of whom had ever been married, 29 percent reported they had not been on a single date in the last year. Among that cohort, pornography use was significant. Thirty-three percent said they had used it in the last day. Fifty-three percent said they had consumed it within the last four. Mark Regnerus, the sociologist, concludes from these numbers that men's frequent use of porn may well be undermining their willingness to try a relationship, to take a risk, to put themselves out there on the dating market with a real-life woman.[17] And it stands to reason, in a certain sense: Relationships are difficult. They are risky. Porn, by contrast, is easy and cheap. It's safe.

I suspect most men, especially younger unmarried men, think of porn the way the industry sells it—as an example of machismo and strength. This is hardly true. Nothing could be more timid or weak, more sterile, than a man, alone, staring at porn on his phone. There is no risk involved, no exposure to hardship or danger in the least. It is, as Regnerus calls it, cheap sex. And it cheapens everyone involved.

Interestingly, staring at porn is one of the few male-dominated activities of which the present-day Epicureans gladly approve. They are happy for men to look at porn all the day long. They defend porn vehemently, religiously, and mock anyone who suggests men should do something else with their time. It makes sense, when you consider it. The modern Epicurean vision embraces self, pleasure—and androgyny. And that is what porn leads to: men as androgynous consumers, beyond manhood, beyond sex even, staring at screens, alone. It is no coincidence that even as men's porn consumption explodes, family formation is collapsing. American men are simply having less sex, in favor of the cheap, virtual substitute.[18] The problem is, men like that aren't really men at all. They are easy to control and order about, focused as they are on their whims and personal safety. Entertain them with bread and circuses, and they do as they are told.

On the other hand: Say no to yourself, discipline your passions, and you begin to develop sterner character. That's what a husband does. And if you are looking for a place to develop the qualities of a husband, a testing ground, ditching porn is a good place to start. Porn is a retreat, like Abraham in Egypt, to which men flee in times of trouble or hardship to avoid real challenges. Making your girlfriend or wife accommodate your porn use is not much different, really, than Abraham asking Sarah to lie about their marriage. In both cases, it's about a man protecting himself and seeking his personal satisfaction to the detriment of others.

Conversely, there is a nobility to be won in rejecting porn, and personal confidence, too. The data shows that men who view porn regularly are less satisfied with their dating partners and less satisfied with their sexual relationships; indeed, it shows they are less satisfied with life in general.[19] Regnerus noted, in his research, a pronounced ennui or apathy associated with significant porn consumption. It deadens.[20] Who wouldn't want something better than that?

But perhaps the greatest reward is one of character. It comes in knowing that you are a man who can abandon security, who is willing to face difficulty, especially for the benefit of someone else. The kind of man who can live for others is the kind of man who can also stand up for himself and what he believes. That's the kind of man America needs. That's the manhood of a husband.

VOW

What else must a man do to acquire the character of a husband, to become a man who can receive God's promise of family, home, and Eden? He must be willing to commit, to vow. And having vowed, he must endure.

God asked Abraham to vow, famously, as a condition of receiving God's blessing. "When Abram was ninety-nine years old the LORD appeared to Abram and said to him, 'I am God Almighty; walk before me, and be blameless, that I may make my covenant between me and you, and may multiply you greatly'" (Genesis 17:1–2). A covenant in the ancient world was an agreement between a partner of high status and a servant—a lord and a vassal, if you like—sometimes conveying land, sometimes title.[21] Here it is all of the above: God is inviting Abraham to be his servant in the pattern of Adam, to "walk before him" as Adam was meant to walk with God in the garden. In return, God promised to give Abraham a family that would establish a new Eden, a new temple.

What is the nature of the covenant between God and Abraham? It is all-encompassing. God asks for Abraham to commit his life to God's work and ways. To become God's servant. God in turn promises to go with Abraham—to guide him, to secure his future. The covenant is a binding of one to the other.

Abraham's vow is made to God, but notice that it involves his wife. For at the center of God's covenant with Abraham was a son. Abraham frequently complained to God that he had no heir. "O LORD God, what will you give me, for I continue childless, and the heir of my house is Eliezer of Damascus?"[22] Without an heir, Abraham could not continue his family line. He could not preserve his family name, the only form of immortality he expected. He could not, in short, anticipate a future. Without an heir, his life would be, in the end, meaningless.

God reassures Abraham that he will have a son, and with Sarah. That promise, which God repeats over and over again, is the basis of the vow between Abraham and God. And it throws fresh light on the meaning and significance of the vow Abraham has already made to Sarah.

For a marriage, too, is a covenant—a promise made and a vow taken, only in this case, between equals. Still, like the covenant between lord and servant, the marriage vow binds the parties together. In taking Sarah as his wife, Abraham had pledged his loyalty. In vowing to be her husband, he had pledged his life. God affirms these vows. In fact, God incorporates them into his own covenant with Abraham: God will use Abraham's marriage to deliver God's promised future. He draws Abraham's covenant with Sarah into Abraham's covenant with God, and in so doing binds Abraham in a new way, with a new promise, to his wife.

What are we to learn from this? A husband is a man who can take a vow, who can commit himself, body and soul, to another. This is not so easy to do. To vow, after all, is to risk. That is the very nature of it: vowing means pledging something of value. In the case of Abraham's vow to God, as in the case of his vow to Sarah, that something was his life. All he had. And that required fortitude and determination. It required bravery.

Fewer and fewer men are willing to vow like that. Marriage is in recession in America, and it deepens by the year. The marriage rate in the United States has dropped by 50 percent over the last century, with the sharpest declines coming in the last three decades.[23] As recently as the year 2000, most Americans between the ages of twenty-five and thirty-four were married, or had been: 55 percent of them, to be exact.

Just over a decade later, those numbers had shifted dramatically. By 2014, more than 50 percent of Americans between twenty-four and thirty-five had never been married, and the marriage trend line continued downward.[24] When men do get married, they are waiting longer and longer for it. The median age for marriage in 1970 was twenty-three. By 2021, it was thirty.[25]

Perhaps this is not so surprising. Vowing of the kind marriage requires—putting at risk one's life, one's emotions, one's future—is discouraged in this Epicurean age. Nothing could be more contrary to the Epicurean ethic than to make such an unbounded, unconditional promise to a spouse, to bind your life to hers, before God. But the willingness to commit, to put everything at risk, is central to what a man is. It is why men have long set such store by their word and celebrated as heroes the men who keep it. Vowing is what husbands do.

ENDURE

And having vowed, a husband must endure.

There came a time in Abraham's life when his commitment to his vows ran thin. I've mentioned it already. Years after God first visited him, years after he promised him a son, Abraham still had no heir. So he had a child by another woman, Hagar, and asked God to make that child the promised heir.

This is, in a way, a familiar tale. Abraham's marriage once seemed to carry great promise—the promise of a new and better world, even. But now that promise appears to have faltered. God has promised a son by Sarah, but there is no son. Nothing any longer looks certain. Abraham can't quite see how he will realize the potential of his marriage after all. Maybe you can relate.

Sarah can't see a way through, either. Interestingly, Sarah is the one who suggests seeking a solution elsewhere—beyond their marriage, outside God's promises. Perhaps she was reacting to Abraham's deep disquiet, or perhaps she had reasons of her own. In that culture, a childless woman was pitied at best, and more likely scorned. Whatever the cause, Sarah too appears to have lost faith.

No matter what we do, struggle will always find us. There may come a time when the promise of married life fades. The dreams that you shared together falter. The bills pile up or the kids are sick, or you can't have kids at all.

Even if you are not married, the same pattern holds. Perhaps you thought you would have found a spouse by this time. Maybe a long-term relationship ended suddenly. Or the job that seemed so promising is suddenly gone.

I have had my own experiences with this. I have a tradition of taking my two boys out for doughnuts, usually of a weekend, typically on Saturday morning. My boys are nine and seven now, but I started the practice years ago, when my younger son was barely two. It gave my wife a respite on a weekend morning and allowed me time with just the boys. Some will no doubt question my choice of activity—pumping them full of sugared confections followed by sugary chocolate milk. They loved it. And I loved the time with them, and still do.

One winter Saturday I had the boys out with me for sugar and there was, unusually, quite a crowd at the local Dunkin' Donuts. This meant we had to wait in line, never easy for wriggly, impatient little boys. I was holding my younger son, Blaise, mostly to keep him from grabbing at the display of coffee mugs and other alluring items situated just at his level, while my older boy Elijah stood in front of me, chattering about what kind of doughnut he would order, the relative merits and demerits of his leading options, and the holiday décor still on display in the shop that he found outdated. (It was January.) It was about then I noticed, as the line inched forward, that Elijah was dragging one leg. At first, I thought it was just how he was standing, or maybe my vantage point. I watched a little longer. No, he was definitely favoring his left leg. In fact, as we finally approached the cashier, I saw that it was a pronounced limp. "Did you hurt your leg?" I asked him a moment later when we sat down. He said no. "Does it hurt now?" I asked. He said no again.

I reported my observations to Erin, who promptly called the pediatrician. His reply was not encouraging. "You never like to hear about a limp," he said. "We had better see him." He directed us to bring Elijah in for an appointment the following Monday.

And then we entered every parent's nightmare. We had hoped the cause might be a subtle bruise or a pulled muscle, or maybe even a reaction from the flu, which both our boys had struggled through recently. Instead, the pediatrician was sufficiently concerned to send Elijah to a specialist, and the first diagnosis we received was, in a word, startling. The doctor thought he had a rare disease that inflames the joints of children, leading to pain and significant loss of mobility. It is often lifelong. He informed us Elijah might be unable to walk as an adult and might well suffer degeneration in multiple joints—shoulders, knees, and so on. We were horrified.

So began a repeating cycle of tests and blood draws and X-rays and MRIs. Elijah had little or no idea what was happening; Erin and I told him only that his hip was hurt and we needed to figure out how to fix it. I remember one series of tests at the local hospital that required Elijah to be sedated. Erin sat with him on the hospital bed and I held his hand, watching his eyes blur and then close. He was only five. I wondered whether he would run again, or know again the joy of roughhousing with his brother, or of swimming or biking or a million other taken-for-granted things.

This was not how I had imagined my family life would go. It was not what Erin had imagined either. It was difficult for us both individually and as a couple. In addition to everything else, we were in the middle of a fiercely contested political campaign, which demanded considerable time and travel from me. A gloom settled over us. The promise seemed to fade.

It was my mother who, in the end, helped me find what I needed to weather the storm. I was on the phone with her, walking beneath a leaden winter sky. And she said to me: *You will endure.*

And there it was. In the face of uncertainty and disappointment, fading hope and looming fear, my job was to endure. It was to hew to the vows I had made. It was to keep to the promise of marriage and home. That is a husband's job, having made his vows, having taken his pledge: to endure. That is what a husband does. He chooses to set his course not by how he feels but by what he has vowed, and by the promise that attends the vow. He chooses to believe.

Abraham was tempted to abandon the promise of his marriage and seek for solace elsewhere. He gave in, for a time, to his doubt and despair. And yet Abraham did not give up, not ultimately. He found his nerve. He pressed on. He honored Sarah and returned to his covenant. He waited for her child as his heir. And in time, God rewarded him and Sarah with a son.

As for us: after batteries of tests and meetings with many doctors, we finally learned Elijah suffered from Perthes disease, a rare disorder that was causing his left hip to degenerate. The socket was crumbling away, bit by bit. Thus the pain and limp. Strange as it seemed, this was a somewhat better diagnosis than the first, insofar as the degeneration seemed to be localized to one hip and was not affecting other joints. And there was a chance for recovery. The doctors were confident Elijah's hip would in fact regenerate: the question was to what extent, and when, and whether permanent damage would result. We did all we knew to do. We told Elijah everyone had challenges in life to overcome. This was his, and we would help him all we could. And we prayed. I have rarely prayed so concentratedly in my life. Today, I am happy to report, Elijah can walk—and run—without pain or inhibition. Soccer is currently his favorite sport.

Through the storm, Erin and I grew closer. We learned to trust one another even more. We came to understand one another better. And I came to see a little more clearly that sometimes promise is found on the other side of pain, that hardship can reveal blessing. That is why once a man has vowed, he endures.

PROTECT AND PROVIDE

You remember that Abraham once lied about Sarah being his sister, not his wife, to keep himself safe. He did it again, later. Abraham and Sarah again found themselves on the move and ended up again in unfriendly territory, where Abraham—again—tried to pass Sarah off as his sister. As before, God intervened to do what Abraham should have done. He protected Sarah and provided for her. God warned the local chieftain in a dream that Sarah was another man's wife, and threatened to kill him if he so much as touched her.

To protect and provide is an obligation laid upon husbands from time immemorial. The anthropologist David Gilmore notes that "[f]or a group to maintain itself over time, people must have a minimum number of children and must socialize them properly—not an easy task." He goes on: "At the same time someone must feed and protect children and their mothers, both of whom are too otherwise occupied to hunt or fight wars."[26]

That "someone" is, traditionally, a man. Specifically, a husband. And what was true in traditional societies is also true today, though the emphasis may be less on hunting and physical prowess than on providing a paycheck and a measure of security. Sociologist William Julius Wilson has written about the concept of "marriageability," which he defines as the ratio of employed men to all women of similar age.[27] The basic insight is that women are careful about whom they marry, more careful than men, and one thing they consistently look for in a man is his ability to contribute to the family. In other words, they look for a man with a job. The data, to say nothing of common sense, suggests women do not generally care to marry men who are little more than overgrown children. When they are looking for a mate, they are looking for someone who can contribute.

The economist Gary Becker made a similar point in a famous article about economics and marriage in 1973. He called it "A Theory of Marriage," the essential claim of which was: marriage is a market based on gains from trade.[28] Men and women decide to marry when each party concludes, rationally, that the other person can contribute something to the partnership, making the marriage "profitable." A gain from trade. For men that means: you have to bring something to your marriage. Generally, that means the ability to support a family.

Of course, marriageability can include more than a decent job. Other traits might help make a man marriageable: temperament, dependability, and so on.[29] But however you dice it, men must contribute. They are expected to provide *something*.

One reason for the declining marriage rate in America is that fewer and fewer men are working and providing. As men do less, go to school less, work less, and risk less, they become less suitable as husbands. It's a simple fact: the number of marriageable men in America is on the wane.[30]

There is no reason that should include you. You can be a provider and protector, and you can start by producing something. Get a job. Keep it. Then pay your bills. Then save some money. These small steps go long distances toward making you the kind of man who can be a husband.

More broadly, become someone who can be counted upon. Consistency can be learned. It can be cultivated. You can become someone who keeps the promises he makes, who does what he says he will do, who shows up when people need him, who helps lift burdens from others rather than creating them. That's the pathway to the character of a husband.

THE CHARACTER OF A HUSBAND

In many ways, the only thing at which Abraham was consistent as a husband was failure. Still, in the end, he received the promise he had long waited for. The story concludes, "The LORD visited Sarah as he had said, and the LORD did to Sarah as he had promised. And Sarah conceived and bore Abraham a son in his old age. . ." (Genesis 21:1–2). His marriage succeeded. His family took root. Because he was perfect? Hardly. Because he made no mistakes? He seems to have made just as many toward the end as at the beginning. But all this is encouraging news, since no man alive is perfect. Here is what Abraham did do: He toiled over the years to acquire something he initially did not have, character. Through the wanderings and the setbacks and the challenges and the trials, Abraham acquired the character of a husband. He learned to risk himself, to vow and endure, to provide and protect. As he did, he shouldered Adam's mission. He advanced God's purposes. He stepped out toward a new Eden.

MANHOOD

CHAPTER SIX

FATHER

My wife and I lost our first child in a miscarriage just a few days after Erin watched the baby's heartbeat for the first time. She described the heartbeat to me in vivid detail the evening after her checkup, a small rhythmic bubble on the sonogram screen. I put my ear to her stomach right there at the dinner table and listened myself, hearing nothing, of course, but we laughed all the same and marveled at the life inside her. We were moving at the time, from a small rental house to the first home we had ever owned, on a piece of land in the country about ten or fifteen miles south of Columbia, Missouri. This is when we both had teaching jobs at the University of Missouri as law professors. We had just started, in fact, and moved to the area around the first of July. Now it was October, and unusually warm for mid-Missouri. The realtor kept warning us we were going to lose the young trees around the house before we even moved in—"You need to go over there right now and water," she said—but we were too excited at the prospect of our first home, and our first baby, to worry about much of anything.

Erin had found the house herself. A child of a cattle ranch in rural New Mexico, she loved the part of the listing that read, "horses permitted." There was actually a horse barn on a neighboring piece of land, and you could see the horses out in the pasture, grazing, from the patio of our new place. Her ambition was to get the baby up on a horse as soon as possible, just as her mother had done with her. Erin had been in the saddle alongside her mom when she was less than a year old.

In addition to my work teaching, I was also practicing law with a nonprofit firm that specialized in First Amendment cases, particularly religious liberty cases. As it happened, we had our first big argument at the U.S. Supreme Court the same week as our move. So I packed my suitcase at the rental house on the eve of moving day, shoving in various extraneous items we hadn't found space for in boxes, flew to Washington, attended the argument (which went well), and returned the following day to the new house, where the movers had relocated our cargo.

We started unpacking. My memory is we started in the kitchen. We ate our first dinner in the new house that night, take-out pizza, atop moving boxes. Packing and unpacking is tedious work, as anyone who has done it knows, but we were happy doing it and the work seemed to go fast. On the second or third day after I returned we were mostly finished, and that's when Erin suddenly became alarmed. I remember her walking into the bedroom where I was rifling through yet another box and saying, *Something's not right. There is too much blood.*

What do you mean? I asked.

I shouldn't be bleeding like this, she said.

Not knowing what else to do, I tried to reassure her. *I'm sure it will be okay*, I said. She called the doctor's office, and they didn't seem overly concerned. The nurse told her to monitor her symptoms. It must have been toward evening, because when we went to bed, I remember feeling encouraged and Erin seemed, to me, somewhat less anxious.

But she had been right. She woke me the next morning in tears. *I've lost the baby*, she said.

Are you sure? I asked. *Are you still bleeding?*

No, she said. *But I feel fine.*

That's good, I said.

No, she said, *that's bad*.

Erin had suffered from morning sickness from the earliest days of her pregnancy, yet on this morning she suddenly felt no nausea or pain. We went to the hospital together a short time later, and after a few moments with the sonogram, the nurse shook her head. *I'm sorry*, she said. *But the baby isn't there.*

We never learned whether our child was a son or daughter. Erin always believed the baby was a girl, and she would know better than anyone else. She had carried the child for nearly three months and felt her, or his, life intertwining with her own. The loss for her was tangible and profound. The baby's life was something missing deep inside her. She could *feel* it, feel the deprivation.

I could not. The entire train of events seemed somehow surreal to me. Before, when Erin first told me she was pregnant, I could hardly fathom we were going to have a baby, wonderful as the news was. Now I could hardly fathom that he, or she, was gone. There had been no moment at which I met my child; now there was no moment to say goodbye. It was almost as if none of it had ever happened. I found it difficult to grieve or to feel much of anything. It was like watching a movie of someone else's life.

Never having met our child, we didn't feel able to choose a name. We didn't know what to do, or if there *was* something to do. The thing about miscarriages, we soon learned, is people rarely speak about them. It's not the sort of thing one shares with those who don't already know about the baby's impending arrival, and since our miscarriage occurred relatively early, that wasn't very many people.

Still, however surreal it seemed to me at first, in the weeks that followed a colder reality began to set in. The doctors pointed out, in a regretful sort of way, that mothers who suffer miscarriages are at greater risk of miscarrying again—and this is especially so when the first pregnancy miscarries. I distinctly remember stopping to ponder this piece of information. It had an edge to it. What did this mean—that we might never have children?

That question cut me. From the time I was a teenager, maybe even before, I had wanted to be a father. I think I associated it with being a man. Virtually all the adult men I admired—my grandfather, my coaches, my own dad—were fathers. But it went deeper than that. I wanted to share my life with someone else, to share the important parts of me. I imagined doing with my future sons all the things I as a boy loved to do: reading and swimming and hunting for buried treasure. (I once led a band of neighborhood children in digging up portions of our backyard, on the supposition that treasure allegedly abandoned by Union soldiers in the Civil War might be secreted there. My mother was not amused.) I imagined helping my future boys through hard days and encouraging them when they were confused.

As I look back on it now, I suppose what I was doing was learning to father myself. Picturing myself as a dad was me learning to grow up. But whatever the origins, the dream of fatherhood took deep root, and now confronted with the distinct possibility that I might not be a father after all, that none of it might come to pass, I realized I had taken my childhood dream for granted. Or maybe more exactly, I realized my dreams about fatherhood were in many ways childish. I had simply assumed that I could be a father if I wanted, that it was something bound to happen in due course—and that being a father was simple enough. Now I saw there was more to fatherhood than that, more contingency than that, and though I only barely glimpsed it, more pain to it, and sacrifice. Fatherhood was not something I could control. And it was not an ornament to decorate my life. Not something to possess, but something that would possess me. Not something I could use to complete my life, but a role that would transform my life into something altogether different and new.

I began to ask myself what it would take to be a father—to truly father a child, to give myself over to the work, to give my soul to it and bind my future to another person for the whole of my life. And I began to see, at the same time, that the opportunity to do this, to give and to sacrifice and be claimed in this way, was itself a gift. Not a guarantee, but a gift.

The waiting and wondering in those months after we lost our baby forced me into a new position of humility and dependence. Fatherhood was something beyond me. I had to wait for it and hope for it. And if I were given the chance, I would need help to meet its challenges.

Three months after we lost our baby, Erin discovered she was pregnant again. We held our breath through the early weeks. I found I was subconsciously counting the days to week ten, when we had lost our first. But that week came and went, and the baby grew.

He came to us at long last on November 3, a bright, brilliantly clear day in another warm autumn. He was born about ten in the evening. In the final moments as I stood beside Erin and gripped her hand, I felt the raw voltage of emotion I hadn't been able to feel the year before. Emotion may not be the right word; it was stronger than that, deeper and more visceral—I was between laughing and shouting when my son arrived and they handed him to me for the first time. I called him then, and have most days since, my long-awaited Elijah. And as I held him I realized the moment was, for me, both an end and a beginning. I felt released, at last, to say goodbye to the child I had never seen. And I felt an overwhelming gratitude for another opportunity to be a father. The wait was over. In one sense.

But in another way, if waiting means acknowledging your limits, if it means humility, my son's birth was just a beginning. The posture of humility that our first baby's loss forced on me was, I came to learn, the posture of fatherhood. In the years since, I have come to understand that being a father means being imperfect. It means feeling out of control. It means confronting all the ways in which you yourself are flawed. Yet for all that, fatherhood is the invitation of a lifetime, the invitation to a different kind of life, because to be a father is to realize perfection is not the aim. And you are not the center of the universe. Fatherhood is an invitation to discover grace, and the character it makes possible.

Maybe you are a father. Maybe you are not. But it seems noteworthy that the first Adam story in the Bible we come to after Adam himself, the story of Abraham, centers on fatherhood. That says something to today's America. Maybe this: we need fathers to confront the chaos and darkness around us, and we need men who have the character of fathers.

Many Epicureans these days want to insist that mothers and fathers are interchangeable or better replaced by the state. The Bible says no. The mission of manhood is bound up with fathering.

THE CRISIS OF FATHERHOOD

We live amidst an epidemic of fatherlessness. More children are growing up without their fathers than ever before in our history, and fewer and fewer men appear interested in fatherhood. According to the Census Bureau's statistics on families, approximately 18.4 million children now live without a father in the home. That's one in four children in this country—double the number since the 1960s.[1] The figures are particularly striking for boys. Fully 32 percent of boys under eighteen now grow up without their biological father present.[2] Most of these boys live with a single mother—a few others live with grandparents or other relatives or with a mom who has remarried.[3]

What is perhaps even more striking is what an outlier these numbers make the United States around the world. A Pew Research survey of over a hundred countries and territories revealed that "the U.S. has the world's highest rate of children living in single-parent households."[4] Globally, about 7 percent of children live in households with just one parent. In America, that number is more than three times higher.[5]

Our epidemic of fatherlessness has spawned a series of related pathologies, among them poverty, delinquency, drug use, and depression. Children in homes without a father present are more likely to live below the poverty line than children in two-parent households.[6] Here is another measure of the same phenomenon: kids in homes with only a single mother have a poverty rate approaching 50 percent. For married-couple families, it's nearer 10 percent.[7]

This poverty often becomes intergenerational. Boys who grow up without fathers are considerably more likely to be idle and without work by their mid-twenties than young men with dads. Even controlling for race, age, the mother's education, and the family's income growing up, young men who come of age without their fathers are fully twice as likely as their peers to be out of the labor force in their twenties.[8]

The absence of a father costs in other ways. Children without dads at home are at far greater risk for sexual assault, especially if they are girls. And both boys and girls suffer much greater danger of physical abuse when their father is absent. To put a number to it, kids in single-parent households are about twice as likely to suffer abuse or neglect as kids who live with their mom *and* dad.[9]

Then there's crime. Crime is a predominantly male activity, and psychologists note, as a threshold matter, that boys with absent fathers often experience higher levels of anger and even rage, and criminality is one consequence.[10] By age thirty, fatherless boys are twice as likely to have spent time in jail, a correlation that holds true even when researchers control for factors like household income, race, and the mother's education.[11] One recent study summarized the data: "Boys in single female-headed families are particularly at risk for adverse outcomes across many domains, including high school dropout, criminality, and violence."[12]

On the other side of the ledger, a father's presence in the home means healthier kids, both physically and emotionally; better academic performance; less depression; less drug use; less violence in the community; and less crime.[13] Perhaps Genesis was on to something, then, those many thousands of years ago, when it portrayed fathers as an answer to the darkness of the world.

A WORK OF SACRIFICE

According to our modern-day Epicureans, you are only really an individual if you throw off constraints and choose your own life path. Discard whatever holds you back—family, religion, tradition—and do as you please. Satisfy yourself. That's the Epicurean way at the heart of modern liberalism and, by extension, modern culture.

What it amounts to in practice, however, is choosing to live for yourself—or for a very peculiar version of yourself. It is a version of you divorced from your history, your family, your home, and traditions—in short, from the things that help make us "selves" to begin with. What are any of us when we put away our family stories and the obligations that come with them, the places we grew up in and the ways they shaped us, and the thousand and one other things that we didn't choose at all, yet that together make us who we uniquely are? We are no persons at all. It is impossible to imagine yourself without these things—just try it—because they are the very components of personhood. And they are virtually all unchosen. The problem with the liberal, Epicurean idea of being an individual is that it refuses to acknowledge the things that make us individuals, the things that give us a foundation for what we believe and what we prioritize. Instead, modern liberals pretend the world can be remade entirely around our unfettered personal choice.

Fatherhood stands as an impediment to this misguided ethic. This is because fatherhood is a work of sacrifice. It is all about surrendering your life to someone else, giving someone else first priority. Think again of Abraham. The call to become a father became the call to leave his kindred, his place of safety and all that was comfortable and familiar, and set out toward something new. Something he had not himself chosen or planned. Whatever ideas Abraham may have had for his life beforehand were upset and overturned by God's call to become a father. As a consequence, the rest of Abraham's life would be spent looking beyond his wishes, living for more than his desires, and giving of himself until he was spent entirely. Fatherhood would claim him and direct him outward, toward others and toward the future. His purpose would no longer be to preserve himself or indulge his whims, but to give himself away so that his children might flourish and the mission he served outlive him. Fatherhood is the business of replacing yourself.

Another way to think of it is this. Epicurean liberalism tells you to live for yourself moment by moment: the self of this instant. Fatherhood aims a man, instead, at the future. It asks him to consider himself in ten years, in twenty years, or thirty—to ask what his children will need from him in those times to come, and how he can be ready for it. It directs him away from what he wants now, in this moment, toward who he might be many years in the future and what legacy he might leave beyond himself.

I remember our son Elijah's first night at home from the hospital. The room we had converted into a little nursery adjoined our bedroom, so we could hear his every sound. I remember lying there in bed, listening to his various little noises—and feeling the weight of being responsible for this small life. And not just for the next few months, not just for the next few years, but always. Multiple times that first night I got up and treaded softly into his room, just to see him there and watch him breathe. Watching over him, tending to him, preparing a future for him—this was my life now. In a word, my life was no longer my own.

This is often a hard fact for men to accept, young men in particular. It is one reason they delay marriage and fatherhood and difficult life choices generally. But it is a vital place to come to, the true beginning, the Bible suggests, of significance, of a life that really matters.

I spoke not long ago to a former student of mine, whom I will call Eric, who was considering a change in jobs. He called to ask my opinion about his options, and we visited for a time. He is in his thirties now, has been married for ten years, lives these days in Colorado, and is, to be frank, perpetually discontent. I gradually discovered as the conversation went on that his wife, also a lawyer, was opposed to his changing jobs, which might involve a move to another city. He told me the issue was not her own work. Her law firm had an office in the city where he was considering a new job. No, the issue was she wanted to take some time off from her work to start a family. When I suggested this was an exciting possibility, he demurred. It's not a good time, he said. I asked why. He was financially secure, with a good job. He had extended family nearby to help. But he said he wasn't quite ready to have a kid. It would require so many changes. It would impose so many... limits. In other words, he would no longer be able to live for himself. Fatherhood meant unwelcome responsibility.

This is a common attitude, encouraged by our Epicurean culture. And those who hold it are right about one thing: fatherhood does constrain. It rewards, even requires, self-denial rather than self-expression.

It promotes service to others rather than personal choice. But those attitudes and decisions are not, contrary to what our culture may say, the death of individualism. They are the gateways to responsibility and lasting significance.

THE VALUE OF HUMILITY

The Abraham story highlights another aspect of the transforming power of fatherhood. Genesis says God made Abraham a father by a miracle. What does this mean? It means he made Abraham confront his limitations. He made Abraham humble.

The thing about Abraham, the really notable thing given the whole thrust of the story, was that he didn't have children. He was old—"as good as dead," in the vivid words of his wife—and, at seventy-five when God called him, well beyond the usual age to father offspring or strike out on new paths. Yet God insisted his future depended on being a father. In short, it appeared God was asking Abraham to do the impossible.

And that is fatherhood in brief, to take the seemingly impossible step of accepting the responsibility for another life, from the moment of its very conception. It is a rolling invitation to discover our limits and failings. When, as a boy, I imagined myself as a father, planning out my adventures with my hypothetical children, I never imagined any shortcomings on my part. If I thought of shortcomings at all, I imagined all the ways I would improve on my own parents! I suspect this is a common pastime of children. When my own children were born, however, I began to see things rather differently.

I remember one occasion when Erin and I were in the midst of a disagreement and I was refusing to admit I had done anything remotely objectionable. I was standing opposite her, like a lawyer facing a witness in the courtroom, rehearsing all the reasons I was right about whatever it was, I now forget. I remember feeling a certain sense of satisfaction that I was winning the argument (I thought), when I caught a stray flick of movement out of the corner of my eye. I paused and looked over. Our two little boys—Blaise had since come along, two years after Elijah—had heard our voices and snuck into the room where we were, and now were standing in the corner watching, wide-eyed. I was appalled. I stopped talking immediately. And I saw in a flash what a fool I had been. I was focused on winning an argument (that didn't matter), irritating my wife (which did matter), and making a spectacle of myself before our children in the process. I remember thinking to myself, *This is the worst. This is the kind of thing I said as a child I would never do. How could I have been so stupid?*

I wish I could say that was the only stupid thing I have done as a father. The truth is, there has not been a day since my first son was born that I have not sought forgiveness for failing at something, or for a situation I bungled, or for an action I regretted. Not one day.

Fatherhood exposes your own inevitable weaknesses and imperfections and forces you to own them. And it reminds you, forcibly, that many of the most important things in life are beyond your power or control. So you venture forward humbly and, like Abraham, trust in God.

When God first gave Adam his mission in the garden, he did it with a command. "Be fruitful and multiply and subdue the earth," God said. But with Abraham, interestingly, God began with a *promise.* "I will bless you," God says, "I will make of you a great nation," and "I will make your name great, so that you will be a blessing."[14] Note the prominent use of "I." In the Abraham story, the mission of manhood, of family and future, comes to depend on God's initiative and God's promises.

The Bible is making a point by way of a contrast. Adam placed himself at the center of the universe. He behaved, when put to it, as if he had created himself, as if he belonged only to himself, as if it was unnecessary for him to defend Eden, protect Eve, and obey God's commands. His arrogance led to his downfall, and others' with him. God begins his dealings with Abraham by signaling to him that he must not do the same. He must display a different kind of character. Abraham's story begins with God telling Abraham, in effect, that he must rely on God to fulfill his life's purpose. He must accept God's grace. The path of manhood is the path of humility of soul.

We are not omnipotent. We do not know all. And however appealing it may from time to time appear, we simply cannot live as if we are the only persons who exist in the universe. That is the way to ruin. The man who cannot admit his weakness or acknowledge his failure is a man who cannot grow, who cannot change, who cannot make amends. That is a man who will cut himself off from love or from challenge and grow progressively weaker because of it. It is a paradox not just of the Abraham story but of life that the way of significance and strength is the way of humility and dependence. In the end, we must all depend on God's promises or end up like Adam, cursed and alone.

Fatherhood beckons us to these truths and to this kind of character. But it also encourages us with this reality, that the purpose of our lives and the success of our children does not depend finally on our perfection. To acknowledge our failings and need is to make space for what the Bible calls grace. And it is grace that will, if we are humble, rule the day.

There is a certain heroism in living according to this promise. Indeed, it is Abraham's acknowledgment of his limits, of his need, that propelled him forward to a new land, to a new family, and ultimately to a legacy that has endured across time. It's what the Bible calls faith, this combination of humility and trust. It is what Adam did not have. It is what fatherhood calls us to.

A LEGACY TO LAST

All men want to matter. The moral of the Abraham story in this regard is simple. If you want to build your piece of the world into a place of beauty; if you want to make it a little better, a little more what it could be; if you want to leave it a place of excellence and opportunity and hope, cultivate the character of a father.

Fatherhood in the Bible is not necessarily limited to begetting sons and daughters, as important as that is. Fatherhood in the Bible is an ethic. It is a way of living your life: sacrificially, oriented towards others, humbly. That is why the Bible depicts the virtues of a father as prominent among those a man must acquire if he wants to take up his mission, the project of Adam.

For those who fear that becoming a father means giving away the chance to do something meaningful, to achieve something lasting, the Abraham story says this: fathering is temple-building. It is about constructing the most lasting thing one can.

"I will make of you a great nation...so that you will be a blessing," God says as he promises Abraham a son and many descendants.[15] God then says something arresting about those descendants, Abraham's family. "[Y]our offspring," he says to Abraham later, "shall possess the gate of his enemies."[16] This is unusual language. The image is at first hard to conjure. The scene is of a conquering force battering the gates of the enemy stronghold, about to overrun it. It is an image of victory.

What does it mean? Abraham's family will overcome their enemies. And who might those enemies be? Well, among other things, given Abraham's role as a new Adam, they are death and darkness themselves. The evil let loose in the world after Adam's failure will be overcome by Abraham's family.

That is, building his family is how Abraham will build the temple God started in Eden. His family will be the temple, or a part of it, part of the restored creation: an emblem of what the world could be. And God's purpose, we are told, is that this family, this little outpost, should grow and expand and carry the light of faith with it.

What was true for Abraham can be true for us. A man's family can be a garden in the wilderness, a place of safety, of flourishing, where there is order and predictability and hope for the future. This is not speculation. This is fact. Researchers have amply documented that families with involved and present fathers are the greatest vehicles for human advancement known to man. Children from intact families with present and involved fathers have higher IQs—intelligence being, we now know, a developmental fact as well as a genetic one.[17] They acquire language earlier and start school more advanced and better prepared than their peers who lack fathers in the home.[18] The trends continue as the children age. Kids are 43 percent more likely to earn primarily A grades, and a third less likely to repeat a grade, if their dads are present.[19] They are twice as likely to graduate from college.[20] In a similar vein, boys with fathers are less likely to engage in criminal behavior, while girls with an active dad are far less likely, by half, to get pregnant as teenagers. And kids of both sexes are significantly less at risk for depression if dad is around.[21]

The presence of a father is so profound, one study found that having a few fathers present in a neighborhood, not even necessarily in every home, "strongly predicted black boys' outcomes irrespective of whether their own father [was] present."[22] In short, families with a father, and neighborhoods where fathers live, are safer, wealthier, and in better health.[23]

Fathers may be mocked by popular culture. They may be lampooned and derided. One recent study found television sitcoms of the last twenty years depicted fathers as fools or boors over half the time.[24] But the idea that fathers are irrelevant louts is truly fiction. The truth is that to be a father is to build a better world. And it is to build something that will last.

One famous consequence of Adam's fall in the Genesis story is the appearance of death. The first deaths—of animals, then humans—occur only after Adam abandons his post as God's servant. From that point on, every person in the Genesis story knows his own life will not last. The way back to Eden with its tree of life is closed. Death is a certainty.

And yet God tells Abraham his influence will extend beyond his years, until all the world is blessed by him. How? As a father. The promise of the Abraham story is that fatherhood works against the curse of death by drawing our lives into the future. If fatherhood is an enterprise of sacrifice, it is sacrifice that makes the future possible. Fatherhood is in fact a constant choice for the future, a choice for hope and possibility. And in this way, it connects our lives with those who will come after us, and with those after them, so that the work of temple-building goes forward, a partnership of meaning across the generations.

Though I must say this: when it comes to fatherhood, there is nothing better than the here and now. The other night I found myself sitting with my younger son Blaise on the couch in our basement, waiting for the kickoff of the Thursday night NFL game. Blaise, age seven, is a sports enthusiast, both as player and fan, and football is, at the moment, his first love. He had talked me into letting him stay up past his bedtime on this night to watch the kickoff and opening drive. Or at least, that is what we agreed to beforehand. As the fateful moment drew nearer—8:20 p.m. Eastern, for the uninitiated—he began to bargain for a little bit more. Maybe kickoff and opening drive and then one more series after that, he suggested. I resisted long enough to show some effort, but truth be told, it wasn't a hard sell. I loved this time with my son, seeing his enthusiasm, watching him reenact the plays he has just observed, jumping from couch to floor to armchair and back again, telling me all the while of his future as a Super Bowl quarterback.

My older son Elijah came down too, bringing a book to read during the commercials. The boys had arranged themselves on either side of me and there we sat, the three of us, Blaise narrating the game, Elijah reading his book, his head on my shoulder. And I thought to myself: Where else would I rather be? What else would I rather be doing? Fatherhood may be a vocation of sacrifice; it may be a choice for the future. But it is also the best, most remarkable, most amazing *now* you could ever imagine. "I will bless you," God told Abraham. That is fatherhood.

CHAPTER SEVEN

WARRIOR

The Dry Cimarron is a twisty bend of river that winds its way across the northeast corner of New Mexico, out where the elevation runs six or seven thousand feet above sea level, before dropping down into the panhandle of Oklahoma. Most of the year its waters move unseen beneath the sandy surface, hence the name "dry." Ages ago it helped carve a canyon among the mesas of this stretch of high desert—the Cimarron canyon—and that's where, back in the 1860s, my wife's family went to homestead.

Incidentally, family lore has it that they started in Missouri, perhaps near where I grew up, a couple of brothers named Murphy and their sister, Susan Murphy Sumpter, who was by that time a widow with a small boy named Bud. Susan went west with her brothers but homesteaded her own piece of land in the Cimarron canyon, on the north side of the river and about ten miles from what was then the only settlement in the area, called Madison. The Madison settlement is gone now, but there is another village nearby named Folsom, and these days a two-lane road follows the river from Folsom down the canyon and by the ranch, which has been in my wife's family since Susan and Bud settled it those many years ago.

New Mexico was the frontier at that time, a vast land of mesas and mountains and *vegas*, or grasslands, largely unpopulated and lawless. To be out there was to be on your own, in most every way imaginable. When they arrived, Susan and Bud began to farm and raise cattle. They built a small wood-frame house back up against a mesa, for protection from the elements. What they did not have protection from were marauders and bandits, of which there were plenty. On the frontier, as in life more generally, where there is chaos and disorder, danger gathers. From the Sumpter ranch, the nearest military outpost was Fort Union, New Mexico, about 125 miles to the west and south; there was another military fort in Colorado 150 miles north. Neither was within a day's ride, or even close. And what Susan and Bud could not have realized when they chose the homestead site was that their new ranch, though remote, was right along a route favored by the region's most notorious outlaw, Captain William Coe.

Coe was a cattle thief and sometimes train robber who patrolled a swath of territory from New Mexico to present-day Oklahoma. A former Union army captain in the Civil War, he was reportedly a charismatic leader, in a malevolent sort of way. He boasted a gang of approximately fifty outlaws under his command. They were killers. They made their headquarters along the Cimarron River a day's ride from the Sumpter ranch, where Coe built a low-slung fortress made of rock, which the locals called Robber's Roost. It had no windows, but it did boast twenty-seven portholes—for firing on uninvited guests. Coe's typical modus operandi was to raid ranches and wagon trains (the Santa Fe Trail was nearby) in New Mexico or Oklahoma or Texas, then rebrand the stolen livestock and drive them to sale away east, in

Kansas or Missouri. His gang once raided an entire town in Colorado, mercilessly gunning down any who attempted to interfere.

It was quite an operation, this gang of Coe's, and Susan and Bud Sumpter ended up accidentally in the middle of it. Coe discovered the Sumpter ranch as he and his gang rode along the Cimarron. Taking advantage of the absence of a grown man, he began imposing himself as a regular, if uninvited, guest. Bud Sumpter would later recall seeing him ride up to the ranch with stolen mules and other livestock. Coe and his gang would rest at the Sumpter place, sometimes overnight—demanding dinner for themselves and feed for their horses—before carrying on to Robber's Roost.

For a time, Bud and Susan acquiesced to this arrangement. To resist, after all, would be to court severe retribution. But eventually they came to resent Coe's intrusions and affronts, and as one year of Coe's visits stretched into two and Bud neared thirteen or fourteen years of age, he decided to become the man his mother needed. He would protect his mother and their ranch. He decided to put himself between the things he loved and William Coe.

Sometime in 1867 or 1868, Coe and his gang descended on a camp of sheep herders pasturing a flock of nearly 1,700 head just a few miles south of Robber's Roost. When the herders unexpectedly put up a fight, Coe and company killed three of them and made off with the sheep. The herd's owner was an affluent and influential rancher in southern New Mexico, and his outrage finally galvanized federal action. The commanding general at Fort Lyon in Colorado dispatched a squad of soldiers who rode directly to Robber's Roost, only to find it empty. Coe had gotten wind of their pursuit and sought cover elsewhere. Undeterred, the soldiers took a cannon to the hideout and razed the building to the ground. Then they turned in pursuit of Coe.

Now Coe was truly on the run, no hideout, no base of operations. For months the soldiers tracked him, joined at some point by reinforcements from Fort Union in central New Mexico. The Coe gang splintered as they ran, and the soldiers managed to capture several members, who in turn provided information on the whereabouts of their fugitive chief.

With the law closing in, where did Coe turn but to his longtime hideaway, the Sumpter ranch. In the spring of 1868 he came riding up one morning, whether alone or with a man or two in tow is unclear, and found, as usual, only Susan and Bud at home. Lore has it that Coe was bedraggled-looking, his beard and hair grown long, his features gaunt, weary from months on the lam. One can surmise he was also desperate. The story goes that he rode up with a rifle laid conspicuously across his lap. Susan Sumpter greeted him evenly and served him breakfast, and any others with him. Then Coe announced he would take a few hours' sleep in the bunkhouse, as was his habit.

But Susan had had enough. She devised a plan. Once Coe and his men were sleeping, Bud might be able to slip away unnoticed and find the detachment of soldiers scouting for Coe. She went to her son. Would he do this? Would Bud risk his life for his mother and their ranch?

He would. He did.

While the outlaws slumbered, Bud saddled his pony from the back pasture and led it quietly to the road, skirting the bunkhouse. Then he mounted up and rode. Hours passed. As they did, the danger grew. If the outlaws woke and found Bud gone, they would almost certainly kill Susan—or worse. Still, she held her nerve, and waited. Finally, as the day waned, Susan saw dust rising in the canyon. Bud had found the soldiers.

Coe and his men meanwhile had slept for the duration, and they woke to a different scene than they had expected. The bunkhouse was surrounded by riflemen. The soldiers took Coe and his cronies into custody, and the story goes that as they departed, the commanding officer thanked Susan and saluted Bud, one man to another. Coe supposedly remarked, "I never figured to be outgeneraled by a woman, a pony, and a boy."

My wife's family has cherished that story for a hundred years and more. It has been told and retold down the generations. It is a story about many things—a woman defending her ranch, the trust between mother and son, the perilous life of the frontier. But it is also the story of a young man becoming something every man is called to be—a warrior—by choosing to face the darkness, choosing to take up responsibility and the risk that comes with it, to venture out into the dangerous and unknown. Bud Sumpter's choice is one faced by every boy who would become a man.

This is what men are called to do, to assert themselves and their power to uphold the right. They are called to acquire the character of a warrior.

Predictably, that is not how today's Epicurean liberals see it. Instead, they openly condemn male assertiveness and warn of the dangers of male power. Their views now define our cultural norms. Yet the Bible—and the traditions of the West—says something different altogether. We would do well to heed the ancient wisdom of the warrior virtues.

THE DARK FRONTIER

The Bible discloses the character of a warrior in the story of Joshua, who faced dark forces to build a new Eden. The Bible tells us that each man must do the same.

By the time we get to Joshua in the Bible, Abraham is dead and gone. He became the father and husband God called him to be. He started his family; he set up an altar in the wilderness. But he is dead. And for four long centuries, the family of Abraham has been imprisoned in Egypt.

Then comes a turn. Abraham's family is released. They journey, haltingly, fitfully, toward their ancestral home, led by Moses. And as they come finally to the borders of the land of Canaan, the site of Abraham's first altar long ago, the moment of consequence arrives. The man named Joshua must now take up Abraham's mission, which was Adam's mission before him, to build and extend God's temple. He must confront the chaos and subdue it. He must clear a path for the light. Here is the start of his story.

> [T]he LORD said to Joshua the son of Nun... "Now therefore arise, go over this Jordan, you and all this people, into the land that I am giving to them, to the people of Israel.... Be strong and courageous. Do not be frightened, and do not be dismayed, for the LORD your God is with you wherever you go." (Joshua 1:1–2, 9)

The Bible encourages us to see our story in Joshua's. The task before him was daunting. The story says the land before him and the Israelites was filled with enemies—the monstrous Rephaim and Nephilim, names that in ancient Hebrew evoke the shades of the dead.[1] Hebrew spies sent to search the land reported that giants dwelt there. And the scripture says elsewhere that the breadth of the place was filled with wild beasts. It had become the province of dark powers. It fell to Joshua to confront those powers and do battle with them. He had to dare. He had to fight. He had to become a warrior.

Our world is not so different from his. Evil runs rampant. Chaos abounds. And to do his part, every man must become a Joshua and acquire the character of a warrior. If today's Epicureans demur, it may be that they have forgotten, or have never understood, the reality of the world as it is: They do not appreciate the presence of evil. And they do not understand a man's role in answering it. In fact, today's Epicurean liberals cast men themselves as the problem.

REMAKING MEN

Today's liberals do not want men to take up the warrior virtues. Their agenda for forming men's characters runs in the opposite direction. The left tells us the warrior character traits are symptoms of "traditional masculinity," which it calls a form of false consciousness from which men need to be liberated. Leftists warn that men's proclivity for strength and aggression is exactly what is wrong with them. They see every man as William Coe (or worse), and no man as Bud (or the cavalry). They say men must be educated to abandon competition and their instinct to be tough. They must learn to discard "emotional stoicism."[2] And they want this character reeducation to begin as early as elementary school, with programs to socialize boys out of "masculinity norms"[3]—or medicate them to enlightenment, if necessary. They do not want to encourage men to be "strong and courageous." They want men to abandon masculinity altogether.

This project usually takes one of two forms, though both lead to the same destination. Some leftists argue that the real problem with male power is the (warrior) ideology that animates it. Men are trapped, they say, in a "suffocating, outdated model of masculinity, where manhood is measured in strength."[4] Men are socialized into aggressive and dominant behaviors, they contend. The American Psychological Association has advised practitioners along these lines, telling them to beware traditional "masculine ideals," which the organization says include "expectations of dominance and aggression" and the "restriction of emotional expression."[5] This traditional masculinity "limit[s] males' psychological development, constrain[s] their behavior, [and] result[s] in gender role strain and gender role conflict."[6]

This same "ideology" supposedly menaces social peace. Traditional masculine ideas incite men to violence and anger, allegedly. The American Psychological Association, once again, warns that "masculine ideals" may "heighten the potential for boys to engage in general acts of violence including, but not limited to, bullying, assault, and/or physical and verbal aggression."[7] Or as Brown University recently advised its students, "Men will often resort to violence to resolve conflict because anger is the only emotion that they have been socialized to express."[8]

The cure is character formation of a different kind: get men to think differently, to reject outmoded stereotypes for more modern, enlightened notions. Adjust the ideology, in other words. Teach boys that aggressiveness is not linked to biology, and that the notion of masculine assertiveness is just another—and dangerous—social construct.[9] Help men find a different set of masculine ideals that don't lionize the warrior virtues or the soldiers and cowboys who practice them.[10] Socialize men out of competitiveness. The leftists who take this line recommend intervention strategies like curbing competition in schools, which they claim only provides "critical fuel for training males to dominate."[11] They advocate instead educational curricula that will confront, and dismantle, traditional masculine thinking.[12]

But another, perhaps more candid, set of critics contends the problem with male power is not merely masculine ideology, not "toxic masculinity" as such, but "the idea of masculinity itself."[13] It is masculinity in general, manhood in general, that is "firmly tied to climate change" and "militarism"—and to rape and domestic violence and school shootings and murder.[14] It is masculinity itself that has made Western society the concatenation of injustices that it is. And it is masculinity itself that must be overcome.

This explains the campaign in many American schools not so much to educate boys as to subdue them, to wring out of them any proclivity for aggressive play and adventure, to rid them of their boyishness. It starts early. One study found half of preschool teachers interrupted or altogether stopped boys' "dramatic" play on a regular basis, deeming it unsafe. Less than a third, meanwhile, reported interrupting girls' play in the same way.[15]

The worst of these interventions may be the "zero tolerance" policies found in many schools which treat boys' mere *interest* in aggressive play as a problem. In New York in 2010, Patrick Timoney—age nine— was threatened with suspension for bringing a Lego minifigure, armed with a tiny plastic rifle, to the school cafeteria. The school summoned his parents and demanded the young boy promise never to bring a "weapon" to school with him again.[16] In Tennessee, fifth-grader Nicholas Taylor was punished for displaying a slice of pizza chewed into the shape of a gun.[17] And these zero-tolerance policies range well beyond toy weapon misdeeds. In North Carolina, a nine-year-old was suspended for "inappropriate behavior." The offense? Calling his teacher "cute" in a conversation with another student.[18] For defenders of these policies, not only should boys be prevented from taking risks or playing with toys supposedly linked to aggression, but they also shouldn't even be *thinking* like boys in the first place.

If boys don't comply, they are drugged. Childhood diagnoses of ADD and ADHD have soared in the last three decades, concentrated overwhelmingly among boys.[19] Research indicates that nearly 10 percent of elementary-aged boys are on Ritalin or some similar drug.[20]

The process for diagnosing ADHD doesn't favor boys. For one thing, boys' brains simply mature later than girls' brains do[21]—so it makes no sense to expect them to behave exactly the same way in school classes segmented solely by age. Diagnosis rates also appear to be skewed by age differences *within* school class years. One study, which evaluated nearly a million elementary-age children, found a 30 percent gap in ADHD diagnoses between the youngest boys in a school class and the oldest.[22] Another study found a 50 percent difference in stimulant drug prescription rates between children in the bottom third of their class age-wise and children in the oldest third.[23]

It gets worse. A 2019 study found that therapists evaluating boys are prone to see evidence of ADHD where it doesn't exist. In the researchers' words, "even a child who presents no characteristics of ADHD is rated more severely if participants thought the child is a boy."[24] For some clinicians, the very boyishness of boys is now something to be controlled and medicated away, rather than channeled in constructive directions.

And as for recess? Forget about it. Despite recommendations that kids in elementary school spend 150 minutes each week on physical education—just 30 minutes a day—less than 5 percent of American school districts meet that bar.[25] When they're deprived of any healthy physical outlets, it should surprise no one that boys periodically act up in class.

As you might expect given this environment, boys are dropping out of school in alarming numbers.[26] Researchers found a 71 percent increase in just twenty years of the number of male high school seniors who say they don't like school.[27] No wonder: schools are increasingly places that don't like boys.

Whether manhood's critics blame ideology or masculinity proper in the end doesn't matter much. The left's ultimate aim is to separate men from manhood, to create "a new breed of men" who view gender as a spectrum of choice rather than anything rooted in reality—and masculinity as a construct individuals can pick up or discard at will. Leftists aim to create a generation of androgynous individuals whose signal character trait is their dedication to self-expression.

And to consuming stuff. Let's not forget that. The corporations that cater to men may attack masculinity—Gillette, for example[28]—but they want those same men, er, *persons*, to keep on consuming. This is the

Epicurean left's new ideal, a nation of androgynous consumers who don't rock the boat and don't question much (and certainly not those in power) but buy plenty of cheap paraphernalia to keep the corporations profitable. In the words of one leftist commentator, "The spectrum of gender affords so many expressions of self, and that freedom can be intoxicating. Men can be whoever they want, whenever they want, and those new identities are limitless...."[29] Why be a man when you can invent your own identity? It is the Epicurean self again, this time as an out-and-out replacement for manhood.

What today's Epicureans fail to consider is the possibility that manhood is real and biological, that men have all that drive and ambition for a purpose. Maybe evil is real, too, and lodged in the recesses of the human heart, where men and women must confront it in themselves. Maybe evil is not, as today's Epicureans have it, a mere matter of adjusting the social systems. And given all that, maybe male power is necessary. Maybe we need strong men to protect the garden of civilization. Maybe we need strong men to win a place for the light.

"STRONG AND COURAGEOUS"

The Bible gives counsel to today's men altogether different from that of the Epicurean liberals. "Be strong and courageous," God tells Joshua. In case we miss the point, he repeats the admonition to Joshua three times over, and punctuates it finally with this promise: "Do not be frightened, and do not be dismayed, for the LORD your God is with you wherever you go."[30] A man needs strength and courage. He needs the character of a warrior.

All of us confront evil in our lives, things that menace us and other people. The appropriate response—the response that *redeems*, that cuts a path for the light to break in—is not androgyny but personal, manly courage.

Joshua had much to fear. He had the giants and beasts he knew were there. He had his past. He had spent four decades as Moses's number two, following the great man around, watching, waiting, but rarely leading himself. The reconnaissance expedition he had organized to this very land years before hadn't ended well. His report and counsel had been soundly rejected by the people, the ones he now had to lead in battle. He had much to be concerned about.

Every man knows how that goes. The same is true in our own lives, always. There are the giants of the world around us. Our health. Our bills. Our marriage and children and work. There are the giants within. Our own wickedness, our bent toward selfishness and strife. Our desire to get our own way, and our tendency to do what we must to have it. These are all wild beasts that threaten.

Why does God repeatedly admonish Joshua to be strong and courageous? Surely it is not so hard to see. Facing these things—facing the ever-present darkness—is not an easy business. Throwing oneself into chaos, into controversy, running toward the monsters of your life, requires firmness of mind and will. It requires courage.

And courage is rare. This is yet another point where the Epicureans are decidedly, pointedly wrong. True courage is not something men must be educated out of. True courage is a virtue men must be encouraged to acquire. There is a reason for that. Courage runs contrary to our instinct for self-preservation. It runs contrary to our drive to minimize the pain in our lives. This is entirely natural, and the instinct of fear—fight or flight—is no reason for shame. Every creature seeks to preserve its own life. Life is worth preserving.

The question is, what does it mean to preserve it? The philosopher John Locke built an entire philosophy around *self*-preservation. Man's instinct for keeping himself safe, Locke said, was the beginning of his rights. Since life was man's most precious property, he had a right to safeguard it.[31] The first right of nature is the right to protect yourself.

Modernity has perhaps learned too much from Locke. Modern society's focus on self (self-care, self-fulfillment, self-preservation) obscures larger truths. Start with this one: Virtually every other society we know has pushed men forward—brave men, courageous men, warriors and soldiers—to stand between danger and civilization, even at the cost of their lives.[32] Why? Because preserving life is not always found in avoiding conflict. And your life is not always the most important one to preserve. Sometimes survival depends on action, on confronting evil, on fighting those who would do us harm. Sometimes survival depends on the aggressive and competitive spirit today's Epicurean liberals want to destroy. Sometimes a man must give his life to enable other lives to go on.

The Greeks called a man's ambition and drive *thumos*, spiritedness. They believed it is what motivated a man to press beyond his merely biological instincts and go to the site of danger. They believed *thumos* is what drove a man to stand in the face of death, to risk reputation and honor, to brave insult and evil.[33] Male spiritedness was the beginning of courage.

Can that spirit be disruptive in the classroom? Yes, certainly. The ancients knew that too. It is one reason Plato prescribed physical training for young men, discipline of the body to match education of the mind. *Thumos* can lead boys to draw pictures of guns and toss imaginary hand grenades. It can provoke fierce competition and the occasional fistfight.

But properly channeled, it is the strength of civilization, and we kill it at our own peril. Courage is necessary precisely because life is fragile—we are fragile. We live ever in the shadow of death. Yet that same fragility is also what makes courage praiseworthy. It is what makes courage a virtue. In the words of the Catholic philosopher Josef Pieper, "without vulnerability, there is no possibility" of true courage because there is no need for it. "An angel cannot be brave, because he is not vulnerable," Pieper said.[34] In a similar way, a man who behaves wildly but does not actually risk anything is not courageous. Courage is present only when it costs a man something, when a man confronts the possibility of loss or even death. "To be brave," Pieper wrote, "actually means to be able to suffer injury."[35] And the most praiseworthy kind of bravery is bravery for the sake of the good. Any idiot can get himself hurt. That is not courage. That is stupidity. Courage risks pain and worse in order to do what is right.[36] This is what male spiritedness is good for. To drive a man to suffer injury, to take a risk for righteousness, to become courageous.

As God admonished Joshua, so we should be admonishing men to forsake focus on self and comfort and to seek after courage. Turn toward the giants in your life. Run toward the darkness that threatens your family. Risk injury and harm. Be strong and courageous.

As Josef Pieper understood, "an injury suffered in fighting for the good confers an intactness" of soul that is more valuable "than all purely natural serenity."[37] There is a kind of character that comes only by courage.

GET CONFRONTATIONAL

As Joshua's story goes on, he musters the armies of Israel and crosses the river Jordan into the land of Canaan. There the Israelites ready for battle. Then one night, on the outskirts of a major garrison city, on the eve of the first engagement, Joshua encounters a strange visitor. "When Joshua was by Jericho, he lifted up his eyes and looked, and behold, a man was standing before him with his drawn sword in his hand. And Joshua went to him and said to him, 'Are you for us, or for our adversaries?' And he said, 'No; but I am the commander of the army of the LORD. Now I have come.'"[38]

The man is an envoy from God, sometimes styled an "angel." He brings a message. "Take off your sandals," he instructs Joshua. "The place where you are standing is holy."[39]

This is no ordinary piece of land where Joshua is. God is going to do something special with this ground. This is to be the site of a new Eden—and Joshua has a role to play. His task is to redeem it. Clear it. For God's purposes to be accomplished, Joshua must rid the land of the giants and the monsters that have taken control. He must break a path for the light.

The same is true for us in our lives, and above all in our characters. Joshua's story is not just about Canaan. Canaan is a place, but it represents more than land. It stands for the whole of the earth, and for our lives as well. God has made the world to be holy; he has made our lives to be holy. And the two go together. In the story, Canaan is overrun with wild beasts and enemies. Our souls can be like that. To clear the ground of our lives for a garden, we must break new paths of character. The path to the world's renewal runs through our souls.

Where do we begin? With confrontation. The Epicureans condemn confrontation and hold up "politeness" as a principal virtue. But politeness alone will not stop evil. Confrontation has its place, beginning in our souls. If we are to acquire the character of a warrior, we must stop compromising with evil.

The Bible implies the beasts and darkness came to Canaan because the inhabitants permitted them there, welcomed them, even. We do the same. By our choices, we can welcome evil, disorder, and chaos in our lives. We can turn our souls into a wasteland. So we must make other choices. We must do what Joshua did: drive the darkness out.

What evil have you compromised with in your life—allowed to slither in, by slow degrees, a little here, a little there? Maybe it's laziness. Have you stopped giving your full effort, at work or with your family?

Are you getting up late, showing up late, doing a lackluster job? You used to care; but now it's easier not to. You're not investing the time with your girlfriend or wife or kids. You're doing what's easy. You're prioritizing you.

Is it anger? When you started dating, you said you would never yell at her that way, but now you find yourself doing it all the time. You said you would be patient with your kids, but now you too often vent your frustrations on them freely. You find yourself on edge night and day.

Is it envy? Do you resent what others have—the girl, the wife, the car? Maybe you resent their success or what they wear, how they talk and how they treat you. Have you allowed yourself to become mired in the thought that life has been cruelly and uniquely unfair to you? Otto von Bismarck, the famed German chancellor of the nineteenth century, once remarked that he lay awake all night, hating.[40] That is what a life given over to envy looks like.

Maybe it is money. You started by saying only a little more, just enough to get by; now it's all you think of. It's the only thing that will satisfy you, the only measure you have that your life matters, the only way you can prove to yourself that you're worth something. Or perhaps it is pleasure, that most Epicurean of vices. Your greatest passion is leisure. Do you live for the next high and whatever can give it to you—sex, alcohol, drugs? Or perhaps you're more careful and more measured, not so gauche. You call it "self-care." But it's become your life.

These are evils we permit in our souls by degrees, like wild beasts stealing into the land. We compromise and choose not to challenge them. Slowly, by inches, we turn our souls over to them and come to love them, after a fashion. Soon enough, they own the place.

There is only one solution. Stop compromising. Start confronting. Choose an evil in your life and drive it back. When you retake ground, hold it. Activate your *thumos*, your drive, for something other than self-promotion. Activate it against evil, for the battle of your soul.

WAR ON PRIDE

The call of a warrior prompts a man to confront the evils of his life. Ultimately, it forces a man to choose between two entirely distinct ways of living. At the heart of every vice, of every sin, is pride. A man can either live for his selfish pride or he can make war on it, sacrifice it, count it loss, as a warrior does, and give himself for God and others. Only one way is the path to character.

Pride takes many forms, but in our age, it is warmly embraced and fervently practiced in the guise of the never-ending, relentlessly pursued quest for *status*. The late novelist Tom Wolfe accurately noted that the pursuit of status is the throbbing heart of modern society. Every man seeks status honor from other men, which is to say the esteem of other men, and to get that esteem a man labors to acquire the items and trappings our society regards as status-worthy. For instance: a high-toned degree or the corner office or a house in the right part of town. Status can involve money, certainly, but far more than that. Money is only one symbol of status, one ticket to social esteem. As Wolfe explained, "Status honor exist[s] quite apart from such gross matters as raw wealth and power. Family background, education, manners, dress, cultivation, style of life—these, the ineffable things, [are] what gran[t] you your exalted place in Society."[41]

You know what he means. There is not a man alive, not a human being drawing breath on this vast earth, who does not crave status. It is what the Bible calls the pride of life. Practically the whole of modern living is geared around it. Universities promise higher status; advertising sells consumer goods as status symbols; even entertainment has become a form of status. And you can spend your life seeking after it, thirsting and lusting for it—*or* you can live for something other than you. But you cannot do both. Either you live for status—which is living for you—or you sacrifice that life, that entire way of life, for something better.

This is the choice the way of the warrior puts us to. When the messenger came to Joshua before the battle, Joshua asked whose side he was on. "No," came the answer, because Joshua had asked the wrong question. God was not on Joshua's side. He was not there to serve Joshua. He was calling Joshua to serve him. He calls us to the same.

Want to be a warrior? Sacrifice your pride. Give up the quest for status. Stop buying stuff to make yourself feel better. Count it loss, and give your life to others instead. Measure your self-worth by their success, your significance by their joy, and your advancement by the growth in your character.

The anthropologist David Gilmore writes that "[i]n fulfilling their obligations, men stand to lose."[42] We may lose our reputations. We may lose our finances or our jobs. We may lose our beloved social status. But that is loss that gives life.

If Joshua will go as God charges him to go, if he will confront the monsters in the land and clear a path, his life will be multiplied many times over. He will help other people to flourish and new gardens to take root. This is the truth behind the words of Jesus in the Gospel of John: "Truly, truly, I say to you, unless a grain of wheat falls into the earth and dies, it remains alone; but if it dies, it bears much fruit."[43] The death of pride can become a source of new life.

The man who sacrifices his pride will take a lower-paying job to be with his aging parents who need him nearby. The man who sacrifices status honor will trade the company retreat and face time with the boss for a weekend with his children. The man who mortifies his pride will admit he has a problem with alcohol and start tackling it, no matter how many social invitations it costs him. And while each of these decisions implies loss, each multiplies the light many times over. For this is the strange yet marvelous contour of our universe, that by confronting his own evils and sacrificing his own pride a man contributes to the healing of the world.

The Roman playwright Plautus said, "[he] [w]ho dies by *virtus*"—manliness—"nevertheless does not perish."[44] The Bible says something better. He who sacrifices his self-love builds his soul and then the world into a temple.

LOVE AND HOPE

The man who makes war on the evil in his life and sacrifices his own pride opens his life, in the end, to something far more powerful. He opens it to love. Love is the burning center of the warrior's existence and the secret of all true courage. The warrior loves something dearly and passionately more than himself. He loves his wife and children. He loves his nation. He loves God. And that love makes him strong.

Self-regard, by contrast, is a weak affection. It will consume your life, to be sure, as in the story of Narcissus, who loved his image so completely he wasted his life away staring at it. But it cannot inspire. If your life is relentlessly about you, you will never run toward danger. You will never confront the giants that threaten, whether your finances or your boss or an addiction. You won't risk incurring the wrath of the powers that be by speaking the truth. You will always try to keep yourself safe, undamaged. And you will always have everything to lose. That way ends in despair and self-contempt.

A man's conscience is a powerful thing. It will condemn the man who constantly avoids struggle and pain as a coward. But if you will abandon your focus on self, you will find the love that gives courage.

And love, in turn, gives birth to hope.

Sometimes courage is portrayed these days as the refuge of the hopeless. J. R. R. Tolkien puts something that sounds like this sentiment into the mouth of Gandalf in his *Lord of the Rings* saga. "There never was much hope," Gandalf says, as Sauron's darkness grows and the quest to destroy the Ring seems to falter. "Just a fool's hope."[45] Many have interpreted this passage to mean courage is most noble, most true, when the warrior believes he is doomed to fail. But that is not quite Tolkien's point, and not the Bible's either. Tolkien's heroes soldier on not because they are fatalists, content to be mere pawns of chance. Nor because they are nihilists, believing all to be meaningless. They soldier on because they believe right will prevail. And they believe their lives can make a difference in making it so.

I have known men like this, and seen with my own eyes the power of their hope. In the fall of 2019, the Chinese Communist government in Beijing orchestrated a crackdown on the hitherto independent city of Hong Kong. Displeased with Hong Kong's autonomy, and Hong Kongers' (as they call themselves) criticism of the Beijing government, Communist leaders threatened to suspend self-government in the city, contrary to China's own treaty obligations that guaranteed the city's special status. In response, protestors took to the streets, only to be met in return by violent police repression. The protestors refused to back down, and the clashes turned bloody.

I was in my first year in the Senate at the time, watching these events unfold from afar. I learned from sources in Hong Kong that the protests were being informally led—it was in many ways truly a spontaneous uprising—by a group of young, very young, men and women. When I heard the accounts of their courage and listened to their pleas for help, I knew I had to go.

I traveled to Hong Kong in October of 2019 to meet with them and see the protests firsthand. The U.S. consulate in the city was less than delighted with my visit. Consulate staff advised beforehand against the trip. Once there, they strongly urged me to keep to my hotel. I politely ignored this advice. I wanted to see the protestors myself, see their courage and their stand, and lend whatever support I could.

One member of my staff had extensive contacts with the protestors. As soon as night fell, we left the hotel and headed toward where we believed, based on his information, the latest clashes between the government and the Hong Kongers were underway. We hailed a cab, but the driver refused to take us more than a few blocks. Eventually we walked, finding our way to the Mong Kok district, usually a bustling shopping and commercial hub, but on that night a battle-ground. The clashes between pro-Beijing police and the protestors had already turned violent by the time we arrived. A car burned in the street. Protestors were spray-painting "Free Hong Kong" on boarded-up windows. There were people running in every which direction. As we watched, a large group of Hong Kongers began to assemble in the middle of the road, peacefully, carrying signs decrying the crackdown. Suddenly a phalanx of pro-Beijing police in riot gear appeared opposite them, heavily armed. They took to loudspeakers and ordered the crowd to disperse. They threatened to disperse them by force if they did not.

The U.S. government often sends military liaisons with members of Congress when they travel abroad. In this case, at this moment, my military liaison leaned into my ear and said, "Sir, we should back away. If they begin firing into the crowd and we are caught up in it, it could cause an international incident." He was right. But the protestors did not back away. We stayed too. I wanted to see with my own eyes what would happen. The protestors held their ground, and eventually it was the riot police who turned and moved back. All night long the protests continued, with explosions and violent exchanges in many parts of the city.

I met with the leaders of the protest the next morning. It was an honor. They were startlingly young—only in their early twenties, most of them. Several were veterans of earlier protest movements. A few had already spent time in prison. I promised to report what they were doing to people back in the United States, to explain what they were fighting for.

Why are you willing to face prison? I asked them—and though I did not name it, we all knew what else they faced, the other, ever distinct possibility: death. *We love Hong Kong*, they said, *and we want to see it free. We believe we can be a beacon for the world.* They had hope.

They were realistic at the same time. They knew the odds were long. They knew the Beijing government could destroy Hong Kong's freedoms in a moment, if it chose. But they believed their stand was worth making, even if they did not live to see their cause succeed, because they believed their actions would echo and build and—in time—whether in their lifetimes or another's, prevail.

That is the courage of hope. And even now, they go on hoping. After the events I witnessed, the Beijing authorities intensified the repression. They forcibly put down the protests. Many of the young people I met that October were later imprisoned or exiled. Yet their hope endures. And the light of that hope—in the right, in God—cannot be extinguished.

God made the world with a plan, to be something—an Eden. And even now that plan is advancing. Every man can play a part. We are *born* to play a part. That is a hope that pain and death cannot destroy. And a man who gives his life to that hope, and to its Author, will not be disappointed.

THE POSSIBILITY OF TRANSFORMATION

A man who lives by courage and love and hope will be changed. When Joshua first appears in the Bible, alongside Moses, his towering mentor, he says next to nothing and makes little impression. Yet by the end of the battles in Canaan, it is Joshua who towers. He has marshalled the armies of Israel, he has led them into war, he has driven back enemy after enemy from the promised land. And in the battle at Aijalon, he holds back even the sun. "[Joshua] said in the sight of Israel, 'Sun, stand still at Gibeon, and moon, in the Valley of Aijalon.' And the sun stood still, and the moon stopped, until the nation took vengeance on their enemies" (Joshua 10:12–13).

Joshua was transformed. How? He himself gave the clue years earlier, when he returned from spying out the very same land and delivered a report to Moses and the people. "The land, which we passed through to spy it out, is an exceedingly good land," he said. "[D]o not fear the people of the land, for they are *bread for us.*"[46] There is a kind of growth that comes only from confronting your giants. There is a kind of strength that comes only from the battle.

Dave Collins and Áine MacNamara are researchers who studied the career paths and life experiences of "super champion" athletes, to use their phrase—athletes who competed at the highest levels of national and international competition and succeeded, multiple times over. Their findings were fascinating. Collins and MacNamara discovered that the most successful athletes were those who encountered some of the most significant personal setbacks, whether from physical injury or other hardship. The most successful athletes not only survived adversity, but they grew from the trauma. They benefited from it.

The super champion athletes used hardship to develop new personal habits and sharpen their mental focus. They used setbacks to discover new strategies for training. Precisely opposite what one might assume, Collins and MacNamara found that the athletes who did *not* experience trauma were the ones who were impoverished. They missed opportunities to build the personal resilience and habits of mind vital to success in elite competition. Collins and MacNamara famously summarized their findings: "talent needs trauma."[47]

The same is true for us all. Joshua forecast that the giants of Canaan would be bread for those who dared confront them. In our own lives, facing danger may expose us to loss, but it also makes us men we would not otherwise be. It builds qualities of character we would not otherwise possess.

My own career has been full of challenges and controversies, legal arguments and political battles. As a United States senator, making difficult choices comes with the job, and my pledge to the people I serve is that I will always do what I believe is right. I have found myself a lone vote in the Senate on more than one occasion. I have found myself sometimes at the center of great disputes. I am often criticized. But that is the job. I am thankful for the opportunity—to learn, to serve, and to hold fast to the truth, no matter the opposition. I have found, as I know has been true for others, that courage begets courage. If you hold fast in the face of anger and accusation now, you will find the confidence to do it again—and again, and again after that. Taking a stand nurtures your resolve. It feeds resilience. It builds hope. If your cause is just, if it is true, you must defend it. If you stand on holy ground, fight for it.

So choose a giant in your life. Maybe it's the state of your marriage. Maybe it's your relationship with your child or with your parents. Maybe it's an addiction. Maybe it's a habit of telling other people what they want to hear to get your way or to avoid conflict. Whatever it may be, resolve to turn toward it rather than away. Take on the risk of injury and pain. Be willing to sacrifice. Perhaps you will see an immediate change. Perhaps not. But you will know that you are fighting for holy ground, for the purpose and potential of your life and those you love. And that fight is what you were born for. We were born, each of us, to spread the light, feeding it on the kindling of our lives. We were born to have the character of a warrior.

When I was a college student, I spent the fall of my junior year studying in Oxford, England—one of those "semester abroad" programs. It was my first time out of the country. I befriended, while I was there, an Anglican priest, whom I will call Martin. He was a big, bluff fellow, probably in his mid-forties when I knew him, the son of a butcher. He used to take me on walks in the morning through the

Oxford market, where the butcher stands were located. "I love the smell of meat and blood in the morning," he would say.

One day on one of our rambles he steered me toward Balliol College, a towering medieval structure in the heart of the town. He brought me up short in front of the college's main gate, near the intersection of Broad Street and Cornmarket. There, set in the pavement, is a cross of cobblestones, marking the site where two English priests were burned at the stake in the year 1555. Hugh Latimer and Nicholas Ridley were their names. They refused to recant their Protestant faith and submit to the religious dictates of the monarch. In consequence, they were bound and stood atop a pile of wood on October 16, 1555, and while a crowd looked on, set to flame. The last words the crowd heard came from Hugh Latimer to his friend, Ridley, as the flames mounted. "Be of good comfort, Master Ridley, and play the man," Latimer said. "We shall this day light such a candle in England that, by God's grace, I trust shall never be put out."

Martin told me this story and stood there with me for a moment after, looking at the cross in the stones. Then he turned on his heel and walked away, saying over his shoulder as he went, "That's what being a man is about." That is the character of a warrior.

CHAPTER EIGHT

BUILDER

My father is one of three boys in his family, the middle son. His older brother is my uncle Bruce. He and my father are approximately three years apart in age. They had formed a fast bond by the time their third brother, my younger uncle, came along, and the stories of Bruce and my dad's childhood antics are legendary in the family.

For example: My grandfather—not Harold, the farmer, but my dad's father—worked as the manager of a small storefront JCPenney in western Kansas during my father's childhood, back when JCPenney still maintained storefronts in small towns. This was the early 1960s. He put in long hours at the store, and if there was one thing he valued at home above all, it was rest. Sleep. Unfortunately for him, Bruce and my dad shared a room directly above their parents' room. The house, which they rented, was very modest, and the boys' room was too small for two beds, so Bruce and my father also shared a bed (until they outgrew that arrangement and one of them moved to a mattress in the basement). Now as any parent of small boys knows, put two of them together in a room and what you do not get much of is quiet. My dad and uncle were no different. Their nighttime laughter and horseplay frequently woke my grandfather in the room below.

On those occasions, Grandpa would reach for a yardstick he kept by his night table and bang the ceiling with it, warning the boys to quiet down. If that did not produce the desired silence, Grandpa took the yardstick up the stairs and converted it to a switch, swatting the boys' backsides. But without much light, and in his general state of nocturnal confusion, Grandpa often had difficulty seeing just whose backside he was swatting. Bruce took advantage of these circumstances by pulling my father on top of him, or so the story goes, and crying out as if he were being spanked, all while Grandpa was, in fact, spanking my father. Similar stories of pranks and tomfoolery are legion.

Bruce was a smart boy and grew, as an adult, to be one of the most interesting people I know. I remember watching him, when I was a child, sit down to the piano and play entire pieces of music that I recognized from the radio or from church by ear, no sheet music in sight. He can still do it. He has what musicians call perfect pitch. If you play a note for him or hum it, he can tell you what note it is, just from listening. He took up the fiddle later in life and the violin and has played the saxophone some as well. There is no instrument I believe he could not play if he wanted to.

He went to college, played football (and shared an apartment with my dad—like old times), and after graduation moved to Arkansas, where my grandparents had gone from western Kansas after JCPenney closed the little store my grandpa managed. There, in Arkansas, Bruce started his own business, pouring concrete.

It's called Hawley Concrete, first incorporated in 1978 and in continuous operation since. He typically has a handful of employees at a given time. Today his oldest son, my cousin, works the business with him. They pour driveways and patios and foundations; they do stamping and staining and concrete repair. You can see some of Bruce's artistry in what he does: there's an elegance to it, and precision. It's hard work, tough work—hot in the humid Arkansas summers and wet in the winter, and they work all year long. But it's good work too—the kind of work that allowed Bruce to get married and raise a family of six kids, and that has allowed him to live a full life, enjoying his children, pursuing his passions. Contributing. Building.

The truth is that manual work of the kind Bruce does has become less and less valued in our society, not least because the elites who set the cultural tone largely disdain those who work with their hands. The media regularly admonish schoolchildren to go to college precisely to avoid the kind of labor Bruce has been doing for forty years. The tech start-up wizard and the Wall Street maven are liberal culture's beau ideals. (Don't believe me? Just look at the main characters on television sitcoms. You'll be hard-pressed to find many a blue-collar worker.) These "masters of the universe" have advanced degrees and sit in air-conditioned offices and make, in pop culture mythology anyway, massive sums of money. That is what today's elites tell our children to aspire to.

Those who don't want that life or don't have those degrees have watched their work prospects steadily dim over the last five decades, as more and more blue-collar jobs have disappeared overseas or been simply eliminated. In their stead, our political leaders offer government benefits—welfare, dependency. Dependence is in fact a temptation to every man, in every age. It is the temptation to let someone else do it for you. Let someone else plan your future, let someone else provide, let someone else take the risk. Let someone else take responsibility. It's a temptation that came to Adam in the garden, to let Eve deal with the serpent rather than to protect her and guard Eden.

The antidote to dependence is building. The antidote to passivity is work. And work is, according to the Bible and the Western tradition it defines, an invitation that speaks to every man. It is an invitation to do what every man wants to do: *matter*, in the most lasting way possible.

The Bible celebrates the value of work and the character of the men who do it in the story of David, whose life followed some centuries after Joshua and the battle for Canaan. What we learn from David as a builder is this: that a man is born to work and to acquire the character that working brings. This is no small thing. If done humbly and well, work can help make the world what it was meant to be. The man who becomes a builder can help cultivate a little Eden.

GIVE MORE THAN YOU TAKE

Besides being a focal point of the Bible, David's story is one of the grand dramatic sagas of all ancient literature. You may remember some of it. He was born to an obscure family, the youngest boy and least looked for to succeed. Nevertheless, God sent a prophet to anoint him, when he was still a boy, to be Israel's future king. Like Abraham, David was called from obscurity to purpose. Like Joshua, David would become a great warrior. And as we meet him, he is about to build and to display for us the promise and power of work. Here is a key part of his story, from the second book of Samuel, once David has become Israel's king.

> The king and his men marched to Jerusalem to attack the Jebusites, who lived there. The Jebusites said to David, "You will not get in here; even the blind and the lame can ward you off." They thought, "David cannot get in here." Nevertheless, David captured the fortress of Zion.... On that day, David said, "Anyone who conquers the Jebusites will have to use the water shaft to reach those 'lame and blind' who are David's

enemies." That is why they say, "The 'blind and lame' will not enter the palace." David then took up residence in the fortress and called it the City of David. He built up the area around it, from the supporting terraces inward. And he became more and more powerful, because the LORD God Almighty was with him. (2 Samuel 5:6–10 NIV)

The story begins with David clearing the land of evil in the manner of Joshua. The Jebusites, interestingly, were some of the ancient peoples that Joshua and his army had failed to expel. The story suggests that even now, centuries later by the Bible's reckoning, some sort of evil omen hangs over their stronghold, Jerusalem: it was the home of the "blind and the lame"—symbolism for a dark power that guarded the fortress.[1] David concludes Joshua's work by confronting and defeating the Jebusites.

And what does he do next? He builds. In particular, he builds a city.

Cities held great significance in the ancient Near East, where they were regarded as the creation of the gods. In both ancient Mesopotamia and Egypt, the earliest writers portrayed cities as primordial, existing even before humanity, their foundations laid by the gods as a pattern for the universe as a whole. In fact, ancient peoples believed that the gods maintained order in the cosmos through the cities they made: they ruled from there, their temples were there; the cities were cosmic control centers. The order of the city at once exhibited and helped sustain the order of the universe, an idea one can hear even in Plato.[2]

This was, I say, the prevailing view in the ancient Near East. But not in the Bible. Not in the David story. David does not come to an ancient city that he reveres to pay homage to its god. He comes to a stronghold of corruption and conquers it, and begins to build something new. And here is perhaps the most interesting element of the story. Jerusalem does indeed become, in the end, a city of the divine. David's God, Abraham's God, does indeed take up residence there, famously so. Zion, the city of David, becomes the city of God—and still is, for millions of worshipers worldwide. But notice, David's God chooses to take up residence in a city that *David* has built. The city is not primordial, built by the gods, but by human hands—by David's hands. That is the point. God honors David by blessing and ultimately dwelling where he builds. God honors David's work. Indeed, David's work makes him a partner with God.

The Bible places a premium on work, and on men with the character to work faithfully. From the beginning of the Adam story all the way back in Genesis, the Bible emphasizes that God has called man to be his partner in the divine labor, the making of the world into a temple. Genesis tells of five days in which God subdued the chaos of the universe, then filled it with stars, then with planets and living things. On the sixth day, he created man and charged him to do the same, to "subdue" and "fill" the earth—that is, to continue the work of creation after the pattern of God. Adam's mission as a man called him to labor and to provide. A man is meant to build, to work.

From his studies across cultures, of Micronesia, Melanesia, Africa, the Mediterranean, and the Americas, the anthropologist David Gilmore concluded that the "critical threshold" marking the passage from boyhood to manhood was "the point at which the boy produces more than he consumes and gives more than he takes."[3] In short, manhood begins when a boy ceases to be dependent and becomes someone who can provide and build.

There is something in the character of a man that responds to the character of work. While he labors to shape and manage the world, the labor itself shapes his soul. Studies show that men who work are more confident, more emotionally stable, and, of course, more prosperous.[4] Perhaps this is why the Bible, from Genesis to David, portrays work as godlike, activity after the character of God.

What we can take from this is straightforward. Men are meant to work, and they should. Men who work are more likely to be happy, more likely to be married, and more likely to have children. In America, three-fifths of working men considered "prime aged," that is, between twenty-five and fifty-four, are married. By contrast, a considerable proportion of those men who are out of the workforce are not only unmarried now, but they have never been married at all.[5]

My advice to young men looking for work is to do whatever honorable work is available. It is the same advice I received as a young man. I grew up hearing many a legend from my dad's father, whose name was Norm, the one who banged for quiet on the ceiling with the ruler, about his first job. He was born and raised in Smith Center, Kansas, which he always remarked to me was the precise geographic center of the continental United States. His family was poor. His father, my great-grandfather, worked the railroad. My great-grandmother worked at a local five-and-dime. They lived in a small house with a detached garage. When my grandfather Norm was a boy, in the 1940s, the garage caught fire by some mishap. Firefighters saved the house, but not the car. The family couldn't afford one again until he was well into high school.

As you might imagine given those circumstances, work was highly valued in that family, and every family member was expected to contribute. My grandfather Norm's first job was as a dishwasher at the Bon Ton Café, a local establishment (long since shuttered). In time, he was promoted to short-order cook. The Bon Ton was a diner, with booths in front, I am told, and an open grill toward the back with a deep fryer on one side. Grandpa took up his station there, grilling burgers and ham'n'cheese, chicken sandwiches, and of course French fries—you name it. He would entertain me as a child by rattling through his menu and boasting of his speed on the grill. Once, while standing in the kitchen carrying on in this fashion, he seized a metal spatula, tossed it end over end in the air, and caught it with the other hand. "This is how I used to do it at the Bon Ton," he said. "I tell you boy, I can still smell the grease on the grill."

His stories made a point. Work is a good thing. No work is beneath you. "I never had a job I didn't learn something from," he would say to me. He urged me to work as young as I could, doing whatever constructive work anyone would pay me to do. (When I asked him why he didn't make grilled cheese anymore and Grandma did all the cooking, he would demur. "I got all wore out at the Bon Ton," he would say.)

Contrast that attitude with the line that emerged among the chattering classes in the 1960s, repeated ad nauseam since, that some jobs are simply "dead-end," not sufficiently stimulating or rewarding to be compelling as work.[6] That notion makes the value of work depend on the job's social status, which means, in practice, it depends on what the culture's opinion makers think of it. And the opinion makers don't work blue-collar jobs. This is how we end up with the increasingly widespread idea that manual labor is somehow degrading.

That is not the view from the Bible. God assigned Adam to perform manual labor, as my grandfather did and my uncle Bruce does still, day in, day out. The Bible's view is that all work is worthwhile if it is performed in service to God and others. As long as it is honest labor, every job has a purpose. Every job provides a service. Every job hones a skill.

The Puritans of old, those fervent Christians who would eventually brave a dark ocean to found a new "city on a hill"—America—had a powerfully robust view of work. They regarded everyday work as a "calling," and their test for whether work was worth doing was simple: ask whether it is useful to others and offered to God. If it is, it's meaningful and worthwhile. The social status of the work means nothing. What others think of it is irrelevant. Honest work honestly done dignifies the worker. The sixteenth-century Puritan Joseph Hall said it like this: "The homeliest service that we doe in an honest calling, though it be but to plow, or digge, if done in obedience, and conscious of God's Commandment, is crowned with an ample reward...."[7] That's a view that should be heard in America today.

There is a practical element to all this, too. The sooner you get employed, the more skills you gain. And the more skills you gain, the sooner you advance in the workforce. Studies show the best job training program is, not surprisingly, a job. The best place to learn new skills and cultivate productive habits is in the workforce.[8]

If it is man's mission to be God's representative, doing God's work, restoring and expanding God's temple, man must be a builder. You could say it like this: To become a man, you must work. You must contribute. You must give more than you take.

REJECT DEPENDENCY

The problem in America today is that too many men are not working, and our respect for those who are is waning. Look at the trends of just the last fifty years. It used to be that almost 90 percent of men over twenty worked—or, at a minimum, were looking for work. That was true from the turn of the last century until about the late 1950s. Then began a long, abysmal decline. By 2015, only 68 percent of men over twenty were in the workforce, or trying to be—meaning that the proportion of men without paid work doubled, from 14 to 32 percent.[9] The COVID-19 pandemic made matters even worse: in early 2022, the percentage of prime-age men neither working nor looking for work was *three times larger* than in 1965.[10] Today, a smaller percentage of prime-age men are working in the labor force than in March 1940, at the tail end of the Great Depression.[11] These numbers are the lowest seen since the military demobilization following the end of the Second World War.[12]

The sheer magnitude of the decline of work is often masked by the official unemployment statistics, which fluctuate higher or lower each month. But those reports are misleading in one key sense: they include only those who are out of work *and actively trying to find a job*. In the last fifty years, millions of men have decided not to try for work at all. These are the men the unemployment statistics do not record, the millions of missing men who have disappeared from labor. Here's another way to get at the size of the problem: if the same percentage of men worked today who did a century ago, there would be ten million more workers on the job in America right now.[13]

In case you have doubts, life without work is not a good life. It is, for one thing, often an existence bereft of close family or companionship. Men without work are more likely to live alone, less likely to be married, and less likely to have children. When they do have kids, they are less likely to see them: an unemployed father is considerably less likely to live with his children than a father who goes to work every day.[14] That's only the beginning. Unemployed men are more frequently divorced.[15] Approximately half of men without work are on painkillers.[16] And these same men suffer higher rates of depression and suicide than men in the labor force.[17]

And it's not as if declining to go to work frees up all sorts of time for productive activities. In fact, men who aren't working seem to do very little at all. They don't, on the whole, volunteer or pursue education or take care of children or others in need. They don't go out much.[18] Most of what they do is sit and watch screens—television, the internet, video games—to the tune of two thousand hours a year.[19] Those are numbers equivalent to a full-time job. There is also crime. Among unemployed men between thirty and thirty-eight years of age, for example, the majority have been arrested at least once, 40 percent have been convicted once, and fully 20 percent have been to prison.[20]

Why are so many men in this country not working? Economists have fumbled for explanations. Surely one reason is the policy choices made by elected officials in Washington over the span of the last five decades. Both parties have embraced a program of globalization, to include liberalized trade, liberalized immigration laws, and lavishly favorable treatment for multinational corporations. This has exacted a heavy toll on American workers, especially American men. There was a time in this country when a man could support his family on the wages of blue-collar work, particularly in the manufacturing sector. Most of those jobs have gone overseas now. Some celebrate this development as good for consumers—more cheap stuff to be had—or as a form of "gender justice": men can no longer rely on their physical strength to get a leg up in the job market, the logic goes.[21]

Many left-wing policymakers argue that blue-collar jobs in manufacturing, farming, and energy are too dirty, too noxious for the climate. They prefer an economy built on white-collar service jobs that produce nothing tangible and require the expensive degrees favored by the leftist intelligentsia. Don't have one of those degrees? You'll just have to make do in a lower-end hospitality or administrative job, which, not incidentally, pay considerably below the hourly average a man could earn in manufacturing. The median manufacturing job pays approximately $22.50 an hour. For hospitality, the median is $13.70 an hour; for administrative services, it is $17.50.[22]

Other liberals cluck their tongues and say of course men could improve their station, if they would just change careers—and interests. These liberal "experts" cast the loss of blue-collar work as a necessary evil, a painful stage on the path to a more efficient economy. They tell men to adjust their attitudes, to give up their outdated attachment to physical labor and production and to embrace gentler roles. One liberal researcher recently argued for pushing men into what he calls "HEAL" professions—Healthcare, Education, Administration, and Literacy.[23] He wants more men to work as home health aides, for example, and as teachers and social workers. There is nothing wrong with those careers, of course: to take just one example, many boys benefit from having

male teachers as positive role models.[24] But the fact is, men are historically less interested in these fields and less educationally prepared to
take them on. Some liberals find men's hesitancy on this score vexing.[25]
Naturally, they blame traditional "gender role" stereotypes and call for
more government spending to get men into so-called HEAL careers.[26]
Change the men, in other words. No surprise, the institutional culture
of many of these fields—such as education—is shot through with the
notion that men and masculinity are problems that need to be fixed.[27]

To the experts safely ensconced in their think tanks, I would just
say this: Is it really too much to ask that our economy work for men as
they are, rather than as the left wants them to be? Is it too much to ask
that men be able to find decent work on which they can support a family
without having to pay six figures in college tuition to acquire a dubious
academic credential, or leave their family home for some distant locale,
or take up a career path in which they have no interest? Men who have
an aptitude for blue-collar work and enjoy it shouldn't be pushed by
policymakers onto career tracks for which they're ill-suited. And they
shouldn't have to apologize to anyone. There is more to life, and to a
successful economy, than learning to code. And an economy with far
more private-sector manufacturers and far fewer public-sector
paper-shufflers should be welcomed, not scoffed at.

Let's tell the truth. The loss of high-paying, blue-collar work for
men has been a catastrophe for this nation and for men, robbing them
of employment, family, dignity, and hope. We should be doing everything we can to reverse it.

Our work crisis is not only economic, however, but also cultural.
It reveals a growing culture of dependency. Researchers report that the
number of men who don't work because they can't find a job is stag-
geringly small, a mere 6 percent in one survey. Fully three quarters of
men out of the labor force say they do not *want* a job.[28] That is, they
would prefer *not* to work. Consider this: in 2014, only 12 percent of

nonworking but able-bodied men between the ages of twenty-five and fifty-four said they were even open to the prospect of working.[29] And indeed, statistics show that men who can't find jobs account for relatively little of the decline in the labor force over time.[30]

Many men are content, apparently, to be dependent. And our political leaders have encouraged it. The response of the modern left to the crisis of work is particularly telling in this regard. Leftists have advocated expanding welfare payments and "disability" insurance, to the point one need not actually be disabled to claim government support. More recently, they have championed universal basic income. This latter idea would have the federal government guarantee every adult in America an income stream generous enough to live on, whether he works or not. One liberal candidate for president recently ran an entire campaign on it.

The message is that work is optional, replaceable, that a check is just as good as a job. And what that means in practice is a check is just as good as a man. Because if government can supply everything a father or husband once did by working, what is the point of manhood? The culture of dependence destroys men's agency and their sense of self-worth.

WORK AND LIBERTY

Dependence also makes men less free. It makes them servile. There is a long tradition of political thought, running back to ancient Rome and Greece but really originating with the Bible, that sees personal independence as a precondition for personal liberty. You can't be free if someone else pays your bills. You can't be free if someone else controls your livelihood, especially if that someone else is the government. You can't be free if you don't work. Why not? Because if someone else controls your livelihood, he controls you. That is the ancients' insight, and they were right.

The Bible elucidates this in the story of the Exodus, when God delivered the Israelites from Pharaoh. Egypt was, for the Israelites, a place of bondage, the "house of slavery," the Bible says. The Israelites worked, indeed—but not for themselves. They worked at the command of another, and the fruits of their labor were taken by others. They subsisted, but not by their labor, only by what they were *given*. This made them slaves, in a political sense and in a personal one, too. They had no meaningful control over their lives, no real ability to shape their futures or influence their fate. Above all, dependence denied them the ability to follow God, to shoulder the mission he had appointed for them. They could not do what he had created them to do. The only person whom they could obey was Pharaoh, the one who gave them bread.

Depending on others for your needs brings you under their influence. If you look to others for your bread, you serve them. They have power over you. That is servility, not freedom. The Bible makes this point by saying that in the promised land, the new Eden, the Israelites were to serve no human master—but, and this is an important addition, that did not mean they could do whatever they pleased: that would be to trade one form of bondage for another, dependence on Pharaoh for slavery to their flesh and passions. Rather, the Israelites were to serve the purpose God had written into their natures, that is, to be his representatives. For men, that meant—and means—"cultivating" and "guarding," making gardens in the wilderness. This is true freedom: to realize and live the fullness of one's humanity, to become God's servant on earth. If you are going to shoulder that mission, if you are going to realize that freedom, you cannot refuse to work. You cannot depend on someone else. You must have independence of character.

Dependence can take forms other than failing to work, of course. It can mean sitting back at work when you know you could do more. Passivity and mediocrity are, in this sense, forms of dependence. It can mean relying on others financially when you could support yourself. It can mean failing to make plans for your future.

When I was a law professor, I knew a student, let's call him Brian, who steadfastly refused to make any settled plans beyond graduation. After he got his diploma, he arranged a trip overseas, backpacking and generally goofing around for several months, then drifted back to the university area looking for some sort of employment. But not anything, mind you, that would tie him down for more than a few months. And nothing that would require more than strictly eight hours of his day, five days a week—at most. He was forever talking about "quality of life" and the importance of maintaining work-life balance. I pointed out that one must first *work* to have a problem with work-life balance, but he was undeterred. I pressed him on what he wanted to do—not just in the next two months or three, but in the next two or three years. Or ten. Or fifteen. He couldn't answer. And while he had a poor relationship with his parents and was not, technically, dependent on them, his refusal to take responsibility for his own future was in fact a form of dependence. He depended on chance, if nothing else. He pursued a life of deferred maturity. In his mind, career, marriage, and fatherhood could wait, maybe forever.

Against the temptation to dependence comes the call to work and build. And the Bible invests that call with the most powerful significance possible. It says that God waits upon our work and cooperates with it. There are things he chooses to accomplish only by our working. There is a future he creates only by our building. He uses our work to renew the world.

REJECT NIHILISM

That message sharply contradicts another group of leftists who claim men's work ruins rather than improves the earth. These are the

climate-change fanatics. They equate human production with despolia-
tion, the use of the earth's resources with environmental rape. For them,
environmental fear now stands in for religious commitment. As one
observer put it, on the left "apocalyptic environmentalism is a kind of
new Judeo-Christian religion, one that has replaced God with nature."
In the Bible, "human problems stem from our failure to adjust ourselves
to God. In the apocalyptic environmental tradition, human problems
stem from our failure to adjust ourselves to nature."[31]

Recall how, in the Genesis story, Adam and Eve are told to exercise
dominion and expand the garden—to cultivate the wild world and
order it to the glory of their Creator. The religion of environmentalism
preaches a very different message: leave the world well enough alone,
in all its unformed chaos, or suffer terrible consequences. Human efforts
to order creation will only do harm, because humans are the villains.

The left routinely blames men for our planet's supposedly imminent
climate doom. The climate crisis, leftists say, is born from Western
society's thirst for power, for dominion over the earth. And men run
Western culture: it's "the patriarchy." So they say. On this telling, men's
assertiveness and desire to build are symptoms of Western imperialism;
the idea of taming the wilderness to build a civilization is merely a
self-serving argument for pushing aside indigenous peoples. The climate
radicals teach that men must accept that their work upon the world
nearly always makes things worse, not better; destroys, not builds up;
robs and deforms. Merely by being male, men do damage. Truly, men
are the problem.

Patricia MacCormack's recent book, *The Ahuman Manifesto*,
provides the starkest imaginable statement of this bizarre creed.
MacCormack, professor of continental philosophy at Anglia Ruskin
University and a self-described "occultist magician," argues that human
beings, and men in particular, have so damaged the nonhuman world
that their only ethical responsibility is voluntary self-extinction. For

MacCormack, "the death of the human species is the most life-affirming event that could liberate the natural world from oppression...."[32] To bring about that goal, she calls for "death activism" intended "to end the human and open the world" to the nonhuman.[33] Notice the exact inversion of the Genesis teaching on men and work. Men do not order the creation and help make it all it could be; men only destroy. Rather than the Bible, MacCormack calls for enlisting the support of "Luciferianism"—that is, Satanism—and "modern witchcraft" as intellectual resources.[34] The biblical tradition is far too focused on those noxious humans, she writes, far too oriented to "the self-serving/God-serving subject that oppresses."[35] Whatever that means.

Credit where it's due, though: MacCormack, more than most, is perfectly clear about the implications of her claims and how sharply they diverge from the Genesis story. She, at least, understands that the logical end point for much contemporary environmental activism is the abolition of men.

This nihilistic theology is having an effect. A 2020 poll found that fully a quarter of childless American adults said climate-change fears deterred them from having children.[36] That number is likely to keep going up: according to one recent analysis, the choice "to not have children owing to fears over climate change is growing and impacting fertility rates quicker than any preceding trend in the field of fertility decline."[37]

There's now an entire genre of "climate fiction" focused on the anxieties of those who foresee total destruction in the near future. "What will be the safest place?" worries the heroine of Jenny Offill's critically acclaimed novel *Weather*. "I can't seem to escape that question."[38] Not to be outdone, Lydia Millet's novel *A Children's Bible* offers an allegorical retelling of the Old Testament against the backdrop of climate-driven civilizational collapse: "New kinds of animals evolve. Some other creatures come and live here, like we did. And all the old beautiful things will still be in the air. Invisible but there. Like, I don't know, an expectation that sort of hovers. Even when we're all gone."[39]

Some on the left are going beyond mere brooding and acting out their fears. As I write this, environmentalist activists around the world have been conducting a campaign of vandalism against famous works of Western art, such as Johannes Vermeer's *Girl with a Pearl Earring.*[40] In an effort to raise awareness about the stakes of the climate crisis, they've been variously gluing their hands to famous paintings or hurling food at them.

What is the message to men in all this? That their work is not only insignificant, but deeply destructive. And if that is true, why bother to work at all? For that matter, why not forgo family and child-rearing and any other act of consequence that expresses some shred of hope for the future, and instead collect a government check? Why not just do nothing? This is where the left's anti-human, anti-work climate theology ultimately leads: to nihilism, to nothingness. But the Bible has something better to offer. A man can be an agent of renewal. His work can matter. He can build.

WORKING WITH GOD

The city of David, Jerusalem, became, in the Bible's description, a place where heaven touched earth, where God himself took up residence, as in Eden of old, where "silver [was] as common…as stones, and cedar as plentiful as sycamore-fig trees in the foothills."[41] The city was a foreshadowing, a foretaste, of what all the world might be if men would carry the light into all the world. And David became an emblem of what a man might do, what he might amount to, if he lived the mission God gave him. David became an agent of life and renewal.

In the Bible, God charges man to help him build creation into a temple, to make it fully what God intends it to be. There is an illuminating contrast on this score with other creation stories from the ancient world. In most of these, the creating gods—be it Marduk or Baal or others—delegate manual labor to humans because it is beneath a god's status.

The Bible, however, says nearly the opposite. God appoints Adam to work not so God can be done with working, but to make Adam a partner in temple-building. Adam's labor, his common, do-it-with-your-hands work, is God's way of bringing his creation into order and fullness. According to the Bible, God designed the earth to respond to man's labor. When Adam abandoned that task, God did not abandon the world. He delegated the task to other men—to Abraham, to Joshua, to David. To us.

This is the Bible's answer, by the way, to the myth of the dead-end job. This is the reason work—all kinds of work—is worth doing. No job that is performed with diligence and intention is a dead end, because all diligent, honorable work brings forth something new in the world. Something better. The world is great with potential. But it needs labor to draw it out.

And everywhere we look, man's labor makes the world come alive. Every discovery, every innovation, every invention and improvement, from the electricity we enjoy to the machines that transport us on the roads or by air, is the product of labor.

The results need not be spectacular for the principle to hold true. My wife, Erin, is a great lover of horses, growing up as she did on a ranch. In that spare, stark country, one needs a horse to move cattle from one place to another. Erin learned to ride almost before she could walk. She has told me many times that a highlight of her youth was a summer she spent working with a horse trainer who lived nearby. He was, she said, a master of his craft. The summer days in the desert are grueling, so the trainer and Erin would ride the horses in the early morning and again in the twilight after sundown, when the creatures could better take the work. In this way, over hours and days, they broke the horses to the saddle and reins. By their work, they made the horses productive beyond their natural instincts, to be of use to the rancher.

Whether it's horse training, or pouring concrete like my uncle, or working a short-order grill, the labor of man helps sustain creation and make it what it could be. The Bible says this is sacred work because when a man produces something that's useful to himself and others, he demonstrates the goodness of creation—that it can bring forth good things. And that in turn demonstrates the good character of the God who made it. That is temple-building.

We can see this effect in our own lives, in our own characters. If you work at it, you can bring a measure of order to your life. Maybe not perfect order, maybe not paradise, but improvement. You can get to work on time, you can work diligently while there, you can do something that benefits someone else, even in a small way. Part of the meaning of the Adam stories is that the world responds to this kind of effort. Not perfectly, often not immediately. Genesis says a curse lies on the ground, after all, and much of the time a man's work brings forth only "thorns and thistles." And yet. The world still answers a man's labor, and what that labor can bring forth is remarkable.

When I was nineteen and a sophomore in college, I thought I might grow up to be an economist. (That phase quickly passed.) In order to major in economics, I had first to take a particular course in calculus. I found I wasn't very good at it. I remember waking up in the middle of the night after one of my midterm exams in a disoriented sweat, convinced I had failed. I paced the halls of my dorm in the small hours of the morning, working back through the test in my head, trying to guess my score—and agonizing over what it might mean for my future. Oh, for the travails of a college sophomore. Still, it set me asking a set of questions every man does at one point or another: What will I do with my life that will matter? What will I do that will last?

I have come to see the David story as an answer to those questions. David built a city where God himself came to dwell—and not because it was so grandly done, but because God honored the work that David did. The Bible makes much of the fact that both the idea to build Jerusalem as Israel's capital city and the idea to construct a temple there belonged to David. The city was his city, the temple was his work. But because David worked for God, God made them his own. And so Jerusalem became great.

A man finds his agency in working. There are many forces in the world, most of them well beyond our control. From the weather to our genetics, we are powerless. Still, the Bible says that when a man works, he moves the world—and this is true whatever the work, whoever the man. When a man works, God comes to aid him. The work he does, his ability to bring forth something good, something beautiful, something new, is an expression of his freedom and his significance. It reflects his likeness to God. The Bible does not teach the rule of fate, that man is the pawn of the gods. It teaches instead that man truly becomes God's delegate, his representative, his servant, *as he works*. He becomes more free, not less. More independent. More himself. Maybe that is why the long political tradition our founders inherited, the one that has its roots in the teaching of the Bible, has long insisted that to be free a man must be able to provide for himself. He must give more than he takes. He must be a builder.

Hawley Concrete is not a famous company. It will never be traded on the New York Stock Exchange. Most people have never heard of it, and never will, I suppose. But my uncle's work has sustained three generations of family—himself, his children, and now his grandchildren. By his honest labor, day in and day out, he has shaped generations of lives and worked upon the fabric of the world. To put it another way, he has built his own Jerusalem, his own Eden, a place where God dwells. That is the legacy of a builder.

CHAPTER NINE

PRIEST

It was my mother, I think, who first introduced me to Blaise Pascal's "night of fire." I forget how old I was: high school, probably. I had not heard of Pascal at the time. I later learned he was a seventeenth-century polymath—a mathematician, scientist, physicist, and inventor, a prodigy—who made his first major contribution to mathematics at age sixteen, when he authored a theorem on the properties of hexagons and conic sections.[1] It was so penetratingly original that the very famous and insufferable René Descartes, he of "I think therefore I am" fame, insisted that it must have been drafted by the boy's father, also a mathematician. He was wrong. Pascal had, in fact, taught himself the basics of math theory when he was only eleven or twelve, without any instruction on the subject, going so far as to anticipate one of the major theorems of Euclid.[2] (To which facts Descartes replied, "other matters related to this subject can be proposed that would scarcely occur to a sixteen-year-old child."[3])

But for Pascal, that was far from all. He went on to compose groundbreaking treatises on binomial coefficients, barometric pressure, and the equilibrium of liquids.[4] Once, while laid up with a toothache, he sketched an essay on the properties of the cycloid—the curve generated by a point on a circle as it rolls along a straight line—that was so incisive it generated an international essay-writing competition in response.[5] Pascal penned his essay in eight days.[6]

He invented the syringe, the hydraulic press, and the forerunner to the wristwatch, and he is considered one of the fathers of modern probability theory.[7] As a pastime, he also constructed the first mechanical calculator, to help his father, who worked for a time as a tax collector. He was nineteen when he finished it.[8] He named the device after himself, "the Pascaline."[9]

If he was a touch immodest, he had reason to be. Pascal was by any measure a remarkably accomplished man. He was celebrated—and if Descartes is any indication, envied—from an early age. He was also lonely, frequently ill, and depressed. He lost his mother when he was three. Born a sickly child, he grew no better with age. His sister would later write that he spent hardly a day after the age of eighteen without some sort of pain; from the age of twenty-four, he could only rarely tolerate solid food.[10] His health was so poor he was forced to remain at home with his family even as he grew older, living at times as little more than an invalid; his sisters or a nurse were known to feed him his meals.[11] In the face of these difficulties, his accolades and glittering talents appeared to provide him little solace. No one could deny his promise, his genius—but he lacked a purpose to set against the miseries and hardship of his life.

When Pascal was twenty-two, his father slipped on a skiff of ice in the January cold—hurrying to prevent a duel, as it happens—and badly fractured his leg.[12] The Pascals sent for a bonesetter to tend to his injuries and got two in the bargain: brothers, named Deschamps, who ended up living with the Pascal family for three months. With their arrival, a shaft of light broke in on Pascal's life. The Deschamps brothers were devout Catholics, disciples of a Dutch theologian named Cornelius Jansen, whose teaching emphasized the desperate situation of mankind—isolated, alienated, alone—and the need for deliverance from the outside, for healing, if you will, of the kind the Deschamps brothers delivered to the body, but this for the soul. That deliverance could come only by God's intervention, as an exercise of God's power, Pascal heard from the brothers. And that power, in turn, could be accessed only by surrendering one's life utterly and entirely to God himself and his purposes. Deliverance came from a conversion of the heart.[13]

Pascal was gripped by the Deschamps brothers' doctrines. He spent many an hour in conversation with them during their months in residence, probing their teaching and observing their manner of life. They lived with a resolve he admired. Their lives pulsed with a purpose he longed for. By the time they departed, he had decided to follow their example and become a Christian. He would give his life wholly to God. Still, he was unclear what precisely this amounted to. And after the brothers left, his scientific pursuits cried out for attention, even as illnesses distracted and dogged him. Over time, his initial fervor faded, and the misery of his life dragged on.[14]

Then came his night of fire.

On November 23, 1654, Pascal was sitting up alone, late, in his rooms. According to the church calendar, it was the feast of Saint Clement, an early martyr of the faith.[15] (Legend has it he was thrown into the ocean while tied to an anchor.)[16] Pascal had the Bible open before him. Then, at ten-thirty, he began to see fire. Fire all around him, fire in his soul. He recorded the experience as follows.

The year of grace 1654,

    Monday, 23 November, feast of St. Clement, pope and martyr, and others in the martyrology. Vigil of St. Chrysogonus, martyr, and others. From about half past ten at night until about half past midnight,

    FIRE.

    GOD of Abraham, GOD of Isaac, GOD of Jacob not of the philosophers and of the learned. Certitude. Certitude. Feeling. Joy. Peace. GOD of Jesus Christ. My God and your God. Your GOD will be my God. Forgetfulness of the world and of everything, except GOD. He is only found by the ways taught in the Gospel. Grandeur of the human soul. Righteous Father, the world has not known you, but I have known you. Joy, joy, joy, tears of joy.

    I have departed from him: They have forsaken me, the fount of living water. My God, will you leave me? Let me not be separated from him forever. This is eternal life, that they know you, the one true God, and the one that you sent, Jesus Christ. Jesus Christ. Jesus Christ. I left him; I fled him, renounced, crucified. Let me never be separated from him. He is only kept securely by the ways taught in the Gospel: Renunciation, total and sweet. Complete submission to Jesus Christ and to my director. Eternally in joy for a day's exercise on the earth. May I not forget your words. Amen.[17]

Eight years later, upon Pascal's death at only thirty-nine, a servant going through Pascal's things felt a lump in the breast pocket of the coat Pascal wore habitually. Stopping to investigate, the servant discovered a piece of parchment bearing the written "memorial" of Pascal's night of fire, sewn into the lining of the jacket. Pascal, as it turns out, took the memorial with him wherever he went every day of his life from the night of November 23, 1654, until his death.[18]

The night of fire had been the night that changed Blaise Pascal. It left him a man aflame, imbued with a passion and purpose he had never felt before. He had touched the eternal. He continued his scientific endeavors, experimenting and inventing right up to the time of his death—his prototype for the first-ever form of public transit went into operation the year he died[19]—but now with little regard for his personal fame. He began writing works of philosophical and theological reflection, including one of the most famous works of philosophy in the Western world, the *Pensées* (or *Thoughts*), his apology for Christianity.[20] Even as his health steadily declined, even as he suffered the loss first of his father and then of his younger sister, Jacqueline, Pascal burned. He had met with God, he believed; he had felt the fire of God's presence—and had given his life over to be consumed. His new purpose was to burn for God in the world.

He succeeded. The flame of his life has inspired men down the centuries, drawing my own eye as a young man all those years later. When I read Pascal's "memorial," I was captivated. I wanted his sense of passion and purpose. What man does not? What young man, especially, would not trade almost anything for a "golden, burning moment," as another writer has said, a chance "to stand out, to shine and burn like a flame against eternal darkness"?[21] When I read Pascal, I knew he had lived what I longed for. What I did not know then, but have realized in the years since, is that Pascal lived what every man was born for.

The Bible's Adam saga tells us that man was born to burn in this fashion. He was born to tend the fire of God. The Bible's way of putting it is: he was born to have the character of a priest.

We know that man is meant to build the world into a temple. As a priest, man brings God *to the world*. He carries the fire of God in himself, in his heart and character, and he brings that fire, in turn, where he goes.

The world cannot do without God, try as it might, and try as the left has in this country for decades now. Modern, Epicurean liberalism is fundamentally atheistic, after the pattern of Epicurus himself, who rejected the relevance of "the gods." Modern American liberals have followed his example. Their attack on American society as "systemically" racist, sexist, and oppressive stems in large measure from their atheist ambitions. They denigrate the traditional family, manhood, and even the reality of biological sex for the same reason. Their target is the biblical influence that has shaped much of American life. Their target is the biblical God.

In his place, today's liberals offer a woke religion that demands we renounce manhood, womanhood, Christianity, and other supposed markers of "social power" and submit to the corrective tutelage of the liberal elite. Today's liberals seek to fashion a new sort of person, one beyond male and female, beyond God, who lives to satisfy desire and consume plenty of things but knows no ultimate purpose in life. The atheistic project promises individual "liberty," but what it has in fact delivered is isolation, despair—and a new social hierarchy based on education and income. In short, liberal atheism has been a failure. The world still needs God, which means it still needs men with the character of priests.

THE GOD-BEARER

The Bible's David can, once again, be our example. He conquered Jerusalem, formerly stronghold of the "blind and lame"—site of chaos and darkness—and rebuilt it as his capital. That was David confronting evil and building something good. And what does David do next?

Where darkness was, he brings the light. That is the model for us. Consider this story.

> So David went and brought up the ark of God from the house of Obed-edom to the city of David with rejoicing. And when those who bore the ark of the LORD had gone six steps, he sacrificed an ox and a fattened animal. And David danced before the LORD with all his might. And David was wearing a linen ephod. So David and all the house of Israel brought up the ark of the LORD with shouting and with the sound of the horn. (2 Samuel 6:12–15)

The Ark of the Covenant, symbol of God's presence, finally comes to rest in David's city. According to the Bible, that makes Jerusalem a symbolic new Eden. But one of the most arresting details in the story is who brings God into Jerusalem, so to speak. It is David. David leads the ark to the city. David attends the ark with sacrifices and dancing. What is the story saying? God follows David and goes where David goes.

Now this is a startling statement about the potential significance of a man. He can be someone whom God himself will accompany, whom God himself will attend. Pascal wrote about the "grandeur of the human soul" in his night of fire. What could be a more exalted statement of a man's potential than to say this, that the power of God might follow him to the places he goes—that he might bring the touch of God to every person, to every place, to every situation that he encounters? There is a famous scene in J. R. R. Tolkien's *Lord of the Rings* that my boys love, where the wizard Gandalf stands upon the bridge at Khazad-dûm and blocks the path of the demon creature of the deep, the Balrog. As Gandalf forbids the demon to pass the bridge, he warns, "I am a servant of the Secret Fire."[22] That is the idea. Men are meant to bear fire within them, to forge the sort of character that has the power to transform. How would you like to be someone of whom this is true?

I knew someone like this. His name was Eric Berg, *Coach* Berg to me. He was one of my high school football coaches who guided me on the field for years and became a personal mentor. I never admired a man more. Eric Berg lit up a room. Part of it was his sheer physicality. He had been a linebacker at the University of Missouri and still carried himself like a linebacker does: confident, commanding. But the real spark was in his face. It was bright, somehow, always. Even when he wasn't smiling, even when he was in fact shouting commands on a field, he radiated a rare combination of ebullience and kindness. He also radiated strength—not the sort of strength that made you feel insignificant in comparison, but the sort of strength that built you up. The strength was contagious, it seemed to flow from him to you. He made you feel bigger, better, as if you could do more. He made you *want* to do more. Listening to him on the field, I felt I could run a thousand miles. Listening to him in his office, as we talked over classes and the future, I felt my life could matter.

He was not loud or demonstrative. He was never showy. But he could walk into a place and change its atmosphere. He could inspire. And boys were drawn to him because of it. They performed for him as they did for no one else, and they wanted to please him; they wanted to be like him. All the while he was the humblest of men. He served quietly as a counselor and assistant coach for forty years, turning down head coaching opportunities at large schools, never seeking the limelight. He is still teaching, and has only recently set aside his coach's whistle. His legacy is not fame or fortune, but forty years of boys' lives transformed. Including mine.

As a teenager, I saw in Eric Berg a man I wanted to become, a model of what a man could be, of what a man could do. He wielded a power that changed the fortunes of lives. Upon his papal inauguration, John Paul II prayed, "Christ, make me become and remain the servant of your unique power, the servant of your sweet power, the servant of your power that knows no eventide."[23] Eric Berg had that kind of power.

This could be you. Your character is meant to be a source of renewal in the world. As David did, you are meant to carry the power of God. And the world needs you to do it. There are contributions that only you can make, service that only you can render. There are possibilities only you can awaken in others' lives, as Eric Berg did in mine. You can be a steward of God's presence.

Genesis says God walked in the garden with Adam, that Adam was invited to be in God's presence. By expanding the garden, Adam was invited to take that presence to the world. It is the same offer—and charge—given to every man.

FIRE AND SACRIFICE

But how does a man do this, cultivate a character where God's fire burns?

The David story offers a suggestion. We read that David dances "with all his might" as the ark comes into the city. This is admittedly an odd scene: a king wearing little but a linen overshirt dancing wildly before the assembled throng. But there is more to it than that. "And when those who bore the ark had gone six steps, he [David] sacrificed an ox and a fattened animal."

David dances and he sacrifices. A wife of David objects to this display as deeply indecorous for a king. "How the king of Israel honored himself today," she reprimands him, "uncovering himself today before the eyes of his servants' female servants."[24] The crux of her complaint is that David made himself a spectacle. He was not sufficiently attentive to his social status and the opinions of other people.

But then again, that may be the point. The dancing cost David. It was a type of sacrifice. He sacrificed his dignity as a king to show his utter devotion to God, king of kings. That is what it symbolized. The dancing was what the Bible calls worship.

Edmund Burke was an eighteenth-century writer, philosopher, and statesman who wrote a famous polemic against the French Revolution and the atheism that animated it. In that celebrated classic, *Reflections on the Revolution in France*, considered one of the founding documents of modern conservatism, Burke wrote that man was born to worship, that he is "a religious animal."[25] He explained worship like this: man's nature, he said, is to give himself to something greater than he is. And not just to any cause or fashion, but to that which speaks to the "permanent part of [his] nature."[26]

Man's life is short and often troubled, but his vision—and his hope—reaches beyond his earthly years. Every man knows that history has gone on long before him, and every man, if he is being honest, hopes to do something that will outlast him down the years. In the midst of his transient life, he yearns for what is permanent. And this is how it should be, Burke said. A man's "hope should be full of immortality."[27] Deep calls to deep, as the psalmist says, and what is permanent in a man—his sense of right and wrong, his love for truth, his determination to matter—calls out for what is permanent in the universe, for eternity.

My wife and I visited Sydney, Australia, when we were newly married, and while we were there I read up on a local Sydney legend named Arthur Stace. Stace was an orphan, the child of alcoholics who eventually abandoned him. When they did, he became an alcoholic too. He thieved, he ran lookout for a brothel (his sisters', as it happened), and he got sent to jail multiple times. At thirty-two, lacking any other employment, he volunteered for the Australian Army during the First World War. But little changed. After the war, he was back in Sydney and back to his old life on the streets. Then one evening in 1930 he wandered into a church on Broadway Street and heard the reverend in the pulpit speak of eternity. He couldn't get the word out of his mind. He converted to Christianity that night. "Eternity went ringing through my brain and suddenly I began crying and felt a powerful call from the Lord to write Eternity," he would later say.[28] And that's what he did, for the rest of his life. He rose each morning at four o'clock and took to the streets of Sydney with chalk in his hand, scribbling "Eternity" every place he could—on walkways, doorframes, and the sides of buildings.

He went on doing it for thirty-five years. Workers on the morning shift would see his handiwork as they reported to their factories. Children spied it on their way to school, morning after morning after morning. The chalked word "Eternity" became a fixture of Sydney, and perhaps a beacon. Not until shortly before his death did the press discover his identity, but long before then he was a legend, and the people of Sydney had embraced his word as their credo. They called him Mr. Eternity.

The writer of Ecclesiastes said God has "set eternity in the human heart."[29] This is what Burke meant about man's "permanent nature," his hope "full of immortality." This is why every man longs to burn with some great purpose, to boast some singular accomplishment, if only for a moment. He longs for the eternal; he wants desperately to partake of it. He wants to connect his life to what will last. The men of ancient Greece kept an altar in their homes, which the father of the family tended day and night, feeding a continuous flame as an offering to the family's ancestors. The ancients believed those ancestors resided with the family still in some manner, and that by paying them homage, they might invoke their protection. For the family's father, the ritual meant even more. By honoring the ancestors of his lineage and acting as their priest, he hoped to join his life to those who had gone before him. He hoped to touch the eternal.[30]

That is why man worships. He cannot find eternity in himself. His knowledge, like his life, is limited. And his every accomplishment, no matter how bright, fades; his every moment of fame passes. If he wishes to touch what is permanent, a man must reach out beyond his being. He must find some way to "connect," as Burke says, his "human understanding and affections," his life, "to the divine."[31] He must worship. He reaches beyond his own person, beyond his own knowledge and power, to find the source of his personhood—to find Being itself. He reaches out to be filled.

Worship is an acknowledgment that a man *needs* to be filled, that he needs something more than his own resources. It is an acknowledgment that he is not omnipotent or all-knowing, that he cannot see the end of every path. It is also an acknowledgment that life is difficult, that we are far from perfect, and that even the basic duties of life are a challenge to us.

We don't love as we should. We don't tell the truth as we ought to. We disappoint others and ourselves. At some point in his life, every man realizes that he does not have the wherewithal, emotional, spiritual, or otherwise, to do the things he ought to do—to be the man he ought to be. It may be alcohol abuse or a failed marriage or a lost career that does it. It may be an estranged child or a tragic accident. For me, it was the death of my friend Jake at twenty-two. Life, we realize, is fragile. It can seem unforgiving. It can be harsh. And we ourselves are brittle, all too easily overwhelmed. We are broken. This is the human condition. Our efforts, alone, unaided, will not change any of that. Our efforts alone will not change us.

Worship will. Worship brings aid. The Bible says God created man with the purpose of helping him, forming him, filling him with God's own strength, God's own presence.

When you think on it, one of the most remarkable things about the Adam stories is that God bothers with men at all. Men create a lot of work for God. They lie. They cheat. They destroy things. They are constantly failing and fighting and fiddling away what he has given them, generally doing the opposite of what they should do. Yet God presses on, determined to work *through* men rather than around or without them. He pours his being into theirs to accomplish his purposes.

That is why the story has David dancing before the ark. He is giving over his short, imperfect life to the enduring source of all life. He is acknowledging his need and inviting God to pour his being into David's own so that David can do what he was meant to do. So that he can be who he was meant to be. He is offering a sacrifice so fire will fall in his soul.

And make no mistake, worship requires sacrifice. Most men know this instinctively. They sacrifice for things all the time. They put in extra hours at work, sacrificing their free time; they sacrifice personal recreation to spend time with their kids; they train their bodies and discipline their minds to get better at a sport or hobby. Those are sacrifices in pursuit of good things. What about pursuit of the highest good, eternity? What would you sacrifice to receive the fire of God in your character?

The ancients had a keen sense of the power of sacrifice. About four hundred years before the birth of Christ, the Roman Forum was devastated by a mysterious chasm which suddenly appeared in its center, disrupting civic and social life. The city's augurs reported that the chasm was the work of the gods, a warning—and the price of the republic's survival was the sacrifice of that which Rome held most dear. A young warrior named Marcus Curtius offered the thing dearest to him: his life. He outfitted his horse in battle attire and donned his full battle armor, then mounted up and rode straight into the chasm.[32] For his homeland, he was willing to give all he had.

Fire falls on sacrifice. In the story of David sacrificing his status and pride before God, we find sacrifice's deepest meaning and greatest power. When a man worships, when he gives his life over to God, he opens his soul to the source of all Being. He opens his character to the source of all life. He is changed. He takes on the character of a priest.

THE ATHEIST PROJECT

Today's Epicurean liberals will have none of this, of course. They believe, like their ancient instructor, Epicurus, that "the gods" are noxious and anti-human. Epicurus said trying to fathom the gods' ways is futile. Trying to please them, impossible. The only sure result of religion is to render humans constant supplicants, scraping and bowing and begging for this or that, without ever knowing if they will get an answer. Better to live as if the gods didn't exist and ignore them entirely. Control what you can control, which is your happiness, Epicurus said.

Epicurus argued that what man gets out of this approach is peace of mind and, crucially, liberty. He wins back control over his own life. If man banishes the gods, he can do as he wishes. For Epicurus, that meant living a quiet life of personal fulfillment, but modern liberals harbor more exalted ambitions. With God out of the way, their aim has been to remake man, and the world.

The modern liberal program in this regard began in earnest with the French Revolution. Informed by Epicureans like Jean-Jacques Rousseau—whom Edmund Burke once called "the insane Socrates of the National Assembly"[33]—the French revolutionaries adopted a campaign of wholesale atheism. Not only, they said, was the Catholic Church a corrupt institution responsible for many of the political abuses they aimed to rectify, but the very idea of God was oppressive. God himself was a tyrant. The notion of God limited man; it suggested man was not the author of his own creation. Accordingly, the revolutionaries aimed to destroy France's Catholic establishment and remove all traces of Christianity from French society. That meant no more monasteries and churches, no more Christmas and Easter, no more church festivals. Moreover, it meant no references to God in public, no public expressions of worship, and no public preaching or other discussion of religion not sanctioned by the revolutionaries themselves, who were by this time busily guillotining people at an alarming rate.

Indeed, for a program allegedly centered on liberty, the revolutionary agenda soon turned violently illiberal. Because the revolutionaries had no use for God, they had no use for personal conscience. Which meant they had no regard for freedom of speech or assembly to express that conscience, not if it was in opposition to the revolution. They were perfectly willing to use the power of the state to stop religious expression and speech to which they objected. On their logic, they had to: people might end up believing the wrong things, like in God, who was a threat to liberty. To the revolutionaries, the church was part and parcel of the old regime's system of oppression and injustice, and those who insisted on worshipping God were enemies of the revolution. For the sake of the public good, the state had to eradicate all such "disinformation," as American liberals would later say.

The revolutionaries went further still. They eliminated (or tried to eliminate) references to God and the Bible in French culture, pulled down Christian statues, and destroyed Christian art. They aimed at nothing short of a complete remodel of French society. In place of France's biblical heritage, the revolutionaries set up a new, alternative religion called the Cult of Reason—and mandated all citizens take part. The revolutionaries believed what Rousseau had once said, that man must be forced to be free.

Their larger ambition was to remake men themselves, not into priests but into atheists. Lacking any belief in God, the revolutionaries lacked an understanding of man's permanent nature. To them, man was the creature of his own creation, and could be made and remade at will—either his own will or the will of the state. And the revolutionaries were not shy about using the state. By abolishing Christianity, rewriting French history, and ending free speech, they sought to fashion a new man free of the "superstitions" and "prejudices" of the past, one who would live entirely by reason, as they defined reason. That was their notion of liberty.

The new French state was notoriously unstable, of course, with the revolutionaries soon fighting, betraying, and killing one another. They cycled through one state religion after the next—first it was the Cult of Reason, then the Cult of the Supreme Being, then the cult of Napoleon Bonaparte—and one constitution after the other. The only constant was the expanding power of government and the withering away of freedom of every kind, public and personal. What started out as a quest for liberty degenerated into one of the most repressive regimes in the history of the world.

That dreary record has not stopped modern American liberals from pursuing a similarly themed agenda. One of the godfathers of today's woke liberals was a 1960s intellectual named Herbert Marcuse, who picked up not far from where the French revolutionaries left off. Marcuse was Marxist—he believed the economic and social structure of the West was systemically oppressive—and he spent a good deal of time pondering why Marx's long-predicted revolution of the proletariat had never come to pass. He concluded that in America, at least, God was largely to blame.

Working people were in many ways the most oppressed members of American society, Marcuse thought, beaten down as they were by the capitalist system he detested, but they were also among the most religious. In a break with Marx, Marcuse decided that economics wasn't destiny after all. Culture was. American culture was shot through with Christianity, and the Christian influence was preventing the revolution America needed.[34]

Marcuse's solution was to transfer his hope for revolution from the working class to a group of people more willing to reject God, namely, the educated elite. Marcuse became an intellectual patron of 1960's student radicalism, which shifted the Marxist emphasis from the working class to a new form of identity politics focused on race and sex and students opposed to the Vietnam War. Student radicals, he decided, often the children of the upper classes, would be the ones to give America what it needed, a thorough de-Christianizing. Only when American culture had been cleansed of biblical influence, biblical talk, and biblical ideas could there be true "liberation." He pressed for a thoroughgoing Kulturkampf, a culture war, to oust the influence of the Bible, including using the power of the state to advance the cause. Marcuse famously advocated what he called "repressive tolerance."[35] Like the French revolutionaries before him, Marcuse believed in forcing citizens to be free. He had no use for free speech for ideas he disagreed with, ones that would hold back "true" liberation.

As Marcuse's intellectual heirs have come to positions of power, they have pursued his aims—really, the aims of the French Revolution—with gusto. For years now, liberal intellectuals have worked to curtail the free exercise of Christian belief. They have argued that citizens should not make arguments about public policy on the basis of their religious convictions, or even using religious language.[36] They have pressed courts to prohibit elected officials from invoking God or the Bible when deliberating about laws. In rhetoric eerily reminiscent of Rousseau and the French radicals, today's liberals demand citizens confine themselves to "public reason" when debating the issues facing society.[37] By which they mean, reasons that do not mention God, the Bible, or Christianity.

More recently, liberal officials have targeted churches and synagogues for unfavorable treatment. For example, during the COVID-19 pandemic, some states and cities allowed secular businesses and entertainment venues to open while keeping houses of worship closed or tightly restricted. They have attempted to teach grade school students that the true American founding happened in 1619 with the advent of the slave trade on the North American continent, rather than in 1776 with the Declaration of Independence that celebrates "unalienable rights" given by the Creator, not the state.[38] In place of the old, patriotic story of colonists arriving to these shores in search of religious liberty, spreading freedom and republican government across the continent, they say American history is about the spread of slavery and oppression. They have insisted, under the official auspices of the Smithsonian, no less, that Christianity is an artifact of "white culture" and therefore, we are to infer, oppressive.[39] The museum said the same about the nuclear family.

All the while, the left decries as "disinformation" views that challenge its own, and increasingly attempts to use the power of government and the media—especially the major technology companies—to silence voices it dislikes. Marcuse would be pleased.

Like Epicurus, today's left speaks in terms of liberty. More accurately, leftists long for liberation from God, from the history and culture of the West that reflects him—and from anything permanent, including human nature. This is one reason they are so fervently opposed to the notion of immutable biological sex. It is why they demand schools teach young children that they are not boys and girls but androgynous individuals with a "gender identity" that changes at will. It is why they demand these same children get access to puberty-blocking drugs without their parents' consent. Biological sex, male and female, *cannot* exist in the modern liberal mindset. It *must* not. It suggests something fixed, something immutable, outside the control of government or man. It suggests permanence. Perhaps even God. And that, to today's left, can only be oppressive.

In the end, the progressives' agenda amounts to a campaign of nihilism. They seek to destroy the traditions and structures of American society that reflect a biblical influence so they can remake American society and the people in it. Theirs has been a decades-long effort to erase the sense of eternity from the public square. But while they speak reverently of liberty, their program has not made America noticeably freer.

On the contrary, liberal atheism has instead made our society more hierarchical and elitist. The liberal Epicureans have given us a new aristocracy, as forecast by Marcuse—one organized around education and the social status awarded by institutions now governed by the left.

Their own doctrines have unraveled the American commitment to equality and respect for the common man. If human nature is permanent and given by God, all people share an equal claim to dignity, whatever their education or manner of work. The mechanic, for example, is entitled to every inch of respect the college professor enjoys. This was once a bedrock conviction of American society.

But if the left is correct and human nature is pliable, and if the educated elite—meaning the left—know best what human progress means; if working people suffer from cultural delusions they are too dull to recognize, from which only the elite can free them, then there is no true equality between persons. There is the elite—Marcuse's vanguard—and everyone else. There is hierarchy.

Convinced of their cultural superiority, today's leftists have imposed a new hierarchy on America. To a remarkable, historically unusual extent, America's cultural institutions are now dominated by a small, homogenous class of individuals who graduated from the same coterie of elite schools and share the same Epicurean, mostly atheistic worldview they learned there. In today's America, education is class, and the liberal educated class now runs the giant corporations, staffs the news

media, captains the entertainment industry, and, of course, steers the
major universities. They set the cultural tone. They hand out the accolades. They control who is favored and not. And while they profess to
believe in meritocracy, they define "merit" in a way that benefits them,
by reference to educational attainments they hold and social prestige
they assign. Not surprisingly, today's global economy works best for
them, too, while common men, workaday laborers, lose their prospects
and their futures.

All this is bad enough. But the consequences of the liberal atheist
program can be observed in other, tragic ways: in the widespread
anomie and discontent that suffuses American society, in the loss of
hope for the future and for life itself. In the last thirty years, drug abuse
in America has set new records. Alcohol abuse has reached highs not
seen since the start of World War I.[40] Opioid deaths number in the
hundreds of thousands.[41] Suicide rates have climbed to the stratosphere,
approaching Great Depression–era levels.[42] On the other hand,
record-low numbers of survey respondents tell pollsters they believe the
lives of today's youth will be better than those of their parents.[43] And
the number of Americans getting married and starting families has
fallen precipitously. These are not the signs of a society hopeful for the
future. These are the groanings of a society cut off from eternity.

These are the results liberal atheism has delivered to America. Not
liberty, not progress, but hierarchy and hopelessness. As for men: when
the left is not castigating them for "the patriarchy" or blaming them
for America's "structural" injustices, it catechizes them in a philosophy
of nihilism, with no larger story or purpose to inspire them and no hope
of eternity to beckon them on. This is the place where numberless men,
young men especially, find themselves in our culture today. The modern
Epicureans tell them that without God they are free to chart their own
destiny and live without fear. In fact, the Epicureans leave men impoverished. They leave them longing to find the permanent things but told

that no such things exist. They leave them longing to touch eternity but told that eternity is a mirage. They leave them longing to burn but with nowhere to turn for fire.

During my teaching days, I had a student, I'll call him Tim, who was in his later twenties and his first semester at law school. Originally from Mississippi, he had worked a job or two between graduating from college and starting on his law degree, and I had the impression he had been reasonably successful. He had done something in finance, if memory serves. We were only a few weeks into the semester when he came by to talk, and my sense of Tim to date was that he was talented. He was sharp. He understood the reading and could think on his feet when called upon. But he was not always the best prepared. He sometimes seemed a little foggy on the details of the cases we discussed. I chalked this up to the morning hour at which the class met. Some people are simply not morning people. I soon learned the true situation was otherwise.

"I love your class," Tim said. "I love law school. I feel challenged by it. I really want to do well."

"Good," I replied. "You will do well, if you want to. You have talent. You can succeed if you apply yourself."

Then he averted his eyes. "I really want to get this right," he said, "but I'm having trouble."

I was slightly confused. He didn't seem to be having any difficulty understanding the content. Then he said: "I'm having trouble showing up to your class sober." Now he looked me in the eye. He had clearly resolved to lay it all out. "I drink a lot," he said. "I may have a problem. And I show up to your class hungover sometimes because it's in the morning. Actually, I show up hungover every morning. And I don't want to, because I care about this."

In the course of our conversation, which went on for some time, it became clear to me that Tim did indeed have a serious drinking problem.

He wanted to stop drinking but couldn't. But what was equally heart-breaking was that our class and the chance of succeeding at law school appeared to be the first things that had made him want to quit drinking in a long time, maybe since he had started. He had drifted toward alcohol abuse at least in part because he felt no particular purpose for his life. He felt he had nothing to live for that would matter in the end. He was a talented kid with all his life before him, with the potential to change many lives and leave the world a better place, but he didn't see any of it. He saw just hardship and pain and meaninglessness.

Burke warned that the French revolutionary program would cut men off from the generations who had gone before them and destroy any sense of purpose that spanned time and place. "No one generation could link with the other," he predicted. "Men would become little better than the flies of a summer."[44] That was how my student felt—isolated, adrift. That is life today for many men in America.

It need not be so. Men are not flies of summer. They do not exist alone, random creatures abandoned in the universe. They are meant to matter, and the work of their lives is meant to endure. They are meant to be like priests who touch eternity and bring the knowledge of it to earth.

"A SON TO ME"

The story of David bringing the ark of God to Jerusalem has an interesting coda, an afterword of sorts that casts not only the preceding story in a new light, but perhaps all the other Adam stories that have gone before it.

The ark is now safely in Jerusalem, installed in a grand tabernacle, a kind of elaborate tent. David meanwhile is securely installed as king. But he begins to worry, as he sits in his palace, that perhaps the resting place for the ark is insufficient. David has a great house: Should not God have a house of his own?

David tells the court priest, Nathan, that he wishes to build a proper house for God.

He asks Nathan to consult God as to how to proceed. The answer Nathan brings back is surprising. You are not to build anything further for God, Nathan reports. God wants to build something for you. Nathan goes on: God will be with you and your descendants forever, even beyond death. He will transform you by his presence. And of David's heir, God promises: "I will be to him a father, and he shall be to me a son."[45]

A son. This is a first in the Adam stories,[46] but perhaps where they have been leading all along. God calls men to build the world into a temple and to be his servants in that world. But this call to mission turns out, in the end, to be an invitation: the invitation to become a son. Here lies the deeper meaning of the statement we first encountered in Genesis that God made man "in his own image." That means to *do* something, certainly, as we have seen—to husband, to father, to fight and build, to rule. But it also means, more fundamentally, to become *someone*, a man of a certain kind of character: a man who reflects God, a man whom God knows.

The contrast with the atheist vision is sharp. The Epicureans say man is alone in the universe and he must make of his life what he can. The Bible says God knows you individually, and wants to do for you what he did for David: to build you something—a life, a purpose. It may seem, in God's call to men to labor with him, that men are serving God. And that is right and true. But upon closer inspection, the mission God gives men involves him doing something for men, for you. The Eastern Orthodox tradition speaks of a union with God (through Christ) that leads to a man's "divinization." Not that man becomes a god, to be clear, but that he begins to reflect God, to look like him, in his soul. The fire that falls on sacrifice is a fire that transforms the heart.

This is a mystery every man must explore and experience for himself. I remember when I first did, my own personal night of fire. It was some time after I first read Pascal's memorial. In the summer before my senior year of high school, my dad got a call from his employer telling him they were moving him to a new town. It was a good opportunity, a promotion. Knowing I was anxious to finish my senior year at my high school, my parents arranged for me to remain in our hometown with a family friend, a widow who had been a surrogate grandmother to my sister and me, while my dad, mom, and sister moved to Springfield, Missouri, three hours away. When school started in the fall, my mother divided her time between the two locations—two or three days with me, the remainder of the week with my dad and sister in Springfield. I thought little of it at the time. Now I see better the sacrifice she, and the rest of the family, made on my behalf.

During football season, the family would drive up for my Friday night game, and afterwards we would frequently make the three-hour trek back to Springfield, together, so we could spend the weekend in one place as a family. It was on one of those nights, after one of those games and the subsequent drive, that I was at home in my bedroom at my parents' new house, up late, reading. It had to have been two or three in the morning. My window was open—it was an October night. I would have been seventeen, a magical age, in many respects: the responsibilities of adulthood beginning to open before you, but childhood's sense of endless possibility still at hand. And yet I wondered, as many seventeen-year-olds begin to do, what it was I would do with my life. What it would amount to. What *I* would amount to. Did I have what it takes to matter, to mean something? Would I be good enough?

That night I had picked up a collection of essays we had in the house by the church reformer Martin Luther—my mother was raised a Lutheran—and had turned to the essay titled "The Freedom of a Christian." And as I read there about God's purposes for mankind and how Jesus had given his life for mine, I suddenly felt, with a force and clarity I had not known before, that God knew me, me personally. That across the expanse of the universe, he saw and recognized me. And he loved me, as a son. I sensed, in a way I cannot explain but could only feel, that he was with me, there, in that small room, and was inviting me to hazard the rest of my life for him. The sense of it, the power of it, came so suddenly and so strongly that I dropped the book. And I just sat there, overwhelmed, for who knows how long.

It was not quite the rapturous fire of Blaise Pascal, but it was a burning moment for me nonetheless, one where I first began to understand, however dimly, what it means to have the character of a priest. And what it means to be called a son.

America needs more men who are like priests. It needs men who will write "eternity" every place they visit, who will renew the promise of eternity everywhere they go. The men of ancient Greece and Rome may have been on to something with their ritual tending of the family hearth. They sensed that men have an obligation to draw their families toward the sacred, to teach their children what eternity means. America needs men who are priests to their families like that.

America needs men who will defend our history as a nation, shaped by the Bible, and the institutions, from the family to the church, that preserve our perception of the permanent things. America needs men who will guard the institutions that, as Burke had it, "connect the human understanding and affections to the divine," that teach us as a society to look not "to the paltry pelf of the moment, nor to the temporary and transient praise of the vulgar, but to a solid, permanent existence, in the permanent part of [our] nature, and to a permanent fame and glory."[47]

In the end, we need men who know how to worship, how to give their lives to God, and who will, as a consequence, bear his imprint on their characters. We need men who are sons of God. We need men who are priests.

CHAPTER TEN

KING

From the time I was five or six, my father would take me pheasant hunting every year on the season's opening weekend, which was usually the first or second Saturday in November. I say pheasant, though typically we shot quail, too. We gathered at my grandparents' farm in northern Kansas—on my mother's family's side, the Hammers. The Hammer men had been hunting opening weekend together time out of mind, and when my dad married into the family he joined them. He would take off work on the Friday before and we would drive out there, my mother and sister with us. Mother usually made a brisket to serve the hunters. I remember this vividly because she cooked it overnight in the oven—we didn't have a smoker—and added liquid smoke for taste. That ingredient in tandem with whatever seasoning rub she used on the meat, roasted over long hours, produced a distinctively pungent smell my sister and I disapproved of as children. My bedroom was in the basement, and even there I could smell it from approximately 2:00 a.m.

forward. "It's the stinky brisket," my sister would say upon waking. Still, that smell meant pheasant hunting, so it was all right by me. Pheasant hunting was a highlight of my year.

By the time I was accompanying my dad to the fields, the annual hunt had swelled to the status of family reunion: fathers and sons and cousins and nephews—and neighbors and family friends and out-of-towners. It was an event, a holiday that in the universe of my childhood occupied a space on par with Thanksgiving and just below Christmas. On the Friday night beforehand, my grandmother served dinner at her house for the assembled kin and guests. Then on Saturday morning we would start, early, before first light. I remember my father sitting on the hearth in the living room, carefully sliding the red-cased shells for his 12-gauge into the elastic loops on his vest. I also was allowed to carry shells, on my vest or in my pockets, and I would walk importantly alongside my dad in the field, handing shells over to him when he called for more.

My main job in the fields, however, in those years before I could carry a shotgun, was to tramp into brush and scare out the birds. We didn't hunt with dogs; we lined up at the edge of a field, twenty or more men across, ten or so feet between each man, and walked the rows of stubbled cornstalks, or sometimes milo. Another group of men stood at the other end—blockers, they were called—to prevent the pheasants from simply darting out and away as the walkers advanced. Pheasants, I soon learned, are wily birds. I also soon learned to stay in line with the walkers and not run ahead, at the risk of getting pelted with buckshot in the back, a point my father emphasized. So I'd walk there with my dad, tramping through brush when needed, shouting "Rooster!" when a male bird was sighted—the hens were off-limits, and the game warden was a frequent visitor on opening weekend—and loving every minute.

We would walk field after field, hour upon hour, from sunup until noontime, at which point we'd stop to eat my mother's brisket and other assorted meats and baked goods, standing around with paper plates in the Quonset shed, where my grandfather stored his tractors and equipment. Then back out into the fields until sundown. In the evening, we would gather back at the shed to clean the birds, and in the years I remember, we had quite a few to clean. It wasn't unusual to see ninety or a hundred birds piled into the beds of the trucks. The state limit back then was four birds per hunter, and we often had thirty or more men in the company.

The men would clean birds and tell jokes and the children among us—myself, my cousin Jeff, and maybe one or two other small boys—would pester their fathers to hurry so we could go have pizza. It was a festive, jolly atmosphere. And at the center of the festivities was my grandfather, the family patriarch, Harold Hammer.

I never knew my grandfather as a young man: he was in his forties when my mother, his youngest child, came along, and well into his seventies by the time I remember him. But he never seemed younger than he did on those hunting weekends and on those Saturday nights. Most of the logistics of the weekend—where to start, who would drive—he had long since delegated to one of my uncles, but like Charles Dickens's character Fezziwig in *A Christmas Carol*—the jovial employer of the young Ebenezer Scrooge and great thrower of Christmas parties—my grandfather orchestrated the merriment. There he was, going from person to person as we cleaned birds, shaking hands, slapping backs, telling stories. There he was in the shed, handing around the Jack Daniel's. There he was offering up pickled herring, that Scandinavian specialty he claimed as a personal favorite. And I remember him with me like it was yesterday, taking my small hand in his large one and, by the light of the single yard lamp, showing me how to hold the cleaning knife and slice along the bone.

He was in his element, and truthfully, we were there, all of us, because of him. It was his farm, but more than that it was his tradition.

It was his family. He was the linchpin for us and somehow, with him in place, at the center, everything settled into order—three generations of his family there together, representing past, present, and future, laughing and carrying on and renewing the years. There were plenty of strong personalities in that assemblage, and Grandpa did not domineer. That was never his way. Like old Fezziwig, his power lay "in words and looks; in things so slight and insignificant that it is impossible to add and count 'em up"—and yet, "the happiness he gives is quite as great as if it cost a fortune."[1]

And on across the years the tradition went, until I grew old enough to carry my own gun and bring my own friends to join the fun. "This is amazing—like Christmas," one buddy from Oklahoma said after visiting. Grandpa was ever in the middle of it. As he aged, he walked the fields less, and by the last years he only left the pickup now and again to stand at the end of the field as a blocker. But he was still there, still presiding, still holding the generations together right up until the last, when strokes claimed his mobility and, in time, his life.

In the ancient Near East, at the center of society and civilization stood a king. According to the ancient myths and traditions, the king joined together the human and divine realms. It was his duty to sustain the divine order on which society was built. He was to personify that order, to embody it, and on pain of his life to defend it. So central was the king to the well-functioning of society that some cultures of the Near East treated him as almost divine, a man who stood above all others.

The Bible, too, speaks of kings. It begins with one—Adam, called to rule on God's behalf from the garden temple. And the Adam stories culminate with another, Solomon, on the throne of his father David in Jerusalem, a new Eden. But the Bible never speaks of kings as a special class of humans who stand above the rest. No, the Bible says every man is called to lead and, equally significant, to take up the *responsibilities* of leadership. Every man is called to use his influence to help bring the world into order, which begins with bringing his own life into order, and by doing that, to discover true freedom for himself and others. Every man is meant to be a king. This is the crowning role of the mission of manhood.

The left today warns shrilly that male leadership can only ever amount to domination. The Bible says it can bring liberty, for a man and those around him; it can bring flourishing—if a man is willing to do what liberty and flourishing require. Our problem today is not that too many men lead, but that too few do. Too few men are willing to subordinate their immediate wants and desires to serve a greater purpose, not least because they've been indoctrinated to believe there is no greater purpose. Too few are willing to bring order to their own souls. The Bible's Adam stories end with a lesson in paradox: the more a man limits himself, the more freedom he finds. The more he serves others, the more influence he gains—and the greater legacy he leaves behind. Character is the gateway to legacy and to liberty.

Solomon, son of David, began his reign humble, eager to serve, aware of his limits, asking God for wisdom. His choices, and the kind of character they produced, helped make him and his nation prosperous and free, for a time. The Bible holds him up as a picture of what Adam in the garden was meant to be, and what my grandfather, in his way, was: a king. It is what each of us can be, if we are willing to order our souls and take up the responsibility of manhood.

A MAN'S DOMINION

The Bible's story of Solomon's reign begins with what sounds like paradise. "Judah and Israel were as many as the sand by the sea. They ate and drank and were happy," it says. And they were rich. "Solomon's provision for one day was thirty cors of fine flour and sixty cors of meal, ten fat oxen, and twenty pasture-fed cattle, a hundred sheep, besides deer, gazelles, roebucks, and fattened fowl." Finally, they were safe. "And he had peace on all sides around him. And Judah and Israel lived in safety, from Dan even to Beersheba..." (1 Kings 4:20–25). All of this as a result of what the Bible calls Solomon's "dominion." All of this because of Solomon's leadership.

The moral is not hard to grasp, though we must say it again in light of the left's misconceptions. It is good for a man to exercise authority—good for him and for those around him, provided he does it well. It is good that a man show ambition, that he aim to do something useful with his life.

The Solomon story touches a universal fact: Every man wants to develop competence in some area or field. He wants to exert some control over his circumstances and have his life matter for something. Every man wants to reign. And he can, to the great good of those in his life, if he will develop the character for it.

The other night at dinner I asked my sons to describe the events of their school day. My younger son, Blaise, focused his report on recess. (He is seven.) He announced that he had launched a digging project to mine for valuable minerals, having recently read a book on this subject. He further reported that he had brought several other boys into his employ and promised them a share of whatever minerals they might find. He assigned each boy a station and a shovel—or hoe or rake—and set goals to measure progress. Based on his nightly updates as the week progressed, all seemed to go well, until the third or fourth day, when he reported digging had slowed "because a couple of my workers were absent. And one wanted to play kickball."

These are the typical antics of children in one sense, but already in my son's play was the distinctly boyish ambition to lead and exercise authority: to have dominion. I applauded him when he told me about his project and encouraged him to keep it up. I want him to grow up to be a king.

Because if dominion is something every man wants and is meant to exercise, the fact is that not every man does. Not every man has the character. Some fear the responsibility it brings and shrink back from taking the initiative. These men become dependent on others, often apathetic, and resentful of those around them who succeed. They come to resent the world in general. This is the man who won't hold a steady job, or ask for a promotion when he deserves one, or ask a woman on a date. This is the man who won't show initiative but wants the benefits initiative brings.

Erin and I have family friends whose youngest son, now an adult, hasn't worked a steady job since he dropped out of high school at age seventeen.[2] His parents are charming people, well-meaning and sincere, and they would do anything for their son. That may be the problem. When he suddenly announced he was quitting high school, they indulged him. When he said he didn't want to get his GED, they went along. When he said the boss at the fast-food restaurant where he was briefly employed was unfair to him, they took his side. Meanwhile, he lived in their basement and ate their food, paying no rent and contributing nothing to the maintenance of the household. By this time he was well into his twenties. He later developed an alcohol addiction, and when the parents finally demanded he stop drinking and seek help or leave the house, he left—only to move in with a wealthy aunt. Where the cycle continues. It is young men like this, who shrink from dominion and its burdens, who become old men full of resentment and regret.

To young men, we should send a clear message: Dominion is good, and you should exercise it. Aim to do something with your life. Aim to exercise some leadership. Aim to accept responsibility for yourself—and others. Aim to have the character of a king.

Some men, of course, desperately want authority for all the wrong reasons. Their model is not the biblical ideal of kingship, serving God and serving others, but the Epicurean doctrine of self-fulfillment. They preen, they abuse, they dominate. They see others as means to their own ends. And why not? This is where Epicurean liberalism leads, its logical end point. If a man is his own god, why should he not do as he pleases? Modern liberals don't like to admit it, but the "toxic" behavior of certain men that they so loudly decry is enabled by their own philosophy. It is fueled by a worldview that says pleasure is the greatest good and you are the center of your own universe. That way of living encourages self-advancement at any cost. It excuses mistreatment of others who stand in your way. It is not the kind of dominion the Bible praises.

Which begs the question, if it is good for a man to reign, if he is meant to be a king, how does he acquire the character to do it? How does he learn properly to exercise dominion?

He can start by recognizing what authority is there for in the first place: to serve the good order that makes his life—all life—possible.

GOOD MEN, GOOD ORDER

In the ancient myths, gods often go to war against the forces of chaos to bring forth order and peace. The motif is so common it has a name, *Chaoskampf*. It is there in the Bible, too, as early as Genesis. In the beginning, God created order from chaos by creating the garden. But the story of the Bible is the story of God continually working *with men*, through men, to defeat the powers of evil and chaos and make all things new. While the quest for order and flourishing is his quest, God has used men to advance it. And the kind of order God calls men to serve reveals something about who he is and how he expects men to lead. Men are to use their power to promote the liberty of others.

In most of the ancient myths, the gods' principal motivation for getting the world into shape is their comfort and convenience. In the Mesopotamian *Enuma Elish*, for example, as the lower gods clamor and fight among themselves, the high god Apsu expresses his frustration to his consort Tiamat. Their petty squabbles are turning the world to chaos, which denies him rest. "Their ways have become very grievous to me," he says. "By day I cannot rest, by night I cannot sleep. I shall abolish their ways and disperse them."[3] Eventually the god Marduk achieves what Apsu mused about and organizes the lesser gods—and the cosmos—under his rule: he achieves order. But he still lacks the servants necessary to serve his wishes and the needs of the junior gods. That is where humans come in. As part of his cosmic order, Marduk creates humans to build temples for the gods' rest and to provide sacrifices for the gods' nourishment. The humans are there to keep the gods happy. The Akkadian epic *Atrahasis*, dating to the eighteenth century BC, reflects the same concept. "Let him bear the yoke," the gods say of men. "Let man assume the drudgery of god,"[4] so the god can do something else. Let men be slaves.

The pattern repeats itself in myth after myth. The gods create order entirely for their benefit. The cosmos is focused on them. They provide humans fair weather, fertility, good harvests, and a measure of peace so that—and only so that—humans might in turn build them temples, bring them food, and provide them rest.[5] Sometimes the gods appoint a king to carry out their commands, and when they do he rules over the rest of humanity as they rule over him: with absolute power and control.[6]

By contrast, the God of the Bible fashions a cosmic order directed toward a very different end. His order is directed toward the good of human beings. Everything God creates in the seven days of creation anticipates human needs. Humans will need light, land, food, habitation, and companionship. They will need time and seasons and agriculture. And so God creates. The functions of the created world are directed towards the needs of man.[7]

And while the Near Eastern gods and goddesses treated humans as slaves, the God of the Bible makes them in his own image, and shares with them his rule. Adam and Eve are permitted to govern the animals; Adam is permitted to declare destinies—typically a divine prerogative—by choosing other creatures' names. Adam and Eve together are given authority over the garden and the world beyond. God does indeed call the man and woman to serve him, but not by meeting his needs: the Bible names no needs of God. Rather, God invites the man and woman to serve him by sharing the work of advancing his purposes for the world.

In this picture, in this order, man and woman are not slaves but figures of authority, and they are free. They are not controlled by anyone, but have purpose and power, delegated by God, that is theirs to use for the good of the world, to join God in helping make the world what it could be.

This divine order reflects what God intends for humans and what he expects men to use their power to promote. The Bible's God wants humans to have personal agency, to be able to do something important with their lives. He wants them to rule and thrive. His order of creation is designed to make that possible. That is the kind of order he has been laboring to achieve across the Adam stories. And that is the order the stories say God expects men, as kings, to serve.

To be a king, a man must learn that we do not create the order of the universe, any of us. We do not set its bounds or arrange its rhythms. God does that. We are the beneficiaries. The Bible makes this point by noting that Solomon inherits his kingdom and its good order from his father David. What we have, we have received. We are to *serve* the order God has made. That is what dominion is for.

Contrast that truth with the claims of Epicurean liberalism. John Rawls was one of modern liberalism's foremost philosophers, and he coined a famous phrase. He said we are, as individuals, "self-originating sources of valid claims."[8] He meant that individuals should and do have the power to choose their purposes and aims in life independent of any preexisting moral order. What makes a claim valid—what makes your actions praiseworthy or good—is the simple fact you have chosen them, not that they comport with or advance a moral order beyond yourself. That is the typical view of Epicurean liberalism.

And it is typically wrong. The effect of it is to render each individual a god unto himself, to imply that he can originate his own being and that there is no permanent, created order to the universe. That road leads, at best, to narcissism and self-indulgence. And narcissism joined to power is dangerous.

Any man who tries to live as if he is a "self-originating source" will soon run up against the reality of other people and their needs and lives. And if he is going to do with his life exactly as he pleases, he must eventually bend these other people to his will. History is choked with men who seized power to impose their will on others, men who tried to create a new order of their own devising. And while Rawls said every individual should be free to make their own choices in life without interference from others, if there is no permanent moral order that guides our choices and grounds our dignity, it is a short step from "self-originating sources of valid claims" to forcing other people to do what you want, for your own "fulfillment."

For modern liberals, this notion that we each create our own moral truth is at the foundation of what it means to be an individual. But no mature, well-adjusted person lives like that. Sooner or later, if you are not a megalomaniac, you grow up and realize you are part of a world with other people in it that you have no right to control.

I have a daughter who is nearly two. She is both the baby of the family and our only girl, and as such the frequent center of attention. But she has also acquired the habit recently of waking at four in the morning—and then shouting from her crib until my wife comes to rescue and feed her. I admire this, in one sense. She has spirit. And that will serve her well in life. But the sleep she is denying the household, and specifically her mother, does not serve anyone well at present. So my wife has been "sleep training," as they say, adjusting our daughter's bedtime in the evening and then lengthening out the time before she liberates our not-so-sleeping beauty from her crib in the morning.

We had to do the same with our boys, particularly our oldest son, who disliked sleep as a toddler. I remember returning him to his small bed in the dark of night, only to hear the pitter-patter of little footsteps five minutes later. Every parent knows the routine. But every child must learn that she or he is not the center of the universe. The natural laws of day and night, waking and sleeping—not to say the needs of others—cannot be remade around the whims of a two-year-old. The same holds true for men.

God gave Adam dominion in Eden to serve the good order God had made, not to serve Adam. If we, as men, want to exercise dominion, if we want to have some control over our lives and influence upon our fortunes, we must serve God—not ourselves—and the people he has placed in our lives. We begin by subordinating ourselves. We acknowledge, in the words of Edmund Burke, the "great, immutable, preexistent law, prior to all our devices, and prior to all our contrivances...antecedent to our very existence, by which we are knit and connected in the eternal frame of the universe, out of which we cannot stir."[9]

Acknowledging this law, God's law, does not make a man impotent. It defines the nature and purpose of his power. The power of dominion, on the Bible's telling, is the ability to bring God's good order into the world—to become its agent—to see it more fully realized and extended.

In short: You have the power to bring order from chaos. God gave it to you. Start using it. Use your influence to encourage: God looked at the world he had made and called it good; you can extend that blessing to your friends, your children, your spouse. Use your power to provide for the people in your life, beginning with your wife and children, if you have them, or other family and those in need, if you do not. Use your power to see that things around you work properly, whether it's improving a system at work or repairing a relationship.

Begin with humility. Ask God for help. That is what Solomon did. In the Bible, the young Solomon famously asks God for wisdom. Soon after taking the throne, he goes to one of Israel's altars and makes sacrifices. Then he falls into a deep sleep, and God comes to him in a dream. God says, "Ask what I shall give you." Solomon replies, "I am but a little child. I do not know how to go out or come in." Solomon goes on, "Give your servant therefore an understanding mind to govern your people."[10] Solomon does not claim to be the author of the universe. He begins with his need. He acknowledges his dependence on God. And as a result of his humility, God speaks to him. He gives Solomon insight and wisdom, such wisdom in fact that Solomon became known as one of the great lawgivers of all time. But what was really happening in Solomon's later lawgiving, according to the Bible, was that Solomon was giving to the world the wisdom of God. By serving God's law, Solomon became an agent of God's order—and his power and influence grew.

The world as we know it is deeply disordered. It needs men ready to use their influence to order it according to God's wishes, not their own—for the good of those they love and the flourishing of the world.

ORDERING THE SOUL

Having said that, it is difficult for a man to be an agent of order and peace if his own life is full of disorder and chaos. Being a king, like being a man, is a matter of character. To rule, a man must first order his soul.

The stories and myths of the ancient Near East portrayed the figure of the king as quasi-divine, as personifying the cosmic order that held together society. The fate of the kingdom depended on him because he held the divine order in his own person.[11]

The Bible also links the fate of the kingdom to the king, not because the king is divine in any way, but rather because his character shapes how he rules. For this reason, shortly before his death, David instructs Solomon to attend closely to his character. And how? By observing the ways of God and keeping his directives.

> When David's time to die drew near, he commanded Solomon his son, saying, "I am about to go the way of all the earth. Be strong, and show yourself a man, and keep the charge of the LORD your God, walking in his ways and keeping his statutes, his commandments, his rules, and his testimonies, as it is written in the Law of Moses, that you may prosper in all that you do...." (1 Kings 2:1–3)

Solomon is to take God's order into his soul. He is to guide his life by God's directives, to order his life by God's will. That is how he will be able to bring order and blessing to others, when his own soul is ordered and blessed. Self-discipline is self-mastery, and self-mastery is strength, and a man's strength, in the biblical view, can bless and empower others.

One summer when I was in middle school my mother announced that every morning she would require my sister and me to rise early and accompany her to the local military academy, which has since closed but at the time had an outdoor track that was open to the public. We would begin each day with a mile run, she said—this was the warm-up— to be followed by other exercises of her devising. I don't recall how my sister reacted to this news, but I protested vigorously. Summer was for sleeping in, I said. I was about thirteen and not yet holding down a full-time job. I did have a small lawn-mowing business, or a lawn-mowing hobby, more accurately, mowing the neighbors' yards and those of a few family friends around town for cash. But that was hardly taxing and consumed relatively little time. I played baseball in the summers, but the baseball season ended in June. So here it was, sometime in middle summer, school over and baseball finished and me at home with only the occasional yard to mow, and all the time in the world. And I wanted to keep it that way.

Neither of my parents were pushovers, but between them my mother was in truth more the disciplinarian. She believed in standards and obedience. Above all, she believed in self-discipline. And as I look back now, I see what she was doing on those summer mornings. She was giving me structure and goals so that I would learn to create structure and goals for myself. She was teaching me self-mastery. I resented her morning constitutionals at first, but soon, despite myself, I began to look forward to them. I enjoyed the running more and the discipline of the exercise. But as much as anything, I began to enjoy the order. My mother's sessions provided structure to my day, and ultimately to my summer. They helped teach me, in a small way, how to order my life.

To teach a man God's order, the Bible contains its own instructions for kings. The instructions are about self-mastery and service to God. For example: The king "shall not acquire many wives for himself, lest his heart turn away."[12] In other words, don't indulge yourself. Don't live for personal gratification. Don't make satisfying desire your life's aim. The apostle Paul says something similar in the New Testament, writing that he disciplines his body so that he will not be mastered by his passions. Are you going out every night? Stop. Are you sleeping in every morning? Get up. Don't surrender your life to the momentary pleasures of alcohol or drugs or intellectual sloth. It's not worth it. Discipline your body. Improve your mind.

The instructions go on. The king shall not "acquire for himself excessive silver and gold."[13] That is, don't make wealth your god. Don't worship social status. Ambition is good and worthwhile, but money for the sake of money is an ultimately empty pursuit. One of my good friends from college became a hedge fund manager in the San Francisco Bay Area. Financial success has always been important to him. He works punishing hours, he's put in his years, and now he earns what must be prodigious compensation. He is married to a wonderful woman and has two children. In addition to their apartment in San Francisco, they own a "country" home in Sausalito, just across the bay. One would think he would be happy with his life. He is not. I met him for lunch some months ago, and he spent much of the time complaining about the cost of living and his children's expenses. *I have to keep grinding*, he said, *just to keep up.* I pointed out that he is a wealthy man in more ways than one, but he demurred. *You might think that*, he said, *but then you see how much these other guys are making and it's not even close.* Money is a hard master.

If not money, what then is to be the king's aim? He is to "learn to fear the LORD his God by keeping all the words of this law and these statutes, and doing them."[14] A man who would be a king must be controlled by a passion for what is right. He must orient his life toward the highest good, toward God. He is to love the truth, to speak the truth, and to live by the truth, always. He is to love the good order that God intends for his universe, and rather than fearing other men—what they might do to him or think of him—he is to fear and respect God. In the New Testament, Paul summarizes the require-ments of a leader this way: he should be "above reproach, the husband of one wife, sober-minded, self-controlled, respectable, hospitable, able to teach, not a drunkard, not violent but gentle, not quarrelsome, not a lover of money."[15]

To lead, a man must master himself. To bring order from chaos, he must order his character. Like the young King Solomon, a man is to do more than observe the order of God as a spectator. He is to make it part of himself, to bring order to his own life by following God's law.

There is an authority that comes from self-mastery. And even a youth can sense its absence. I remember talking with one of my law students once about what job he might take for the summer. He was a little at loose ends—not sure what branch of law he wanted to pursue, not sure what his longer-term goals were. Finally I said, "Have you asked your father?" He waved his hand dismissively. "I don't take my dad's advice on anything," he said. I asked why not. He replied, "He doesn't treat my mom well. He's lazy. He's never tried to do anything at work or get ahead. He's never encouraged me to do anything with my life." He shrugged and offered by way of conclusion: "He's not someone I can look up to."

Self-mastery brings self-respect and the respect of others. And don't kid yourself, its absence is noted. If you want to have influence with your kids, bring some order to your life. Discipline your speech. Organize yourself. Show them how to serve, how to discipline their passions to meet a long-term goal. If you want to have influence at work, do the same. If you want influence in any sphere, in any endeavor, cultivate a well-ordered soul.

THE ORDER OF LIBERTY

All this talk about order rings contrarian in an age that claims to prioritize liberty. But this brings us to another paradox. The Bible claims order and self-command are not opposite to liberty but are liberty's prerequisites. Freedom and character go hand in hand.

There is an interesting line, in this regard, in that same set of ancient instructions for kings. The king must not lead his people into luxury and love of ease—self-indulgence—the Bible says, lest the people "return to Egypt." God warns, "You shall never return that way again."[16] Egypt, of course, was the land of bondage from which God delivered Israel. Israel's king must see to it the nation never goes back.

The idea is that self-gratification and pleasure-seeking do not constitute liberty; they constitute a path away from liberty. Freedom is something more than following one's momentary whims. It is more than doing whatever you please. A man who wants to be free must order himself and his soul, because only then will he have the capacity to do what liberty means to do: *to rule.*

When God set Adam and Eve in the garden, he charged them, as the representatives of all humanity, to rule the earth on his behalf. Notably, God does not single out a special class of individuals to rule. He does not create a rank of demi-gods. He shares his authority, rather, with all humans. The idea that each person can exercise God's authority, can share in his rule, was, and is, a truly revolutionary notion, unknown to the ancient world—and still disputed today. From this biblical claim, and this biblical view of the individual, comes the West's biblical tradition of individual liberty. The ideal of individual freedom and individual rights originates not in the Enlightenment or with the French Revolution but here, in the Bible's teaching that every person can share in the rule of God.

The West's storied tradition of self-government originates here, too. For if all men and women are born to rule over themselves and over creation, then no one man is born lord over another. And no man is born subservient to someone else. The ancient myths portrayed all humans as slaves to the gods, and most humans as slaves to other humans. Such was the supposed order of nature. The Greeks and Romans, similarly, believed some men were born to rule and others—most—born to be slaves. That is not the Bible's view. In the beginning, all humans receive the injunction, through Adam and Eve, to govern. It is part of their purpose and the ground of their dignity. Reflecting on this, the seventeenth-century Puritans concluded that the best form of government was a republic, where free men shared in rule together.[17]

The American founders inherited this tradition—one that flows straight back to the Bible.

The invitation to rule is, from the Bible's perspective, the very heart of liberty. But what does it mean? The Adam stories spell it out. The power to rule is the power to subdue chaos and bring order. It is the power to extend what is good where there is darkness. It is the power to bring forth the hidden potentials of nature, of the physical and animal worlds, to make them productive and beautiful. The power to rule is the power to act upon the world to change it, to improve it—to use our skill and art to bring forth its potential and make it more what it could be.

The power to rule is also the power to order our own lives and improve them. In fact, in our character is where the power to rule—the power of liberty—begins. Human nature is like the rest of nature: it holds great potential, but it must be tended to and developed. Every parent knows this and does it, daily. The other day my younger son demanded to know why he couldn't drink root beer, a particular favorite, at every meal. I explained to him that we discipline our choices in food and drink for the good of our bodies, to develop their potential.

Athletes do the same, constantly. I have a good friend who plays in the NFL. He is the best kicker in the league. And he has not gotten to that station by happenstance. He trains his body rigorously, using weights and drills for muscle development and explosiveness. He manages his nutrition. He carefully tracks his sleep. And he refines his skills with single-minded focus and determination. I was amazed when, at the conclusion of a recent season, he spent weeks breaking down his kicking motion and critiquing it—how did he point his foot, what was the angle of his knee—looking for ways to improve mechanics that were already hugely successful. *Why?* I asked. *Because I can be better*, he said. It was that simple. There was potential there yet to be tapped. And he was determined to tap it. This is "ruling," this is bringing will and purpose to bear on one's own nature—body and mind—to make yourself more what you could be.

The ancient Greeks understood these principles. They spoke frequently of the connection between self-command and liberty. I have already mentioned Plato's *Phaedrus* and the image of the soul as a chariot harnessed to twin horses. Just as the horses must pull together for the chariot to move smoothly, a man's lower and higher passions must be synchronized for a man to realize his full potential. In similar vein, both Plato and Aristotle compared a man's soul to the order of a city: when a man orders himself, he becomes what he could be—and gains new control over his life. He gains liberty.

TWO CONCEPTS OF LIBERTY

Modern liberals disagree. They see no link between character and liberty. Freedom to today's Epicureans depends on there being no moral order, no God, no eternity or human nature—only your needs, which you must be free to satisfy, here and now.

The liberal philosopher Isaiah Berlin wrote a famous essay to this effect years ago, entitled "Two Concepts of Liberty." His conclusion was (though he did not put it quite so starkly) that the ancient, biblical concept of liberty is counterfeit. The Bible's liberty forces a person to accept the existence of some greater moral law and purpose beyond himself. Liberty is available only when the individual orders his life by God's law.[18] Berlin objected. That notion subjects man to a moral system not of his choosing, he pointed out. By definition, it prevents him from doing as he pleases.[19] That cannot be freedom, Berlin went on. True freedom is when you are "unobstructed by others," when you are able "to choose to live as [you] may desire."[20] True freedom is when you satisfy your needs as you see fit.

This is where the left's crusade of nihilism comes in, its campaign of *dis*order. Leftists want to raze the inherited structures of society so individuals can be "free." The biological realities of male and female constrain individual expression, they say, so they must be denied, and traditional gender roles abolished. The traditional family, likewise. And traditional religion, too. All must go so individuals can do as they please. And there are some individuals who must be forced to be free. If you are a traditional Jew or Christian, a defender of the traditional family, or a believer in the reality of male and female, you cannot be left to your own devices. You must be restrained and reeducated, lest you perpetuate intolerance and bigotry.

The Epicureans say those who do what suits them are free. But the embarrassing truth is that some people have more opportunity to do what suits them than others—namely, the wealthy and, in today's society, well-educated. They are the ones with the disposable income and leisure time. They are the ones who have the luxury and the means of curating their "personal brand" and maximizing their life options. If liberty is all about personal choice and self-expression, liberty becomes a luxury good. And the wealthy have a corner on that market. The Epicurean idea of liberty so loudly proclaimed by today's left ends up being the province of the educated upper class, which should come as no surprise, I suppose, since that's where most of today's liberals hail from.

The Bible takes a different view. Man is free not when he shrugs off order but when he embraces it. A man discovers freedom by growing into the nature God has given him and responding to the purpose God has written into his life. The Bible says God freed the Israelites from slavery so they could serve him. Serving him *was* freedom, because serving him was what they were created to do. It's what all humans were created to do; it's what fulfills our nature and makes us truly human. A man is born to be God's servant and temple-maker. He is most fully alive when he does these things. By living into the purpose inscribed on his soul, a man gains control of his life and acquires the power to shape his circumstances and to change the course of the future. That is character. That is liberty.

The left's denial of purpose and order has just the opposite effect to what it promises. Its program leads a man not toward greater strength and independence, not toward greatness of soul, but toward impotence and resignation. For this reason: We are not the authors of our own universes. We do not create ourselves out of nothing, and it is an impossible burden to try.

More and more young men struggle with the basic responsibilities of adulthood—moving out of their parents' home, for example, or holding down a job. One explanation is the incredible fear of failure the leftist view of liberty unwittingly inspires. If you must fill your life with meaning entirely on your own, it can seem safer to some not to try. Failure, after all, would leave your life empty. This is a critical, if often overlooked, difference between the generations. Young men raised half a century ago had the strength of a broadly Christian culture still at their back. They had the confidence of permanent truths handed down to them by their churches and families that oriented their lives and supplied them meaning. They had the bulwark of a social order that directed their ambitions toward marriage, children, and gainful work. Not so today.

Today's young men must concoct their own truth (they are told) and make their own rules, with nothing but their shifting wants and anxieties to guide them. The result is the glaring dichotomy obvious everywhere in our culture between the rhetoric of self-realization on the one hand and loud cries of victimhood on the other. Now we can see why. Denied the truth of his inherent purpose, faced with the burden of forging his own meaning *ex nihilo*, it can be easier for a man to focus on something rather more doable—like getting the government to give him stuff and blaming someone else for his problems. Call it activist victimhood.

Modern liberalism may preach liberation, but it creates victims. Victimhood relieves the lonely, isolated man of the burden of self-creation the modern Epicureans place upon him. Being a victim gives him the right to demand society do something for him, rather than the other way around. It assures him society owes him; victim status excuses his failures. It also gives him a "job," of a sort: the right to be an activist and demand that government fork over what he is "owed" by taking it from his alleged oppressors. And all that brings a certain type of meaning. But it is a pathetic and shallow meaning, built on complaining of one's own incompetence.

Yet this is where modern liberalism leads, to competing cries of victimhood and ever-increasing demands for rights. The left begins by stridently urging individuals to reject moral order and remake reality. It ends by promising them care and protection—and entertainment and comfort—when they cannot. Liberalism's opening note of liberation soon gives way to dependence.

WHO IS GOING TO RUN THE COUNTRY?

Which is exactly how many in today's ruling class want it. Today's liberals believe in government by experts, by which they mean themselves. Their program amounts to telling men to accept the entertainment they are offered, live off the government cash they are given, and let other people run the country. Throw in a dash of activism, if you want; go and tell anyone who will listen that society is systemically corrupt and you are a victim. Post a rant on social media. Make yourself feel good. And then settle down and let the experts fix it, because the experts *agree* that America is oppressive. They wrote that script. It is part of their justification for claiming power and destroying the very things—family, blue-collar work—that permit the common man to get a leg up in life and exert influence in society.

You want to talk about two concepts of liberty? This is how the Epicurean concept works out in the end. It is bread and circuses for the people—the working men and women of this country now rendered faceless and voiceless by liberal policies; separated from family, from work, from church and home—and power for the elite, who will busily continue deconstructing American society to make the common person dependent on them.

The question is, who is going to run the country? The people or the experts? Working men and women, or the self-appointed elite? This is where the Bible's teaching on manhood, character, and liberty gets real, and urgent. The men of this country face a choice. They can turn off their screens and reclaim responsibility for their lives; they can reject the Epicurean siren song of self-indulgence, that soothing lullaby that is really just a means of keeping men distracted and dependent; they can stop taking handouts; they can find a wife and start a family; they can, in sum, get their character in order and reclaim their independence as men. Or not. And if not, the American republic as we have known it will cease to exist. America the nation will go on, to be sure, for a while anyway, and a good many people will go on making a good deal of money; that part won't change. But the American *republic*, Lincoln's "last best hope on earth," will vanish. We will be no longer a self-governing nation because we will not have the character for it. We will be governed by other people, a small group of people with the money and access to whom we have surrendered control—the experts—and not by ourselves.

Isaiah Berlin decided, in the end, that self-rule and liberty had no necessary connection. You do not need to govern yourself in order to be free. At back of this conclusion lurks the modern liberal disdain for ordinary people, the everyday Joe. Modern liberals think little of these men, as we have seen. That is why they want to remake them. They certainly don't think most men—*you*—can be trusted to run the country. For that reason, the liberals insist government is terribly complicated and inordinately complex and must be managed by well-trained experts: *them*. In return, these experts will make certain you are adequately provisioned and amply entertained.

And maybe the left is right that liberty and self-rule have no connection, if liberty is about being taken care of. But if liberty means independence from the experts, if it means the chance to serve God and do something with your years on earth that will matter, then self-rule and liberty are connected in every way. Character and liberty are bonded. Never forget this fact from Genesis: God invites men to share in his rule. He invites every man to be a king. That is where our tradition of self-government comes from. But if a man is going to rule, he must show the character of a king. Self-government requires self-mastery. It requires virtue. And to rescue our republic from decline into a dull and atheistic materialism defined by the rule of the bureaucrats and the few, America needs men of virtue now.

One of the men who understood this best in American history was Theodore Roosevelt. As a boy, I loved Roosevelt, and I still do—the indomitable Rough Rider, the scourge of the giant trusts, the man who spoke so frequently of right and wrong that a Democratic newspaper once sniffed he carried "a pulpit concealed on his person."[21] He understood about men and liberty. Roosevelt once pointed out that in this country, "we are not ruled over by others, as is the case in Europe; we rule ourselves." Consequently, he went on, "we have the responsibilities of sovereigns not of subjects."[22] A subject waits for someone to do things for him. A subject is happy to be entertained. A subject looks to some other person, some government or group, to solve his problems and provide for him. He is passive. He plays the victim. He does as the experts instruct.

The Epicureans have recommended we behave like subjects for years. But that is not the kind of freedom, if it is freedom at all, that the Bible says we were meant for.

We are sovereigns. Kings. And a sovereign must take responsibility for his own life. He orders his passions so that he can govern his soul. And having ordered himself, he brings the blessing of order to those around him: he provides, he protects, he tells the truth, he gives his life for others. That is the way of a king. "We have rights," Roosevelt told the men of his day, "but we have cor[r]elative duties; none can escape them."[23] Our rights are safe only if we are willing to perform our duties—to make difficult decisions, to delay gratification, to refuse dependence. Our rights are safe only if we have strength of soul. Weak men incapable of self-control cannot hold on to any rights at all.

And ultimately, our rights take their meaning from our duties. It's because we have obligations to God and to family, to church and nation, that we have rights to begin with. Our rights follow from what we are called to do and who we are called to be. The power to be a king is the power to take up those duties rather than abandon them. It is the power to shoulder responsibility.

Roosevelt understood that true liberty begins with order in the soul. "We only have the right to live on as free men," he concluded, "so long as we show ourselves worthy of the privileges we enjoy."[24] Freedom is a moral enterprise. Liberty demands character, and only men of high character can live it—and keep it, and pass it on. America's most urgent need politically is not for this or that piece of legislation. It is for men to embrace the call to character, the call to what Theodore Roosevelt termed "righteousness." He never tired of quoting Proverbs to his countrymen: "[R]ighteousness exalteth a nation."[25] He was right.

For too long, too many American men have been content to be entertained. Or they have believed the lies they have been told about the evils of masculinity. Either way: American men, it is time to wake up. It is time to become free men, as your fathers and grandfathers were, to order your souls and answer to God and be what he made you to be: not subjects, but kings.

"I AM IN THE FATHER, AND THE FATHER IS IN ME"

If becoming a king is the summit of a man's journey, then the journey ends as it began: with an invitation from God. The Bible says the good order God brought forth in Eden and asks men to carry into the world reflects, above all, himself. It is a revelation of who he is: just, generous, wise, and good. And so when God tells Solomon as king—and every man after—to follow his ways, he is not telling him merely to follow a set of prescriptions or rules. He is inviting men to become like himself. He is inviting men to take on the character of God.

That is what manhood finally means. "I am in the Father and the Father is in me," Jesus once said to his startled listeners.[26] That is the invitation.

■　　■　　■

The last time I saw my grandfather he was in a nursing home, in Cloud County, Kansas, a county over from where his farm and house were. I was all grown up by then, in law school; I went back to visit him in the summer of my first year. He had suffered several strokes. I remember finding him—with my dad and mother and younger sister—reclining in a cushioned armchair out in the common area, sleeping. Other seniors were gathered at tables here and there, working on crafts. Some watched television. What struck me immediately was how thin he had gotten. He had always been a solid man, perhaps a little rotund. His face was perpetually tanned from the hours and days in the sun. Now he was pale white, and his cheeks were sunken. His hair, or what remained of it—he had been nearly bald since I knew him, with only a ring of brown hair around the back of his head, always combed neatly down—had also gone utterly white and now stood out at all angles. I remember seeing a sketch once of the aging King Arthur, in one of those T. H. White novels, I think: Arthur reclines in the picture, gaunt, his eyes closed, his strength spent. This was like that.

Grandpa stirred when we all gathered around, and sat up. I don't know that he recognized me. He was his usual cheerful self, though, asking about the things he usually did, the crops, the weather. After a few minutes he drifted off again, and was soon snoring quietly as we sat beside him. I realized as I sat there that this was goodbye. And I realized that, more than anyone else I had ever known personally, he was the man I most wanted to be. He had been a model for me of what it meant to be a man—a husband and father, a warrior and builder, a priest and a king.

He always prized a strong handshake. He used to greet me, from the time I was small, with outstretched hand, enfolding my boyish palm in his large one, thick and calloused from his work. And he would say, "Now give me a good firm grip."

He wasn't able to shake my hand that last day. But before we left, I placed my hand atop his, as he rested, and held it there for a moment, just to say thank you. Thank you for being a good man.

OF TEMPLES AND MEN

My son Elijah had his birthday the other day, a sparkling fall day of the kind you sometimes get in the middle part of autumn, crisp, no humidity, bright. Much like the day he came to us. We hosted a party at a park near our house. Elijah began planning it weeks in advance. He started by drawing sketches of the activities the party should include: tree climbing, roasting marshmallows, bonfires, "exploring." These sketches went through several iterations, sometimes in consultation with his younger brother. "You should add football," Blaise advised. Elijah later took to the computer to design a formal invitation, complete with 3D graphics, advertising the various recreational possibilities and promising plenty of cake to those who attended. My wife dutifully sent the invitation to his prescribed list and collected the returns.

The park where we hosted the festivities sits behind two baseball fields and offers a playground and swings, as well as plenty of trees for climbing. There is a covered pavilion with picnic benches in the middle and a fixed charcoal grill, where I lit a fire for the marshmallow roasting. But from my boys' perspective, the chief attraction of the place is the creek that runs alongside the park's eastern boundary and then disappears into a stand of trees on the far side. It is wide and shallow, with plenty of stones for throwing. And whatever the other activities on my son's list, there was never any question where the partygoers would end up. The creek exerts a magnetic, almost magical pull.

Sure enough, hardly ten minutes had passed before both my sons and most of their friends were in the water, soaked to their pant legs, clamoring loudly to each other about the rocks and the current and the lizards they imagined they saw. I could hear them from where I stood at the grill, talking with the other fathers. Or at least, I could hear them for a while. At some point I noticed, with surprise, that I didn't hear anything at all. That's when I realized the boys had gone. The whole lot of them had disappeared down the creek bed.

When they hadn't returned half an hour later, my wife suggested I might want to investigate. Another father and I set off along the creek bank, pushing through fallen leaves and underbrush, calling the boys' names. Two or three hundred yards on from the park, the creek crossed a culvert, the customary boundary to my boys' adventuring. This was the point at which they typically turned back. But they were nowhere to be found.

The other dad and I pressed ahead, making small talk and wondering aloud to ourselves where precisely the creek terminated. And how was it that our sons had managed to get so far afield in such a short time? After a spell of more walking and wading—the creek meandered, which meant that in order to keep a straight course we had to cross it twice—we heard voices in the distance, and then finally met a party of boys coming in our direction, with my son Elijah at the head. "Dad," he called out when we were fifty paces apart, "where are the others?" I said I had intended to ask him the same question. "We got separated," he replied, "we were supposed to meet back up at the culvert but they didn't come. We've been out trying to find them. We have to keep looking!"

I suggested they instead return with the father who had accompanied me, and I would go on looking for the remaining boys myself. Elijah rejected that suggestion out of hand. "No, we have to find them!" he said with fierce urgency. Without waiting for my reply, he turned his little party around and directed them back in the direction they had come. "Let's rescue them," he cried.

It was then I realized that my son was growing up. He didn't want the help I offered. He didn't want to be rescued. *He* wanted to do the rescuing. He wasn't looking for safety at all, but for adventure—he had created the adventure, as a matter of fact, along with his buddies, and now he was going to see it through. He was rehearsing, without knowing it, for the role of his life. That's what manhood is, in the end: an adventure into the unknown, into darkness and chaos, to extend the light and build the garden, an adventure toward character. If too many men seem lost and without purpose today, perhaps it is because they have not discovered that adventure, and the story that tells them who they are.

■　　■　　■

Speaking of which, I have not yet finished the story.

Solomon lived to the end of his days, a man of peace to the last. But only barely. In his latter years he strayed—he loved many foreign wives, the Bible says. In other words: he gave way to self-indulgence and the weakness of the flesh. Upon his death, his kingdom dissolved into bitter civil war, never to be united again. Four hundred years later, foreign invaders carried his people into exile and burned the temple he had built, symbol of a renewed Eden, to ash. All that to say, Solomon's reign represents a conclusion, but not the end. No, that would await another Adam, and a better man than Solomon. That would await a better man than us all.

On the Bible's telling, Solomon's Jerusalem is a portrait of what the world might be, what it will be, when it is fully rescued from chaos and completed: when it is fully and finally redeemed. Solomon's reign was a premonition of things yet to come. The world is still waiting to be made a temple.

Until then, every man has a part to play. And this work is the story of a man's life, the call that summons him to be what he was made to be. He can acquire the character of a husband and father, a warrior and a builder, a priest and, yes, a king. These are the roles toward which a man's responsibilities guide him. These are the virtues that make a boy a man.

We live in an era of astounding affluence, of widespread technology and obsession with comfort and ease. And yet the dominant note of our Epicurean culture is increasingly one of despair. The nagging sense that nothing matters, that everything is meaningless, plays just beneath the surface of our public life. It helps account for the frenzy of entertainment that distracts so many young men and the relentless pleasure-seeking modeled by celebrities and the cultural elite. It helps explain our inability to talk about death and the profound fear of it on display everywhere—in our obsession with youthfulness, in our fixation on health. Men, particularly, get the message delivered to them from the time they're young: the world is an empty place and nothing you can do will change that. In fact, men are told that virtually anything they do, short of renouncing their masculinity, will make the world far worse.

The Bible, that book much maligned by today's cognoscenti yet still the book we cannot do without, tells a different story. The world is not empty; our lives are not meaningless. History is about something, it is headed somewhere, and we can be part of it. What we do, here and now, can matter—for all time. A man can matter.

The Bible is right. The Epicurean liberals are wrong. The world was born with purpose, and history is moving toward that purpose even now. The world may be disordered at the moment and out of joint. It may be chaotic and menaced by evil. But it is made to be something more, much more: a place of peace and liberty and astounding beauty. The creation is a cathedral, magnificent in design beyond all imagining, reflecting its Creator.

And humans are the creatures God has chosen to help bring it on toward that goal.

Every man can be a man of peace, a man of order. He can bring order to his own life. He can choose self-discipline and strive for self-command. He can commit himself to a woman for a lifetime and put her interests ahead of his. He can be a father who will love his children and devote himself to them. He can work with industry and build something honorable. And America needs men who will do these things. In this age of fatherlessness and self-absorption and irresponsibility, America needs men who will start families and build homes and leave legacies of character that will span generations.

Every man can be a man of liberty. He can know the freedom of self-control and the agency it brings—the ability to shape his life and shape the world around him. Put another way, a man can know what it means to rule. He can bring forth the hidden potential of the world through his effort and his work. He can change circumstances, discover new possibilities, create beauty. He can change the direction of other people's lives. And in doing all these things, he can discover meaning and purpose for his own. This is true liberty.

America needs men who understand that liberty is not the flight from responsibility but the movement toward it, who understand liberty is found not in dissolving the bonds of family and tradition and faith, as the Epicurean left instructs, but in forging them stronger.

America needs men who will aspire toward real independence, not the false freedom of self-fulfillment the left uses to keep men preoccupied and pliant.

America needs men who are ready to be more than consumers and do more than be entertained, men not content to let the expert class govern them or have bureaucrats run their nation. America needs men able to govern themselves and to reclaim for our time the liberty of self-government. If we get those kinds of men, with that kind of character, the American republic will endure. And that is how our great experiment in liberty will be judged, in the end: not by the wealth we accumulated or the might we displayed, but by the character of the citizens we produced.

How then does it all end? The Epicureans have their answer. One of the most common inscriptions the ancients chose to place upon their tombstones ran "n.f. f. n.s. n.c."—an abbreviation for *non fui, fui, non sum, non curo*. It means, "I was not. I was. I am not. I care not."[1] There is the Epicurean philosophy in sum. Vanity of vanities, all is vanity.

As for the Bible: well, it ends with another Adam, of course.

The hints are there from the beginning. When God called Abraham to Adam's work, he did not issue a command, you may recall. He made a promise. And that detail turns out to hold the destiny of the world. "I will bless you," God said to Abraham, and "in you all the families of the earth shall be blessed."[2] The work of manhood has ever depended on God's promise. It has ever depended on his grace. No man could fulfill man's mission, not finally. Not Adam, not Abraham, not Joshua or David or Solomon or anyone else. Men are as flawed as the world they inhabit. Every man needs saving, as the world needs saving. God's promise to Abraham reveals God's intention to save it—and us—from the first. He answers our need: He becomes a man, one last Adam. And this Man takes the failures and shortcomings and the malice and pain of all men into himself and gives his life to overcome them. And he offers the new life he has won to all who will receive it. He becomes himself the ultimate temple, where God and humanity are united. And one day, he will unite heaven and earth, and make all the world a new Eden at last. That is where the story is headed.

And that determines how we live now. I have mentioned my own father from time to time in these pages; I think of him again, finally, in connection with grace. He was an athlete as a young man, in high school and college, and he carries himself still with an athlete's grace. I remember, as a child, watching him catch a pass, admiring as he moved smoothly over the distance, extending his arms to catch my throw, light, never labored. He taught me something about how to live like that as a man, to live with grace. He disdained men who blustered and strutted. He laughed at false bravado. He instructed me as a small boy, when I was just beginning to play sports and hunt and enter the world of men, that character is what counts. Live with character, he taught me, and you'll never have anything to prove to anyone. That's how he wore his manhood: easily. He showed me that manhood is not playacting or social performance. It is an invitation to character that God extends by his grace.

■ ■ ■

The night after my son's birthday party, I tucked him into bed and read to him and his brother, as I do most evenings. And then I took his small hands in mine and prayed for him, that God would awaken his heart to the call on his life, to the great adventure for which God made him. "Lord, would you use my son to build your temple and bring your presence to the world?" I asked. May the same be true for every man.

AUTHOR'S NOTE

In the fall of 2021, I gave a speech on the plight of men in America that became the germ of this book. I have been asked many times since when I first became interested in the topic. The answer is easy: when I became a father.

I have two small boys at home and a baby daughter, and I have written about all three in these pages. My daughter is just now a toddler, but my boys are growing up. Thinking about their future, and about my obligation as a father to help them become the men they were meant to be, started me thinking about manhood in earnest and the challenges men face today in becoming men in full. This book is the result of those ruminations. In a sense, it is an open letter to my sons. The wonder of their lives captivates me every day. And I dedicate this book to them with a profound sense of gratitude that I get to be their father. I love you, Elijah and Blaise.

Many individuals have had a hand in this book, and I am grateful to each of them. I want to thank a few of them here by name. John Ehrett and Vijay Menon provided truly exceptional research assistance; I am much in their debt. David Lindell read the manuscript from front to back, as did Zack Kahler, and I am deeply grateful to them both for their timely feedback and lucid insights. I also benefited tremendously from a group of younger men who read the book all the way through and told me plainly what they liked and didn't. Thank you to Chris, Daniel, Chad, Tyler, Pierson, Cal, Josh, and Ryan.

My publisher, Tom Spence, was enthusiastic about this project from the very first. It has been a true privilege to work again with him and his team at Regnery. My editor, Harry Crocker, is the consummate professional and shaped the book in ways that made it much, much better. He curtailed many a bad idea and directed me toward many a good one. Thanks also to Kathleen Curran and the entire Regnery team.

The book would never have made it to print without the excellent offices of my agent, Esther Fedorkevich, and her outstanding staff. I thank them all.

Finally, my wife, Erin. I started out thinking to write a book focused narrowly on fatherhood. She helped me see the relevant questions were truly far broader. She read every word of the manuscript numerous times, commented on draft upon draft, listened to many an evening recitation, encouraged me when I was beleaguered, clarified my muddled thinking, and eventually offered the counsel every writer needs to hear in the end: "Josh, stop writing." This project, like my life, has been illumined by her.

NOTES

CHAPTER ONE: IN THE BEGINNING

1. Erik Hurst, "Video Killed the Radio Star," Chicago Booth Review, September 1, 2016, https://www.chicagobooth.edu/review/video-killed-radio-star.

2. Ibid.

3. Rachel Sheffield and Scott Winship, "The Demise of the Happy Two-Parent Home," U.S. Congress Joint Economic Committee, July 23, 2020, https://www.jec.senate.gov/public/index.cfm/republicans/2020/7/the-demise-of-the-happy-two-parent-home, 20.

4. Philip Zimbardo and Nikita Coulombe, "Young Men and Society: We Will Only Get Out What We Put In," Institute for Family Studies, January 14, 2021, https://ifstudies.org/blog/young-men-and-society-we-will-only-get-out-what-we-put-in.

5. Leonard Sax, "Boys Are Falling Farther and Farther behind Their Sisters: Should We Care?" Institute for Family Studies, September 22, 2021, https://ifstudies.org/blog/boys-are-falling-farther-and-farther-behind-their-sisters-should-we-care-; Douglas Belkin, "A Generation of American Men Give Up on College: 'I Just Feel Lost,'" *Wall Street Journal*, September 6, 2021.

6. Nicholas Eberstadt and Evan Abramsky, "What Do Prime-Age 'NILF' Men Do All Day? A Cautionary on Universal Basic Income," Institute for Family Studies, February 8, 2021, https://ifstudies.org/blog/what-do-prime-age-nilf-men-do-all-day-a-cautionary-on-universal-basic-income.

7. Ibid.

8. See Mark Aguiar et al., "Leisure Luxuries and the Labor Supply of Young Men," *Journal of Political Economy* 129, no. 2 (February 2021); Fabio Zattoni et al., "The Impact of COVID-19 Pandemic on Pornography

Habits: A Global Analysis of Google Trends," *International Journal of Impotence Research* 33 (2020): 824–31.

9. Rob Whitley, "The Silent Crisis of Male Suicide," *Psychology Today*, September 10, 2021.

10. Sally C. Curtin, Matthew F. Garnett, and Farida B. Ahmad, "Provisional Numbers and Rates of Suicide by Month and Demographic Characteristics: United States, 2021," *National Vital Statistics System Report No.* 24, National Center for Health Statistics, Centers for Disease Control and Prevention, September 2022 ("Suicide rates increased for males aged 15–24, 25–34, 35–44, and 65–74."), 1. See also Whitley, "The Silent Crisis of Male Suicide."

11. "Long-Term Trends in Deaths of Despair," U.S. Congress Joint Economic Committee, September 5, 2019, https://www.jec.senate.gov/public/index.cfm/republicans/2019/9/long-term-trends-in-deaths-of-despair.

12. Patrick T. Brown, "Opioids and the Unattached Male," *City Journal*, January 14, 2022.

13. See Eberstadt and Abramsky, "What Do Prime-Age 'NILF' Men Do All Day?"; "Long-Term Trends in Deaths of Despair," U.S. Congress Joint Economic Committee; Lauren Rouse, "Suicide Rates Are on the Rise among Older White Men in Rural Areas," Vital Record, Texas A&M Health, March 29, 2021, https://vitalrecord.tamhsc.edu/suicide-rates-are-on-the-rise-among-older-white-men-in-rural-areas/.

14. Paul Hemez and Chanell Washington, "Percentage and Number of Children Living with Two Parents Has Dropped Since 1968," United States Census Bureau, April 12, 2021, https://www.census.gov/library/stories/2021/04/number-of-children-living-only-with-their-mothers-has-doubled-in-past-50-years.html.

15. Jason DeParle and Sabrina Tavernise, "For Women under 30, Most Births Occur outside Marriage," *New York Times*, February 17, 2012.

16. See National Fatherhood Initiative, *Father Facts*, 8th ed. (Germantown, Maryland: National Fatherhood Initiative, 2019); Erin Pougnet et al., "The Intergenerational Continuity of Fathers' Absence in a Socioeconomically Disadvantaged Sample," *Journal of Marriage and Family* 74, no. 3 (2012): 540.

17. David Gilmore, *Manhood in the Making: Cultural Concepts of Masculinity* (New Haven, Connecticut: Yale University Press, 1990), 226.
18. John Stoltenberg, "Why Talking about 'Healthy Masculinity' Is Like Talking about 'Healthy Cancer,'" Feminist Current, August 9, 2013, https://www.feministcurrent.com/2013/08/09/why-talking-about-healthy-masculinity-is-like-talking-about-healthy-cancer/.
19. See "WATCH: Far-Left Berkeley Law Professor Melts Down When Senator Hawley Asks Her If Men Can Get Pregnant," Senate website for Josh Hawley, July 12, 2022, https://www.hawley.senate.gov/watch-far-left-berkeley-law-professor-melts-down-when-senator-hawley-asks-her-if-men-can-get.
20. See, for example, Phil McCombs, "Men's Movement Stalks the Wild Side," *Washington Post*, February 3, 1991 (providing a critical, but balanced, overview of the "mythopoetic men's movement").
21. See Larry Siedentop, *Inventing the Individual: The Origins of Western Liberalism* (Cambridge, Massachusetts: Belknap Press, 2014), 51–78, 94, 135–36, 296–99, 327–28, 349–63.
22. See, for example, Eric Nelson, *The Hebrew Republic: Jewish Sources and the Transformation of European Political Thought* (Cambridge, Massachusetts: Harvard University Press, 2010), 1–22, 138.
23. See, for example, Carl Jung, *The Red Book (Liber Novus)*, trans. Mark Kyburz, John Peck, and Sonu Shamdasani (New York: W. W. Norton & Company, 2009), 301 (describing the relationship of chaos and uncertainty to growth).
24. See Charles Knapp, "Theodore Roosevelt on the Decadence of Various Peoples, Including the Romans," *The Classical Weekly* 18, no. 15 (1925): 113–14.

CHAPTER TWO: A MAN'S MISSION

1. Genesis 2:7–8. Unless otherwise cited, all biblical references are to the English Standard Version.
2. See John H. Walton, *Genesis: The NIV Application Commentary* (Grand Rapids, Michigan: Zondervan, 2001), 166.

3. Genesis 2:9.

4. See Walton, *Genesis*, 170–85. Geerhardus Vos tellingly refers to the tree of life as a "sacrament." He goes on: "We have here the possibility of an attainment of a higher state [to become like God], but it is conditioned by obedience. The way of the tree of life is the tree of knowledge." Geerhardus Vos, *The Eschatology of the Old Testament*, ed. James T. Dennison Jr. (Phillipsburg, New Jersey: P&R Publishing, 2001), 75.

5. Genesis 3:8.

6. See G. K. Beale, *The Temple and the Church's Mission: A Biblical Theology of the Dwelling Place of God* (Downers Grove, Illinois: InterVarsity Press, 2004), 66–80.

7. Beale, *The Temple and the Church's Mission*, 65 (citing *Enuma Elish* 6.51–58).

8. Genesis 2:2. For a discussion of the similarity and its significance, see Beale, *The Temple and the Church's Mission*, 64.

9. John H. Walton, *Genesis 1 as Ancient Cosmology* (Winona Lake, Indiana: Eisenbrauns, 2011), 101 [citing Dietz Otto Edzard, *Gudea and His Dynasty: The Royal Inscriptions of Mesopotamia, Early Periods, Vol. 3/1* (Toronto: University of Toronto Press, 1997), 82].

10. John H. Walton, *Ancient Near Eastern Thought and the Old Testament: Introducing the Conceptual World of the Hebrew Bible* (Grand Rapids, Michigan: Baker Academic, 2006), 127.

11. On the theme of sacred structures as bridges linking cosmic realms, see Mircea Eliade, *The Sacred and the Profane: The Nature of Religion* (New York: Harcourt, 1957), 32–42.

12. Beale, *The Temple and the Church's Mission*, 88–90.

13. On this point, consider the way the two Genesis creation accounts conclude. The first ends with the comment that on the seventh and final day, "God rested from all his work." Meaning not that God lay down for a nap, but rather "rest" in the ancient Near Eastern sense—that he came to rest upon the place, that is, took up residence there, in his temple. The second account ends this way: "And the man and his wife were both naked and were not ashamed" (Genesis 2:25). That is, it ends with the

images of God, the man and woman, taking God's place in the garden temple. Unlike Marduk or various of the other gods of the Near Eastern pantheon, the God of Genesis "rests" by delegating his authority to his icons. He passes on his work to them. See R. R. Reno, *Genesis: Brazos Theological Commentary on the Bible* (Grand Rapids, Michigan: Brazos Press, 2010), 62 ("The seventh day gives creation its future.... We are animated by an imperative that involves change").

14. Gregory Beale sums up the biblical evidence for this nicely: "There are indications elsewhere in the Old Testament"—meaning beyond Genesis 1 and 2 themselves—"which are developed later by Jewish commentators, that Eden and the temple signified a divine mandate to enlarge the boundaries of the temple until they formed the borders around the whole earth." Beale goes on to cite Numbers 24:5–9; Ezekiel 17, 19, and 31; Isaiah 54 and 66; Jeremiah 3; Zechariah 1 and 2; Daniel 2; and Psalm 72. He also helpfully collects the views of early Jewish commentators, ranging from the Dead Sea Scrolls to Sirach and beyond. See Beale, *The Temple and the Church's Mission*, 123–67.

15. For a summary, see Beale, *The Temple and the Church's Mission*, 154–67.

16. See Genesis 2:19–20.

17. This may be an unfamiliar way of putting things to some, but I humbly submit it is the picture the Bible offers of what God meant the world for. It was always to be his temple, and the humans always had a central part to play. Once the Fall occurs and sin enters the equation, God's project to make the world a temple becomes also a work of salvation. For more on the relationship between eschatology and soteriology, to use the theological terms, see Vos, *The Eschatology of the Old Testament*, 73–76.

18. Abraham Kuyper, *Christianity and the Class Struggle*, trans. Dirk Jellema (Grand Rapids, Michigan: Piet Hein Publishers, 1950), 18–19.

19. Isaiah 45:18 (emphasis added).

20. Kuyper, *Christianity and the Class Struggle*, 18–20.

21. Most especially Titus Carus Lucretius, a Roman poet, whose famous work, *De rerum natura*, was rediscovered in 1417 and well known by the

middle of the seventeenth century, particularly among religious skeptics. See Catherine Wilson, *Epicureanism at the Origins of Modernity* (New York: Oxford University Press, 2008), 2–3, 16–17; N. T. Wright, *History and Eschatology: Jesus and the Promise of Natural Theology* (Waco, Texas: Baylor University Press, 2019), 7–10 (discussing Lucretius's influence).

22. For a summary of the Epicurean tradition's stances, see Wilson, *Epicureanism at the Origins of Modernity* (New York: Oxford University Press, 2008), 4–7.

23. Carlin A. Barton, *Roman Honor: The Fire in the Bones* (Berkeley, California: University of California Press, 2001), 38–39.

24. Ibid., 39 (quoting Cicero, *Tusculanae disputationes* 2.22.53).

25. Ibid., 40 (quoting Seneca, *De providentia* 2.2).

26. "President Demands Railroad Control: Objects to Government Ownership, He Tells Raleigh Audience," *New York Times,* October 20, 1905 (quoting Roosevelt).

27. Theodore Roosevelt, *The Winning of the West* (New York: G. P. Putnam's Sons, 1889), 2:169.

28. "President Demands Railroad Control" (quoting Roosevelt).

CHAPTER THREE: A MAN'S BATTLE

1. I have changed his name for the privacy of his family.

2. The Hebrew word is *samar,* meaning, most basically, to guard or watch over. See G. K. Beale, *The Temple and the Church's Mission: A Biblical Theology of the Dwelling Place of God* (Downers Grove, Illinois: InterVarsity Press, 2004), 69.

3. Ibid., 69–70.

4. Ibid. (quoting 2 Baruch 14:18, in an allusion to Genesis 2:15).

5. John H. Walton, *The Lost World of Adam and Eve: Genesis 2–3 and the Human Origins Debate* (Downers Grove, Illinois: IVP Academic, 2015), 128–36 (adducing examples).

6. Geerhardus Vos, *The Eschatology of the Old Testament*, ed. James T. Dennison Jr. (Phillipsburg, New Jersey: P&R Publishing, 2001), 75.

7. The key words from Genesis 3:8 are *qol* and *ruah hayyom*, traditionally translated together as God walking in the garden in the cool of the day. But the words may also mean, "They [Adam and Eve] heard the roar of the Lord moving about in the garden in the wind of the storm." John H. Walton, *Genesis: The NIV Application Commentary* (Grand Rapids, Michigan: Zondervan, 2001), 224.

8. See Norman Wentworth DeWitt, *Epicurus and His Philosophy* (Minneapolis, Minnesota: University of Minnesota Press, 1954), 68, 232–33, 251, 286–88.

9. See Jean-Jacques Rousseau, *Discourse on the Origins of Inequality (Second Discourse), Polemics, and Political Economy*, ed. Roger D. Masters and Christopher Kelly (Hanover, New Hampshire: Dartmouth College Press, 1992), 34–35. For an overview of Rousseau's Epicureanism, see Jared Holley, "Rousseau on Refined Epicureanism and the Problem of Modern Liberty," *European Journal of Political Theory* 17, no. 4 (2018): 411–31.

10. Rousseau, *Discourse on the Origins of Inequality (Second Discourse)*, 43–55.

11. See William Kessen, "Rousseau's Children," *Daedalus* 107, no. 3 (1978): 155.

12. David Gilmore, *Manhood in the Making: Cultural Concepts of Masculinity* (New Haven, Connecticut: Yale University Press, 1990), 223–24.

13. Carlin A. Barton, *Roman Honor: The Fire in the Bones* (Berkeley, California: University of California Press, 2001), 40.

14. Ibid., 41 (quoting Virgil, *Aeneid* 9.205–06).

CHAPTER FOUR: A MAN'S PROMISE

1. Helen Pluckrose and James Lindsay, *Cynical Theories: How Activist Scholarship Made Everything about Race, Gender and Identity—and Why This Harms Everybody* (Durham, North Carolina: Pitchstone Publishing, 2020), 136–37.

2. Stephanie Pappas, "APA Issues First-Ever Guidelines for Practice with Men and Boys," *Monitor on Psychology* 50, no. 1 (2019): 34.
3. Fredric Rabinowitz et al., *Guidelines for Psychological Practice with Boys and Men*, American Psychological Association, August 2018, 3, https://www.apa.org/about/policy/boys-men-practice-guidelines.pdf.
4. Andrew Koppelman, *Antidiscrimination Law and Social Equality* (New Haven, Connecticut: Yale University Press, 1996), 164.
5. David S. Cohen, "No Boy Left Behind? Single-Sex Education and the Essentialist Myth of Masculinity," *Indiana Law Journal* 84, no. 1 (2009): 186.
6. Arianne Shahvisi, "'Men Are Trash': The Surprisingly Philosophical Story behind an Internet Punchline," *Prospect*, August 19, 2019.
7. Kathleen Elliott, "Challenging Toxic Masculinity in Schools and Society," *On the Horizon* 26, no. 1 (2018): 17–22.
8. See, for example, Robert Moore and Douglas Gillette, *King, Warrior, Magician, Lover: Rediscovering the Archetypes of the Mature Masculine* (New York: HarperOne, 1990), 70–73.
9. See Plato, *Phaedrus*, 246a–254e.
10. Karl Marx, "Economic and Philosophic Manuscripts of 1844," in *The Marx-Engels Reader*, 2nd ed., ed. Robert C. Tucker (New York: Norton & Norton Company, 1978), 71.
11. Judith Butler, *Gender Trouble: Feminism and the Subversion of Identity* (New York: Routledge, 1999), 180 (arguing that "gender reality is created through sustained social performances").

CHAPTER FIVE: HUSBAND

1. Genesis 12:1. For more on the parallel between God's charge to Adam in Genesis and God's call to Abraham (and later promises to his descendants), see N. T. Wright, *The Climax of the Covenant: Christ and the Law in Pauline Theology* (New York: T&T Clark Ltd., 1993), 21–26.
2. Genesis 12:7.
3. Genesis 17:15–16.

4. Lee Brown, "Who Is Andrew Tate, the Incendiary Influencer Arrested in Romania?" *New York Post*, December 30, 2022.

5. Ibid.

6. Katherine Donlevy, "Incendiary Influencer Andrew Tate, Brother Arrested on Sex-Trafficking Allegations: Report," *New York Post*, December 29, 2022.

7. See Joel Khalili, "These Are the Most Popular Websites Right Now—and They Might Just Surprise You," TechRadar, July 13, 2021, https://www.techradar.com/news/porn-sites-attract-more-visitors-than-netflix-and-amazon-youll-never-guess-how-many ("[A]dult websites Xvideos and Pornhub are among the most trafficked in the United States, receiving an average of 693.5 million and 639.6 million monthly visitors respectively."); see also Similarweb, "Top Websites Ranking," https://www.similarweb.com/top-websites/ (accessed November 2022).

8. See Limor Barenholtz, "What Is the Most Searched Thing on Google in 2022?" Similarweb, July 20, 2022, (noting that "pornhub" ranks above "amazon," "gmail," and "nba" in terms of search volume).

9. Mark Regnerus, *Cheap Sex: The Transformation of Men, Marriage, and Monogamy* (New York: Oxford University Press, 2018), 107.

10. Ibid., 114–15.

11. Ibid., 115.

12. Ibid., 113.

13. Ibid., 114–21.

14. Ibid., 131–32.

15. Ibid., 127.

16. Daniel Cox, Beatrice Lee, and Dana Popky, "How Prevalent Is Pornography?" Institute for Family Studies, May 3, 2022, https://ifstudies.org/blog/how-prevalent-is-pornography.

17. Regnerus, *Cheap Sex*, 128–31.

18. Joona Räsänen, "Sexual Loneliness: A Neglected Public Health Problem?" *Bioethics* 37, no. 2 (2023): 101. ("A study published in the *Journal of American Medical Association* [*JAMA*] found that between 2000–2002 and 2016–2018, the proportion of 18 to 24-year-old individuals who

reported having had no sexual activity in the past year increased among men [but not among women]. In another recent study, similar results were reported: American men belonging to the youngest birth cohort who entered adulthood were more likely to be sexually inactive than their Millennial counterparts at the same ages just a few years prior.") See also Samuel L. Perry and Kyle C. Longest, "Does Pornography Use Reduce Marriage Entry during Early Adulthood? Findings from a Panel Study of Young Americans," *Sexuality & Culture* 23, no. 2 (2019): 394 ("higher levels of pornography use in emerging adulthood were associated with a lower likelihood of marriage by the final survey wave for men").

19. See Paul J. Wright et al., "Pornography Consumption and Satisfaction: A Meta-Analysis," *Human Communication Research* 43, no. 3 (2017): 335–36.

20. Regnerus, *Cheap Sex*, 127–28.

21. See John H. Walton, *Covenant: God's Purpose, God's Plan* (Grand Rapids, Michigan: Zondervan, 1994), 13–15.

22. Genesis 15:2.

23. Gaby Galvin, "U.S. Marriage Rate Hits Historic Low," *U.S. News & World Report*, April 29, 2020.

24. Regnerus, *Cheap Sex*, 145–46.

25. Alan J. Hawkins et al., 2022 *State of Our Unions—Capstones vs. Cornerstones: Is Marrying Later Always Better?* (Charlottesville, Virginia: National Marriage Project, 2022), 6.

26. David Gilmore, *Manhood in the Making: Cultural Concepts of Masculinity* (New Haven, Connecticut: Yale University Press, 1990), 225.

27. William Julius Wilson, *The Truly Disadvantaged: The Inner City, the Underclass, and Public Policy* (Chicago: University of Chicago Press, 1987), 81–106.

28. Gary S. Becker, "A Theory of Marriage: Part I," *Journal of Political Economy* 81, no. 4 (1973): 813–46.

29. Regnerus, *Cheap Sex*, 148–49.

30. Ibid., 148–53.

CHAPTER SIX: FATHER

1. National Fatherhood Initiative, "The Statistics Don't Lie: Fathers Matter," 2022, https://www.fatherhood.org/father-absence-statistic.

2. W. Bradford Wilcox, Wendy Wang, and Alysse ElHage, "'Life without Father': Less College, Less Work, and More Prison for Young Men Growing Up without Their Biological Father," Institute for Family Studies, June 17, 2022, https://ifstudies.org/blog/life-without-father-less-college-less-work-and -more-prison-for-young-men-growing-up-without-their-biological-father.

3. Ibid.

4. Stephanie Kramer, "U.S. Has World's Highest Rate of Children Living in Single-Parent Households," Pew Research Center, December 12, 2019, https://www.pewresearch.org/fact-tank/2019/12/12/u-s-children-more- likely-than-children-in-other-countries-to-live-with-just-one-parent/.

5. Ibid.

6. "America's Families and Living Arrangements: 2021," United States Census Bureau, November 29, 2021, https://www.census.gov/data/tables/2021/demo /families/cps-2021.html, Table C8. Poverty Status, Food Stamp Receipt, and Public Assistance for Children Under 18 Years by Selected Characteristics: 2021.

7. ASPE Human Services Policy Staff, "Information on Poverty and Income Statistics: A Summary of 2012 Current Population Survey Data," Office of the Assistant Secretary for Planning and Evaluation, U.S. Department of Health and Human Services, September 11, 2012, https://aspe.hhs.gov /reports/information-poverty-income-statistics-summary-2012-current -population-survey-data-0.

8. Wilcox, Wang, and ElHage, "'Life without Father.'"

9. Jeffrey Rosenberg and W. Bradford Wilcox, *The Importance of Fathers in the Healthy Development of Children* (Washington, D.C.: U.S. Department of Health and Human Services, 2006), 17.

10. Alysse ElHage, "Boys in Crisis: An Interview with Warren Farrell," Institute for Family Studies, March 9, 2017, https://ifstudies.org/blog/boys -in-crisis-an-interview-with-warren-farrell (quoting Warren Farrell: "Boys with dad-deprivation often experience a volcano of festering anger").

11. Wilcox, Wang, and ElHage, "'Life without Father.'"

12. David Autor and Melanie Wasserman, "Wayward Sons: The Emerging Gender Gap in Labor Markets and Education," Third Way, March 20, 2013, https://www.thirdway.org/report/wayward-sons-the-emerging-gender-gap-in-labor-markets-and-education, 49.

13. Rosenberg and Wilcox, *The Importance of Fathers in the Healthy Development of Children*, 13.

14. Genesis 12:2–3.

15. Genesis 12:2.

16. Genesis 22:17.

17. Rosenberg and Wilcox, *The Importance of Fathers in the Healthy Development of Children*, 12.

18. Ibid.

19. Ibid.

20. Wilcox, Wang, and ElHage, "'Life without Father.'"

21. W. Bradford Wilcox, "The Distinct, Positive Impact of a Good Dad," *The Atlantic*, June 14, 2013.

22. Raj Chetty et al., "Race and Economic Opportunity in the United States: An Intergenerational Perspective," *The Quarterly Journal of Economics* 135, no. 2 (May 2020): 717.

23. See Joshua A. Krisch, "The Science of Dad and the 'Father Effect,'" Fatherly, July 11, 2022, https://www.fatherly.com/health/science-benefits-of-fatherhood-dads-father-effect (summarizing benefits of the "father effect").

24. Erica Scharrer et al., "Disparaged Dads? A Content Analysis of Depictions of Fathers in U.S. Sitcoms over Time," *Psychology of Popular Media* 10, no. 2 (2021): 275–87.

CHAPTER SEVEN: WARRIOR

1. John H. Walton and J. Harvey Walton, *The Lost World of the Israelite Conquest: Covenant, Retribution, and the Fate of the Canaanites* (Downers Grove, Illinois: IVP Academic, 2017), 145–49.

2. See, for example, Adam A. Rogers, Dawn DeLay, and Carol Lynn Martin, "Traditional Masculinity during the Middle School Transition: Associations with Depressive Symptoms and Academic Engagement," *Journal of Youth and Adolescence* 46, no. 4 (2017): 710.

3. Ibid., 720–21.

4. Michael Ian Black, "The Boys Are Not Alright," *New York Times*, February 21, 2018.

5. American Psychological Association, "Harmful Masculinity and Violence: Understanding the Connection and Approaches to Prevention," In the Public Interest, Public Interest Directorate, September 2018, https://www.apa.org/pi/about/newsletter/2018/09/harmful-masculinity.

6. Fredric Rabinowitz et al., *Guidelines for Psychological Practice with Boys and Men* (Washington, D.C.: American Psychological Association, August 2018), 3, https://www.apa.org/about/policy/boys-men-practice-guidelines.pdf.

7. American Psychological Association, "Harmful Masculinity and Violence."

8. Brown University, "Unlearning Toxic Masculinity," BWell Health Promotion, https://www.brown.edu/campus-life/health/services/promotion/general-health-social-wellbeing-sexual-assault-dating-violence-get-involved-prevention/unlearning.

9. Elizabeth J. Meyer, "The Danger of 'Boys Will Be Boys,'" *Psychology Today*, March 14, 2014, https://www.theguardian.com/world/2019/jan/15/gillette-metoo-ad-on-toxic-masculinity-cuts-deep-with-mens-rights-activists.

10. Jared Yates Sexton, *The Man They Wanted Me to Be: Toxic Masculinity and a Crisis of Our Own Making* (Berkeley, California: Counterpoint, 2019), 87–88.

11. Ashley Rivera, "Traditional Masculinity: A Review of Toxicity Rooted in Social Norms and Gender Socialization," *Advances in Nursing Science* 43, no. 1 (2019), 2–3.

12. Rogers, DeLay, and Martin, "Traditional Masculinity during the Middle School Transition," 720–21.

13. Sam de Boise, "Editorial: Is Masculinity Toxic?" *NORMA: International Journal for Masculinity Studies* 14, no. 3 (2019): 150.

14. Ibid., 148–49.

15. Mary Ellin Logue and Hattie Harvey, "Preschool Teachers' Views of Active Play," *Journal of Research in Childhood Development* 24, no. 1 (2009). Cited in Christina Hoff Sommers, "School Has Become Too Hostile to Boys," *Time*, August 19, 2013.

16. Christina Hoff Sommers, *The War against Boys: How Misguided Policies Are Harming Our Young Men* (New York: Simon & Schuster, 2013), 45.

17. Ibid., 46.

18. Ibid., 61.

19. See, for example, Guifeng Xu et al., "Twenty-Year Trends in Diagnosed Attention-Deficit/Hyperactivity Disorder among US Children and Adolescents, 1997–2016," *JAMA Network Open* 1, no. 4 (August 2018).

20. "Data and Statistics about ADHD," Centers for Disease Control and Prevention, last reviewed August 9, 2022, https://www.cdc.gov/ncbddd/adhd/data.html. (This is a composite statistic. Thirteen percent of all boys are reportedly diagnosed with ADHD; 62 percent of all ADHD-diagnosed children take medications = 8.06 percent of the boy population is on ADHD meds. My working assumption here is that medication use rates don't materially differ between sexes; if anything, the number may be higher than this.)

21. Thomas Armstrong, *The Myth of the ADHD Child: 101 Ways to Improve Your Child's Behavior and Attention without Drugs, Labels, or Coercion* (New York: Penguin Publishing Group, 2017), 35–36.

22. Ibid., 28–29.

23. Ibid.

24. Megan Fresson et al., "Overdiagnosis of ADHD in Boys: Stereotype Impact on Neuropsychological Assessment," *Applied Neuropsychology: Child* 8, no. 3 (2019): 240.

25. Armstrong, *The Myth of the ADHD Child*, 279.

26. Richard V. Reeves, Eliana Buckner, and Ember Smith, "The Unreported Gender Gap in High School Graduation Rates," Brookings, January 12,

2021, https://www.brookings.edu/blog/up-front/2021/01/12/the-unreported-gender-gap-in-high-school-graduation-rates/. ["In 2018, about 88% of girls graduated on time compared to 82% of boys—a 6 percentage point gap…. The graduation rate for boys is only slightly higher than for economically disadvantaged students (82% v. 80%)."]

27. Catherine E. Freeman, *Trends in Educational Equity of Girls and Women: 2004*, National Center for Education Statistics, U.S. Department of Education (Washington, D.C.: U.S. Government Printing Office, 2004), 45.

28. Alexandra Topping, Kate Lyons, and Matthew Weaver, "Gillette #MeToo Razors Ad on 'Toxic Masculinity' Gets Praise—and Abuse," *The Guardian*, January 15, 2019.

29. Sexton, *The Man They Wanted Me to Be*, 252.

30. Joshua 1:9.

31. See John Locke, *Second Treatise of Government*, ed. C. B. Macpherson (Indianapolis: Hackett Publishing Company, 1980), 11–12.

32. David Gilmore, *Manhood in the Making: Cultural Concepts of Masculinity* (New Haven, Connecticut: Yale University Press, 1990), 223–24.

33. See Harvey C. Mansfield, *Manliness* (New Haven, Connecticut: Yale University Press, 2006), 206–7.

34. Josef Pieper, *The Four Cardinal Virtues: Prudence, Justice, Fortitude, Temperance* (New York: Harcourt, Brace & World, 1965), 117.

35. Ibid.

36. Ibid., 119.

37. Ibid.

38. Joshua 5:13–14.

39. Joshua 5:15.

40. See Alois Atzler, *Deutsche Geschichte seit 1815 bis zur Gegenwart* (Paderborn, Germany: Salzwasser Verlag, 1905), 130–31.

41. Tom Wolfe, "The Human Beast" (lecture, National Endowment for the Humanities, 2006).

42. Gilmore, *Manhood in the Making*, 223

43. John 12:24.

44. Carlin A. Barton, *Roman Honor: The Fire in the Bones* (Berkeley, California: University of California Press, 2001), 43 n.48 (quoting Plautus, *Captivi* 690, cf. 683–89).

45. J. R. R. Tolkien, *The Lord of the Rings: The Return of the King* (London: Collins Modern Classics, 2001), 797.

46. Numbers 14:7–9.

47. Dave Collins and Áine MacNamara, "The Rocky Road to the Top: Why Talent Needs Trauma," *Sports Medicine* 42, no. 11 (2012): 2 (author proof).

CHAPTER EIGHT: BUILDER

1. For an overview of prior interpretations emphasizing this theme, see P. Kyle McCarter Jr., *II Samuel: A New Translation with Introduction, Notes and Commentary (The Anchor Bible)* (New York: Doubleday, 1984), 138.

2. John H. Walton, *Ancient Near Eastern Thought and the Old Testament: Introducing the Conceptual World of the Hebrew Bible* (Grand Rapids, Michigan: Baker Academic, 2006), 275–77. See also Marc Van de Mieroop, *The Ancient Mesopotamian City* (New York: Oxford University Press, 1999), 61.

3. David Gilmore, *Manhood in the Making: Cultural Concepts of Masculinity* (New Haven, Connecticut: Yale University Press, 1990), 226.

4. See, for example, Adrianne Frech and Sarah Damaske, "Men's Income Trajectories and Physical and Mental Health at Midlife," *American Journal of Sociology* 124, no. 5 (2019): 1372–1412 ("Men reported worse mental health when they were…working fewer hours…. Men's ability to earn and sustain a family wage may directly influence their mental health via less exposure to unemployment, a more reliable paycheck, and higher job satisfaction and also indirectly through feelings of self-esteem, autonomy, or self efficacy…"). See also Karsen I. Paul and Klaus Moser, "Unemployment Impairs Mental Health: Meta-Analyses," *Journal of Vocational Behavior* 74, no. 3 (2009): 264–82. ("The average number of

persons with psychological problems among the unemployed was 34%, compared to 16% among employed individuals. Moderator analyses demonstrated that *men and people with blue-collar-jobs were more distressed by unemployment* than women and people with white-collar jobs.")

5. Nicholas Eberstadt, *Men without Work: Post-Pandemic Edition,* 2nd ed. (West Conshohocken, Pennsylvania: Templeton Press, 2022), 92.

6. Oren Cass, *The Once and Future Worker: A Vision for the Renewal of Work in America* (New York: Encounter Books, 2018), 198.

7. Joseph Hall, quoted in Charles H. George and Catherine George, *The Protestant Mind of the English Reformation* (Princeton, New Jersey: Princeton University Press, 1961), 139n. Cited in Charles Taylor, *Sources of the Self: The Making of the Modern Identity* (Cambridge, Massachusetts: Harvard University Press, 1989), 224.

8. Edmund S. Phelps, *Rewarding Work: How to Restore Participation and Self-Support to Free Enterprise* (Cambridge, Massachusetts: Harvard University Press, 1997), 11–15.

9. Eberstadt, *Men without Work: Post-Pandemic Edition,* 49.

10. Ibid., 11.

11. Ibid., 9.

12. Ibid., 7.

13. Ibid., 44.

14. U.S. Congress Joint Economic Committee, *Inactive, Disconnected, and Ailing: A Portrait of Prime-Age Men Out of the Labor Force,* SCP Report No. 3-18, Social Capital Project, Joint Economic Committee—Republicans (September 2018), 2, 22.

15. U.S. Congress Joint Economic Committee, *Inactive, Disconnected, and Ailing,* 12.

16. Alan B. Krueger, "Where Have All the Workers Gone? An Inquiry into the Decline of the U.S. Labor Force Participation Rate," Brookings Institution, September 7, 2017, 1, https://www.brookings.edu/bpea-articles/where-have-all-the-workers-gone-an-inquiry-into-the-decline-of-the-u-s-labor-force-participation-rate/.

17. U.S. Congress Joint Economic Committee, *Inactive, Disconnected, and Ailing*, 19–20.

18. Mene Ukueberuwa, "The Underside of the 'Great Resignation,'" *Wall Street Journal*, January 21, 2022.

19. Council of Economic Advisers, *The Long-Term Decline in Prime-Age Male Labor Force Participation*, Obama White House, June 2016, 24. Table 1 shows that prime-age men not in the labor force in 2014 watched television for an average of 335 minutes per day, or roughly 2,000 hours per year.

20. Anneken Tappe, "Here's Why a Whole Group of Men Is Being Overlooked in the Workforce," CNN Business, February 18, 2022, https://www.cnn.com/2022/02/18/economy/unemployment-criminal-records/index.html.

21. See, for example, World Economic Forum, *The Industry Gender Gap: Women and Work in the Fourth Industrial Revolution*, January 2016, 4, 6 ("Given that career choices are disproportionately affected by prior experience and bias, traditionally male dominated professions often find it difficult to attract women.... According to...predictions, men will lose more than 1.7 million jobs across the Manufacturing and Production and Construction and Extraction job families.... Women will only lose 0.37 million jobs in these two male-dominated job families. . ."). See also Richard V. Reeves, *Of Boys and Men: Why the Modern Male Is Struggling, Why It Matters, and What to Do about It* (Washington, D.C.: Brookings Institution Press, 2022), 22. ("One thing is certain. The long-run shift away from jobs requiring physical strength is going to continue. Fewer than one in ten jobs now require what the Bureau of Labor Statistics describes as 'heavy work.'. . . The goal here is not to bring back brawny jobs for men, it is to help men adapt. Most of the occupations set to grow the most in coming years are female dominated.")

22. All numbers taken from the U.S. Bureau of Labor Statistics, "May 2021 National Industry-Specific Occupational Employment and Wage Estimates," https://www.bls.gov/oes/current/oessrci.htm. For the median wage of manufacturing-sector employees, see the table for Sectors 31, 32,

and 33, "Manufacturing," ("all occupations" line). For the median wage of hospitality-sector employees, see the table for Sector 72, "Accommodation and Food Services" ("all occupations" line). For the median wage of administrative services employees, see the table for Sector 56, "Administrative and Support and Waste Management and Remediation Services" ("all occupations" line).

23. Reeves, *Of Boys and Men*, xiii.
24. Josh Brown, "Male Teachers Provide Important Role Models," EdSource, December 21, 2017, https://edsource.org/2017/male-teachers-provide -important-role-models/591879.
25. Reeves, *Of Boys and Men*, 150–55.
26. Ibid., 157–58.
27. See, for example, Warren Farrell, "The Chilly World of Campus Males," National Association of Scholars, October 27, 2011, https://www.nas.org /blogs/article/the_chilly_world_of_campus_males. ("Professors in engineering and the hard sciences don't speak out much about the politics of male-female issues. What we hear emanates strongly from departments of women's and 'gender' studies and is adapted by psychology; social work; sociology; anthropology; literature; schools of education; and the seminaries.")
28. U.S. Congress Joint Economic Committee, *Reconnecting Americans to the Benefits of Work*, SCP Report No. 5-21, Social Capital Project, Joint Economic Committee—Republicans (October 2021), 14–15.
29. Ibid., 32.
30. Ibid., 14–15.
31. Michael Shellenberger, *Apocalypse Never: Why Environmental Alarmism Hurts Us All* (New York: Harper, 2020), 263–64.
32. Patricia MacCormack, *The Ahuman Manifesto: Activism for the End of the Anthropocene* (London: Bloomsbury Academic, 2020), 141.
33. Ibid., 97.
34. Ibid., 96.
35. Ibid., 102.

36. Lisa Martine Jenkins, "1 in 4 Childless Adults Say Climate Change Has Factored into Their Reproductive Decisions," Morning Consult, September 28, 2020, https://morningconsult.com/2020/09/28/adults-children-climate-change-polling/.

37. Alex Williams, "To Breed or Not to Breed," *New York Times*, December 2, 2021.

38. Jenny Offill, *Weather* (New York: Knopf, 2020), 178.

39. Lydia Millet, *A Children's Bible* (New York: W. W. Norton & Company, 2020), 223.

40. Brian Bushard and Carlie Porterfield, "Climate Activists Throw Black 'Oil' at Gustav Klimt's 'Death and Life'—Here Are All the Recent Protests Targeting Museums," *Forbes*, November 15, 2022.

41. 1 Kings 10:27 (NIV).

CHAPTER NINE: PRIEST

1. Will Durant and Ariel Durant, *The Story of Civilization VIII: The Age of Louis XIV* (New York: Simon and Schuster, 1963), 55–56.

2. Ibid., 55–56.

3. Marvin R. O'Connell, *Blaise Pascal: Reasons of the Heart* (Grand Rapids, Michigan: Eerdmans, 1997), 26.

4. Donald Adamson, *Blaise Pascal: Mathematician, Physicist, and Thinker about God* (New York: St. Martin's Press, 1995), 4–5, 36.

5. O'Connell, *Blaise Pascal*, 171–73.

6. W. W. Rouse Ball, *A Short Account of the History of Mathematics* (New York: Dover, 1960), 233–34.

7. Adamson, *Blaise Pascal*, 13, 33.

8. Ibid., 2, 25.

9. See Matthew L. Jones, *Reckoning with Matter: Calculating Machines, Innovation, and Thinking about Thinking from Pascal to Babbage* (Chicago: University of Chicago Press, 2016), 11.

10. Adamson, *Blaise Pascal*, 1, 15.

11. See Desmond Clarke, "Blaise Pascal," Stanford Encyclopedia of Philosophy, last revised June 22, 2015, https://plato.stanford.edu/entries/pascal/.

12. David Simpson, "Blaise Pascal (1623–1662)," Internet Encyclopedia of Philosophy, https://iep.utm.edu/pascal-b/.

13. O'Connell, *Blaise Pascal*, 49–52.

14. Ibid.

15. See Midge Fusselman, "What Blaise Pascal Saw in a November Night of Fire That Inaugurated a Year of Grace," The Federalist, November 23, 2017, https://thefederalist.com/2017/11/23/blaise-pascal-saw-november-night-fire-inaugurated-year-grace/.

16. See John Chapman, "Pope St. Clement I," *The Catholic Encyclopedia* (New York: Robert Appleton Company, 1908).

17. Fusselman, "What Blaise Pascal Saw in a November Night of Fire."

18. Ed Simon, "Why Pascal's Wager Is Eminently Modern," *Nautilus*, January 26, 2017; Durant and Durant, *The Story of Civilization VIII*, 66–67.

19. Fiona Zublin, "The First Buses in the World Were in Paris (and They Ate Hay)," Ozy, December 12, 2018, https://www.ozy.com/true-and-stories/the-first-buses-in-the-world-were-in-paris-and-they-ate-hay/90088/.

20. See Adamson, *Blaise Pascal*, 9.

21. Michael Meade, *The Water of Life: Initiation and Tempering of the Soul* (Seattle: GreenFire Press, 2006), 198.

22. J. R. R. Tolkien, *The Lord of the Rings: The Fellowship of the Ring* (London: HarperCollins, 2012), 330.

23. Pope John Paul II, "Homily of His Holiness John Paul II for the Inauguration of His Pontificate" (St. Peter's Square, October 22, 1978), John Paul II Foundation, https://jp2.com/homily-of-his-holiness-john-paul-ii-for-the-inauguration-of-his-pontificate-2/.

24. 2 Samuel 6:20.

25. Edmund Burke, *Reflections on the Revolution in France, and on the Proceedings in Certain Societies in London Relative to that Event*, 9th ed. (London: J. Dodsley, 1791), 135.

26. Ibid., 137.

27. Ibid.

28. Christine McTaggart, *Today Is: Daily Inspirations (Volume 2)*, 2nd ed. (Australia: Insight-Freedom Publishing, 2012), 96.

29. Ecclesiastes 3:11 (NIV).

30. Numa Denis Fustel de Coulanges, *The Ancient City: A Study on the Religion, Laws, and Institutions of Greece and Rome*, 4th ed. (Boston: Lee and Shepard, 1882), 29–41. See also Larry Siedentop, *Inventing the Individual: The Origins of Western Liberalism* (Cambridge, Massachusetts: Belknap Press, 2014), 10–13.

31. Burke, *Reflections on the Revolution in France*, 137.

32. Titus Livius, *The History of Rome: The First Eight Books* (London: Henry G. Bohn, 1853), 453. See also Carlin A. Barton, *Roman Honor: The Fire in the Bones* (Berkeley, California: University of California Press, 2001), 42–43.

33. Edmund Burke, *A Letter from Mr. Burke to a Member of the National Assembly; in Answer to Some Objections to His Book on French Affairs* (Paris: J. Dodsley, Pall-Mall, 1791), 33–34.

34. See Herbert Marcuse, "The Historical Fate of Bourgeois Democracy" in *Towards a Critical Theory of Society: Collected Papers of Herbert Marcuse, Vol. 2*, ed. Douglas Kellner (London: Routledge, 2001), 173.

35. Herbert Marcuse, "Repressive Tolerance," in Robert Paul Wolff, Barrington Moore Jr., and Herbert Marcuse, *A Critique of Pure Tolerance* (Boston: Beacon Press, 1965), 81–123.

36. See, for example, Tom Bailey and Valentina Gentile, eds., *Rawls and Religion* (New York: Columbia University Press, 2015) (providing an overview of the debate regarding "public reason" and religious claims).

37. See, for example, John Rawls, "The Idea of Public Reason Revisited," *The University of Chicago Law Review* 64, no. 3 (1997): 765–807.

38. Naomi Schaefer Riley, "'The 1619 Project' Enters American Classrooms," *Education Next* 20, no. 4 (2020): 34–44.

39. Frederick M. Hess and R. J. Martin, "Smithsonian Institution Explains That 'Rationality' & 'Hard Work' Are Racist," American Enterprise

Institute, July 20, 2020, https://www.aei.org/op-eds/smithsonian-institution-explains-that-rationality-hard-work-are-racist/.

40. "Long-Term Trends in Deaths of Despair," U.S. Congress Joint Economic Committee, September 5, 2019, https://www.jec.senate.gov/public/index.cfm /republicans/2019/9/long-term-trends-in-deaths-of-despair, 6.

41. "Overdose Death Rates," National Institute on Drug Abuse, last updated January 20, 2022, https://nida.nih.gov/research-topics/trends-statistics/ overdose-death-rates.

42. "Long-Term Trends in Deaths of Despair," U.S. Congress Joint Economic Committee, 5.

43. Megan Brenan, "Americans Less Optimistic about Next Generation's Future," Gallup, October 25, 2022, https://news.gallup.com/poll/403760 /americans-less-optimistic-next-generation-future.aspx.

44. Burke, *Reflections on the Revolution in France*, 141.

45. 2 Samuel 7:14.

46. Prior to this passage, the Bible uses sonship language for the house of Abraham as a whole. For example, Moses reports the words of God to Pharaoh, "Israel is my firstborn son…Let my son go" (Exodus 4:22–23). As Peter Leithart helpfully sums up, "Sonship was exclusively a corporate idea in the early part of Israel's history. With the Davidic covenant, however, the corporate identity of the 'son' of God was focused in the single person of the Davidic king. The fortunes of Israel would henceforth turn on the iniquity or righteousness of the 'son.'" Peter J. Leithart, *A Son to Me: An Exposition of 1 & 2 Samuel* (Moscow, Idaho: Canon Press, 2003), 218.

47. Burke, *Reflections on the Revolution in France*, 137.

CHAPTER TEN: KING

1. Charles Dickens, *A Christmas Carol* (London: Blackie and Son, 1908), 48.

2. Here again, I have changed a few of the details for privacy while keeping intact the basics of the story.

3. Stephanie Dalley, *Myths from Mesopotamia: Creation, The Flood, Gilgamesh, and Others*, rev. ed. (New York: Oxford University Press, 2000), 234. See also G. K. Beale, *The Temple and the Church's Mission: A Biblical Theology of the Dwelling Place of God* (Downers Grove, Illinois: InterVarsity Press, 2004), 64.

4. John H. Walton, *Ancient Near Eastern Thought and the Old Testament: Introducing the Conceptual World of the Hebrew Bible* (Grand Rapids, Michigan: Baker Academic, 2006), 215.

5. Ibid., 135–40.

6. Ibid., 278–79.

7. See John H. Walton, *Genesis 1 as Ancient Cosmology* (Winona Lake, Indiana: Eisenbrauns, 2011), 176–77.

8. John Rawls, "Kantian Constructivism in Moral Theory," *The Journal of Philosophy* 77, no. 9 (1980): 543.

9. Edmund Burke, *The Works of Edmund Burke: Volume VII* (Boston: Charles C. Little and James Brown, 1839), 116.

10. 1 Kings 3:5–9.

11. Walton, *Ancient Near Eastern Thought*, 278.

12. Deuteronomy 17:17.

13. Ibid.

14. Deuteronomy 17:19.

15. 1 Timothy 3:2–3.

16. Deuteronomy 17:16.

17. Eric Nelson, *The Hebrew Republic: Jewish Sources and the Transformation of European Political Thought* (Cambridge, Massachusetts: Harvard University Press, 2010), 1–22. See also Michael Walzer, *The Revolution of the Saints: A Study in the Origins of Radical Politics* (Cambridge, Massachusetts: Harvard University Press, 1965).

18. Isaiah Berlin, "Two Concepts of Liberty," in *Liberty: Incorporating Four Essays on Liberty*, ed. Henry Hardy (New York: Oxford University Press, 2002), 179–81.

19. See John Gray, *Isaiah Berlin: An Interpretation of His Thought* (Princeton, New Jersey: Princeton University Press, 2013), 50–59, 67.

20. Berlin, "Two Concepts of Liberty," 169, 215.

21. Unidentified Democratic newspaper in Roosevelt Albany Scrapbook, Putnam Papers, Theodore Roosevelt Collection at Houghton Library, Harvard University.

22. Theodore Roosevelt, "Doing as Our Forefathers Did…" (speech, Dickinson, Dakota Territory, July 4, 1886).

23. Ibid.

24. Ibid.

25. Theodore Roosevelt, "History as Literature," *American Historical Review* 18, no. 3 (1912): 489 (speech, Boston, December 27, 1912).

26. John 14:11.

EPILOGUE: OF TEMPLES AND MEN

1. Bart D. Ehrman, *Heaven and Hell: A History of the Afterlife* (New York: Simon & Schuster, 2020), 79.

2. Genesis 12:2–3.

INDEX

A

abad, 23

Abraham (biblical), 56, 63–66, 68, 70–72, 75–79, 81–82, 84, 90, 93, 95–101, 107–8, 132, 134, 147, 154, 210

academic performance, 5, 92

Adam (biblical), 13, 17–19, 21–24, 30, 35–38, 42, 49, 52–53, 55–57, 63–66, 69, 76, 84, 90, 96–98, 100, 108, 131, 134, 136, 144, 147–48, 155, 159, 162, 172–73, 180–81, 186, 188, 194–95, 208, 210

adamah, 17

addiction, 6, 73, 121, 126, 183

ADHD, 111–12

agency, 141, 149, 186, 209

aggression, 51, 109–11, 115

alcohol abuse, 118, 120, 160, 162, 170, 172, 183, 191

American founding, 168

American Psychological Association, 50, 109–10

American republic, 6, 11–12, 30, 200–201, 210

ancient world, 20–21, 24, 35, 65, 76, 147, 194

androgyny, 75, 112–13, 168

Ark of the Covenant, 157, 159, 163, 172–73

Assyria, 21

Atrahasis, 185

authority, 182, 184, 186, 193–94

B

Babel, 38

Babylon, 20–21

Becker, Gary, 83

Beijing, China, 123–24

Berg, Eric, 158–59

Berlin, Isaiah, 196, 200

Bible, 10–13, 17, 19–24, 26,
    29–30, 32, 35–36, 39, 41–42,
    46, 49, 53–57, 63, 66, 69, 90,
    94, 96–98, 107–8, 113, 117,
    119, 121–22, 124, 131–34, 136,
    141–49, 153, 155–57, 160, 162,
    165, 167, 173, 175, 180–82,
    184–86, 188–91, 193–97, 200,
    202–3, 207–10
biological sex, 8–9, 156, 168, 197
blessing, 76, 82, 96, 98, 134, 188,
    190, 202
blue-collar work, 9, 131, 136,
    139–40, 200
Bonaparte, Napoleon, 166
Brown University, 110
builder, 12, 25, 56, 132, 137, 149,
    204, 208
Burke, Edmund, 160–62, 164,
    172, 175, 188

C
Canaan, 108, 116–17, 124–25,
    132
capitalism, 34, 166
Catholic Church, 164
chaos, 11–12, 16–18, 21–22, 24,
    35, 38, 53, 64, 66, 90, 104,
    108, 114, 117, 134, 144, 156,
    184–85, 188–89, 192, 195,
    207–8
character, 6, 11–13, 26, 28–29,
    34–35, 39–43, 49, 52–53, 55–57,
    63, 68, 72, 75–76, 84, 90, 97–98,
    107–10, 112–13, 116–17,
    119–20, 125–27, 132, 134, 142,
    148, 155–56, 158–59, 163–64,
    173, 175–76, 181–84, 189–90,
    192–93, 195–96, 198, 200–202,
    203, 207–11
Cicero, 29
Civil War, the, 88, 104
climate change, 110, 139, 144–46.
    See also environmentalism
coaching, 26, 46–47–49, 67, 70,
    88, 158
Coe, William, 104–7, 109
college, 5–6, 26, 32–33, 45–46,
    70, 99, 126, 130–31, 140, 148,
    169, 171, 192, 211
Collins, Dave, 125
competitiveness, 51, 109–10, 115,
    125,
consumerism, 75, 113, 119, 139,
    210
cosmos, the, 20, 27, 37, 133, 185
courage, 113–16, 121–22, 124,
    126
covenant, 76–77, 81
COVID-19 pandemic, 137, 167
creation, 11, 17–19, 21–22, 24, 27,
    30, 41–42, 64–66, 69, 99,
    133–34, 144–48, 164–65,
    185–86, 194, 199, 209
crime, 6–7, 9, 91–92, 138
Cult of Reason, 165–66
Cult of the Supreme Being, 166

cultivation, 11, 16, 23–25, 38, 83, 98, 119, 132, 137, 142, 144, 159, 193

culture, 10, 12, 26, 28, 34, 36, 39, 50, 57, 64, 66, 69, 79, 92, 94–95, 99, 131, 134, 136, 140–41, 144, 165–68, 170, 180, 198, 208

Curtius, Marcus, 163

D

David (biblical), 56, 132–34, 146–47, 149, 156–57, 159–60, 163, 172–73, 180–81, 186, 190, 210

Declaration of Independence, 168

"deep masculine," 9

delinquency, 91

dependence, 57, 89, 97, 131, 134, 137, 140–43, 183, 189, 199–200, 202

depression, 5, 91–92, 99, 138

Descartes, René, 151–52

Deschamps brothers, 153

Dickens, Charles, 179

disorder, 17, 23–24, 38–39, 52, 54, 104, 117, 189, 197, 209

dominion, 18, 36, 52, 144, 181–84, 186, 188

drug abuse, 5–6, 9, 170

Dry Cimarron, 103–5

duty, 9, 11, 28, 35, 40, 43, 52, 180

duty to guard, 35–36, 42–43, 131, 142

E

Eden (the garden), 11, 13, 17, 19–24, 35–38, 42–43, 49, 52, 55–57, 63–66, 69, 72, 76, 84, 96–98, 100, 107, 117, 124, 131–32, 142, 144, 146, 149, 157, 159, 180–81, 184, 186, 188, 194, 203, 207, 211

Egypt, 20–21, 72, 75, 107, 133, 142, 193

elites, the, 7, 51, 63, 131, 156, 167, 169, 200, 208

Enuma Elish, 20, 185

environmentalism, 144–46. *See also* climate change

Epicureanism, 28, 34, 39–42, 49, 51–52, 54, 64, 66–70, 74–75, 78, 90, 92–94, 107–9, 113–15, 117–18, 156, 164, 169–70, 173, 184, 186–87, 196–97, 199–200, 202, 208–10

Epicurus, 27–28, 39, 50, 164, 168

Eve (biblical), 19, 21–22, 24, 36–37, 55, 64, 69, 97, 131, 144, 186, 194

evil, 30, 34–43, 49–50, 55, 64–66, 98, 108, 113, 115, 117–21, 133, 139, 156, 184, 202, 209

Exodus, the, 142

F

Fall, the, 49, 100

family, 9, 35–36, 41–42, 50, 52, 62–63, 65–66, 69–72, 75–77, 83–84, 91–92, 94, 96–99,

107–8, 116–17, 119, 135,
138–40, 146, 156, 161, 168,
174–75, 180, 189, 197, 200,
202, 210
farming, 15–17, 22, 61, 104, 129,
139, 177, 179, 203
father, 7, 12, 56, 88–93, 96,
98–100, 141, 161, 173, 203–4,
208–9
fatherhood, 88–90, 93–98,
100–101, 143, 214
fatherlessness, 7, 9, 90–92, 209
fertility, 19, 145, 185
free speech, 166–67
French Revolution, 39, 160, 164,
166–67, 172, 194
Freud, Sigmund, 12
fruitfulness, 16, 18, 96

G

Genesis, 17–28, 35–38, 43, 51–55,
63–66, 76, 84, 92, 95, 100,
134, 144–45, 148, 159, 173,
184, 201
Gilmore, David, 7, 82, 120, 134
Girl with a Pearl Earring
(Vermeer), 146
globalization, 139, 170
God, 9–11, 13, 17–30, 32, 35–38,
40, 42, 49, 51–57, 63–66, 69,
72, 76–79, 81–82, 84, 93,
95–101, 107–8, 113–14,
116–17, 119–21, 124, 127,
132–34, 136–37, 142–49,
153–57, 159–70, 172–76,

180–81, 184–86, 188–94,
196–97, 201–3, 209–11
gods, 17, 19–21, 27, 37, 39,
133–34, 147, 149, 156, 163–64,
184–87, 191, 194
grades, 99
Great Depression, 137, 170
Greeks, 27, 29, 54, 115, 194, 196

H

happiness, 27–28, 34, 39, 164, 180
Hawley Concrete, 130, 149
Hayes, Tom, 46, 48
"HEAL" professions, 139–40
Hong Kong protests, 122, 124
Hong Kong, China, 122–23
hope, 25, 28, 30, 38, 57, 81,
98–100, 121–22, 124, 126, 140,
146, 160–61, 167, 170, 200
human nature, 24, 34, 168–69,
195–96
humility, 56–57, 89–90, 95, 97,
189
husband, 12, 56, 63–64, 66,
69–72, 74–78, 81–84, 107, 141,
173, 192, 204, 208

I

independence, 9, 141–42, 198,
200–201, 210
Isaiah (biblical), 25
Israel, 108, 116, 124, 132, 149,
157, 159, 181–82, 189, 193
Israelites, 108, 116, 142, 197

J

Jansen, Cornelius, 153
Jerusalem, 132–33, 146, 149, 156–57, 172, 180, 208
Jesus, 120, 154, 175, 203
John Paul II (pope), 159
Joshua (biblical), 56, 107–8, 113–14, 116–17, 120, 124–25, 132–33, 147, 210
Judah (biblical), 181–82
Jung, Carl, 12

K

Kansas, 15, 22, 61, 71, 105, 129–30, 135, 177, 203
King Arthur, 53, 204
king, 12, 56, 132, 159–60, 172, 180–81, 183–86, 189–93, 201–4, 208
kingdom, 186, 190, 207
Kuyper, Abraham, 24, 26

L

labor, 4, 18, 24, 119, 131, 134, 136, 138–39, 142, 147–49, 173, 186
labor force, 4–5, 91, 137–38, 140–41
Latimer, Hugh, 127
leadership, 49–53, 181–83
left, the, 7–9, 17, 35, 67, 109–10, 112, 139–40, 144, 146, 156, 168–70, 181–82, 197–99, 201, 210

legacy, 93, 97–98, 149, 158, 181
leisure, 5, 118, 197
liberalism, 8–10, 26–28, 39, 41–42, 52, 92–93, 156, 184, 186–87, 199
liberation, 167–68, 199
liberty, 9, 11–12, 30, 54, 86, 141, 156, 164–66, 168–70, 181, 184, 193–98, 200–202, 209–10
Lincoln, Abraham, 200
Locke, John, 114–15
Lord of the Rings (Tolkien), 121, 157
Luther, Martin, 175

M

MacCormack, Patricia, 144–45
Machiavelli, Niccolò, 6
MacNamara, Áine, 125
manufacturing, 9, 139–40
Marcuse, Herbert, 166–69
Marduk, 20, 147, 185
Marius, Gaius, 29
marriage, 63–64, 66–69, 72, 74–75, 77–78, 81–84, 94, 114, 126, 143, 162, 198
Marx, Karl, 50, 55, 166
Marxism, 50–51, 166–67
masculinity, 7–9, 12, 28, 49–51, 57, 67, 109–10, 112, 140, 202, 208
toxic, 7, 51, 67, 110, 184
Mesopotamia, 20, 133, 185
Millet, Lydia, 145
miscarriage, 85, 87–88
misogynism, 49, 68

mission, 11, 13, 21, 24, 26, 29–30, 35, 38, 42, 55–56, 63, 65–66, 84, 90, 93, 96, 98, 108, 134, 137, 142, 146, 173, 181, 210

Missouri, 3, 15, 33, 71, 85, 103, 105, 158, 174

Moses (biblical), 108, 114, 124–25, 190

N
Nathan (biblical), 173

Near East, 17, 19, 36, 133, 180, 186, 189

New Mexico, 71, 86, 103–6

New York Post, 68

"night of fire," 151, 153–55, 157, 174

nihilism, 9, 68, 122, 143, 145–46, 169–70, 197

O
Offill, Jenny, 145

oppression, 7, 9, 41, 50–51, 67, 145, 156, 164–66, 168, 199

order, 11, 17–18, 20–24, 26, 48, 51, 54–56, 99, 133, 144–45, 147–48, 180–81, 184–200, 202–3, 209

Osiris, 20

Oxford, England, 126–27

P
Pascal, Blaise, 151–55, 157, 174–75

patriarchy, 7, 34, 50, 144, 170

Paul (apostle), 191–92

Pharaoh (biblical), 72, 142

Pieper, Josef, 115–16

Plato, 54, 115, 133, 196

Plautus, 121

pleasure, 27–28, 34, 41, 52, 68, 75, 118, 184, 191, 194, 208

pornography, 5, 72–75

poverty, 7, 91

power, 7, 10, 20, 29, 36–37, 49, 52, 54–55, 95–96, 107–10, 113, 119, 121–22, 132–33, 142, 144, 153, 156–59, 162–68, 175, 180, 184–89, 195, 198–200, 202

pride, 119–21, 163

priest, 12, 35, 56, 126–27, 155–56, 161, 164–65, 172–73, 175–76, 204, 208

purpose, 11–12, 16–17, 19, 21, 24, 26–27, 29–30, 38, 54, 63, 65–66, 68, 84, 93, 97, 99, 113, 117, 126, 132, 136, 142, 152–53, 155–56, 161–63, 170, 172–73, 175, 181, 186–87, 194, 196–98, 207, 209

R
Rawls, John, 186–87

Ra, 20

Regnerus, Mark, 73–75

responsibility, 12, 35, 37, 39, 52, 56, 94–95, 107, 131, 143–44, 174, 180–81, 183, 198, 200–202, 208–9

Ridley, Nicholas, 127
Roman Empire, 10, 12, 29, 42, 141, 163, 175
Roosevelt, Theodore, 12, 30, 201–2
Rousseau, Jean-Jacques, 39–41, 50, 164–65, 167

S
sacrifice, 11, 28, 41–42, 64, 69–70, 89, 92–93, 100–101, 119–21, 126, 157, 159–60, 163, 174, 185, 189
Sarah (biblical), 72, 75, 77–79, 81–82, 84
schools, 5, 9–10, 41, 51, 67, 109–12, 168–69
screen time, 5
self-discipline, 190–91, 209
self-fulfillment, 28, 115, 184, 210
self-government, 13, 30, 112, 194, 201, 210
self-gratification, 34, 52, 194
self-mastery, 54, 190–91, 193, 201
self-preservation, 114–15
self-respect, 193
Senate Judiciary Committee, 7
Seneca, 29
serpent (biblical), 23, 36–37, 52, 131
servanthood, 49, 53, 55
service, 52, 56, 95, 136, 159, 191
Seti I (pharaoh), 20
Severino, Tony, 47–48

sex, 8–9, 54, 68, 72, 74–75, 118, 156, 167–68
sexual addiction, 73
sexual assault, 91
sin, 40, 50, 119
single mothers, 91
single-parent households, 91
Solomon, 56, 180–82, 186, 189–90, 192, 203, 207–8, 210
Stace, Arthur, 160
status, 37, 76, 119–20, 136, 147, 159, 163, 169, 192, 199
strength, 6–7, 12, 36, 68, 74, 97, 109, 113, 115, 125, 139, 158, 162, 190, 198, 202
suffering, 40–42
suicide, 4–6, 9, 138, 170
Sumpter, Bud, 103–7
Sumpter, Susan Murphy, 103–7
"super champion" athletes, 125
Supreme Court, 71, 86
Sydney, Australia, 160–61

T
Tate, Andrew, 67–68
Taylor, Nicholas, 111
temple, 11, 19–27, 30, 35, 37–38, 42, 52, 55–56, 63–66, 76, 98, 100, 108, 121, 133–34, 137, 146–49, 155, 173, 180, 185, 197, 207–8, 211
Thoreau, Henry David, 66
thumos, 115, 118
Timoney, Patrick, 111
Tolkien, J. R. R., 121–22, 157

tradition, 9–10, 41, 50, 69–70, 82,
  92, 107, 131, 141, 145, 149, 169,
  179–80, 194–95, 197, 201, 210
transgenderism, 8
trauma, 125
tree of knowledge, 19, 37

U
unemployment, 137–38
universal basic income, 141

V
video games, 5, 68, 138
Vietnam War, 43, 167
violence, 8, 50–51, 92, 110, 192
vir, 29
virtù, 6
virtus, 29, 121
vow, 76–78, 81–82, 84

W
warrior, 12, 29, 53, 56, 107–10,
  113, 115, 117, 119–22, 126–27,
  132, 163, 204, 208
weakness, 7, 49, 96–97, 207
welfare, 131, 141
West, the, 8, 10, 50, 107, 110, 131,
  144, 146, 155, 166, 168, 194
Wilson, William Julius, 82
Wolfe, Tom, 119
work-life balance, 143
work, 4–6, 9, 11, 15–17, 20–26,
  28, 30, 35, 38, 52, 69, 76, 83,
  89, 91, 93–94, 100, 114, 117,

131–49, 163, 169, 172, 186,
  189, 193, 198, 200, 204,
  208–10
World War I, 160, 170
World War II, 137
worship, 21, 52, 134, 160,
  162–65, 168, 176, 191